Visions of Culture

Visions of Culture

An Introduction to Anthropological Theories and Theorists

Jerry D. Moore

ALTAMIRA
PRESS

A Division of Sage Publications, Inc.
Walnut Creek ✦ London ✦ New Delhi

For information contact:

AltaMira Press
A Division of Sage Publications, Inc.
1630 North Main Street, Suite 367
Walnut Creek, California 94596 U.S.A.

Sage Publications Ltd.
6 Bonhill Street
London EC2A 4PU United Kingdom

Sage Publications India Pvt. Ltd.
M-32 Market
Greater Kailash 1
New Delhi 110 048 India

Printed in the United States of America

Library of Congress Cataloging-in-Publication Data

Visions of culture: an introduction to anthropological theories and theorists / author, Jerry D. Moore
    p. cm.
    Includes bibliographical references and index.
    ISBN 0-8039-7096-X (cloth: alk. paper) — ISBN 0-8039-7097-8 (pbk: alk. paper).
    1. Anthropology—Methodology. 2. Anthropology—Field work. 3. Anthropologists—History 4. Anthropologists—Biography. I. Moore, Jerry D.
GN33.V57   1996
301—dc20   96-25386
                                       CIP

    99   10   9   8   7   6   5

Production by Labrecque Publishing Services
Interior and Cover Design by Denise M. Santoro
Editorial Management by Denise M. Santoro

Excerpts from BWITI: AN ETHNOGRAPHY OF THE RELIGIOUS IMAGINATION IN AFRICA © 1982 by James Fernandez; published by permission of Princeton University Press.

Excerpts from EDWARD EVANS-PRITCHARD by Mary Douglas. Copyright © 1980 by Mary Douglas. Used by permission of Viking Penguin, a division of Penguin Books USA Inc.

Excerpts from PATTERNS OF CULTURE by Ruth Benedict. Copyright 1934 by Ruth Benedict, © renewed 1961 by Ruth Valentine. Reprinted by permission of Houghton Mifflin Co. All rights reserved.

Excerpts reprinted with the permission of Simon & Schuster from RACE, LANGUAGE AND CULTURE by Franz Boas. Copyright 1940 by Franz Boas; copyright © renewed 1967 by Franziska Boas Nichelson.

From RUTH BENEDICT: STRANGER IN THIS LAND by Margaret M. Caffrey, copyright © 1989. Courtesy of the University of Texas Press.

Excerpts from A SCIENTIFIC THEORY OF CULTURE AND OTHER ESSAYS by Bronislaw Malinowski. Copyright © 1944 by the University of North Carolina Press. Used by permission of the publisher.

Excerpts from SEX AND TEMPERAMENT IN THREE PRIMITIVE SOCIETIES © 1935, 1950, 1963 by Margaret Mead; published by permission of William Morrow and Company, Inc.

Table of Contents

Acknowledgments

This book was written for students, and various versions of the chapters have been tested on my students at California State University, Dominguez Hills. I want to thank them for their patience, questions, and puzzling looks—and for forcing me to be clear in exposition and intent. When I was writing the chapter on Edward Sapir, I felt an immediate empathy for the Ottawa period in his life when he lacked students; to lack the exchange of ideas with students would be a great loss, and I thank my students for their contributions to this book.

I would also like to thank my colleague Robert Franklin for his anthropological insights, and I would like to acknowledge four of my teachers who taught me anthropological theory as an undergraduate and graduate student: Michael Seelye, Joel Canby, Charles Erasmus, and Albert Spaulding. I would also like to thank Dr. James W. Fernandez for answering my request for information on his anthropological career.

I cannot sufficiently express my gratitude to my wife and colleague, Janine Gasco, who read draft chapters, listened to theoretical and editorial problems, and whose advice was unfailingly sound.

At AltaMira Press, I was fortunate to work with Mitch Allen, whose confidence in this book—even in the face of scathing reviews—is the principal reason this project was completed. I also thank Denise Santoro of AltaMira Press for her editorial assistance. I also appreciate the careful work of Rachel Fudge and her colleagues at Labrecque Publishing. I would also like to acknowledge the contributions made by the six anonymous reviewers who read different versions of this manuscript.

Finally, I would like to thank the student, whose name I never knew, who asked one of the best questions anyone can pose: "What's the goddamn point of it all?" This book is dedicated to him. ✦

What's the Point?

Several years ago I attended a weekend conference organized by a very active group of undergraduate anthropology students from a major midwestern public university. The annual conference was held in a group of cabins on the edge of a beautiful lake. The setting was conducive to serious presentations and also provided an opportunity for professors and students to discuss ideas in an informal environment, an informality enhanced by several kegs of beer.

Towards the end of an exhausting day of dialogue, the discussion turned to theoretical matters. Many of the students were enrolled in Professor X's course on anthropological theory and theorists, and they began to complain about the course, emboldened by beer and the absence of Professor X, who was simply too busy to attend the conference.

A young man stood up and said, "We start off with Edward Tylor, but Professor X tells us that Tylor was just an armchair anthropologist. So we read Malinowski who everyone says was a good fieldworker, but then Professor X says Malinowski was a racist. And then we read Margaret Mead, and Professor X says Mead was a liar."

The young man swayed slightly and demanded, "What's the goddamn point of it all?"

It was a very good question.

It is commonplace to assert that anthropology is in a crisis, but if that is true, it is a crisis of our own making. James Peacock, a former president of the American Anthropological Association, summarized anthropology's potential contributions and reflected on its shortcomings: ". . . poised for victory, we retreat, turn within, luxuriate in ourselves, squander our resources in silly arguments, shrink our vision to the smallest world, fiddle while Rome burns and barbarians are at the gate" (Peacock 1994:1).

In a field as diverse as anthropology, it is inevitable that conflicting opinions exist; controversy is fine. But in the midst of conflict, we lose sight of the intellectual achievements of anthropology and the personal contributions of anthropologists. And worse, we fail as teachers to communicate to our students the legacies of anthropologists who are worthy of attention, scrutiny, and respect.

This book is written for anthropology students. It is an introduction to the principal theorists and theories that shaped and continue to influence modern anthropology. Organized in a series of profiles, I summarize the major theoretical concepts of 21 scholars and attempt to relate those concepts to each scholar's formative influences, anthropological research, intellectual framework, and personal vision.

The chapters are organized into five thematic sections beginning with a brief introductory essay outlining the problems and issues common to the anthropologists in the section. Each chapter introduces a scholar's contribution to anthropology, profiles her/his professional life with an emphasis on fieldwork and publications, and discusses major aspects of the anthropologist's work: Morgan's comparative approach to kin systems, Durkheim's *conscience collective*, Malinowski's theory of needs, Lévi-Strauss' structural approach to myth, Victor Turner's concept of social drama, and so on.

The conclusion is followed by a bibliography of references students can pursue in more depth. I have tried to cite readily available sources, referencing recent republications in collections rather than original publications in more obscure journals. Again, the bibliography is not meant to be a complete listing of each anthropologist's published works, but a representative cross section listing principal bibliographical sources.

Visions of Culture is organized differently from other texts on anthropological theory. First, I have attempted to represent a broader range of anthropological viewpoints than, for example, Adam Kuper describes in his excellent study of British social anthropologists (Kuper 1983). Second, I have attempted to sample more current trends in anthropology than are discussed in Elvin Hatch's (1973) *Theories of Man and Culture*. Perhaps most distinctly, I attempt to provide a balanced, though not uncritical, reading of each anthropologist's contribution to anthropological theory. This simply means that I do not personally advocate a specific theory as Marvin Harris (1968) does in *Rise of Anthropological Theory*; the scholars discussed in *Visions of Culture* are not straw men or whipping boys. Each anthropologist discussed in this book has intellectual merit; they were included because their ideas are important and deserve to be understood.

Finally, I have presented each anthropologist in the context of her/his intellectual milieu; I have not measured each scholar against current theoretical trends in anthropology. Today, for example, cultural ecology and cultural evolution have fallen into disfavor, but they were important theoretical lines of inquiry from roughly 1945–1975. The several variations on functionalism were important to anthropology from the mid-1920s to the mid-1960s, although they are less so now. Because of their impact in the development of anthropological theory, I discuss these works even if some current theorists might consider such positions hopelessly outdated.

Visions of Culture is organized around the women and men who shaped modern anthropology. Other approaches to anthropological theory emphasize ideas over individuals, but I believe there are good reasons for a biographical structure. Ideas do not exist in the ether; they take shape in the experiences of individuals. Obviously, certain ideas become generally held, common properties. The organic analogy, the idea of progress, the function of society, the post-modernist critique, and so on have broad existences; they are not the single-handed creations of "Great Men." In my reading of anthropologists' theories, such broad concepts seem to be generic foundations on which specific scholars build their theoretical structures. Other factors and problems more immediately shape individual anthropologists' ideas.

Preeminent among these is the experience of anthropological fieldwork. Repeatedly, one discovers that anthropologists arrive at their theoretical positions in the process of trying to understand another human culture. Benedict and the Zuni, Mead and the Samoans, Radcliffe-Brown and the Andamanese, Malinowski and the Trobriand Islanders, Evans-Pritchard and the Azande, Steward and the Shoshone, Harris and rural Brazilians, Turner and the Ndembu, Geertz and the Javanese, Fernandez and the Fang—there is a recurrent dialectic that occurs in the context of research. In general discussions of theory, the empirical contexts of fieldwork are too often ignored. This is a shame since ethnographic research is anthropology's most important addition to the social sciences, and our translations of other cultures' experiences are anthropology's most lasting contribution to intellectual life.

Any collection stumbles on a basic problem: "Who should be included?" The selection process is like basketball fans arguing about the perfect "dream team." Magic Johnson, Michael Jordan and Larry Bird—they would be on every fan's list, but what about the other two players? Wilt Chamberlain or Kareem Abdul Jabar? Jerry West or Dr. J? How do you decide?

Obviously, I could not write about every major anthropological figure, so my selections require justification. First, I have considered anthropologists who dealt with central issues, such as: "What is the nature of culture?," " "What is the relationship between the individual and society?," " and "How can another culture be understood by an anthropological outsider?" These are fundamental issues with which anthropologists have struggled since the late-19th century, but not all anthropologists have focused on these theoretical issues. I realize that I have ignored major figures who made significant theoretical and substantive contributions to anthropology, and I apologize to them, their students, and their posthumous advocates. Second, I have not considered scholars whose works were important during their lifetimes, but have since faded in relevance (see, for example, Ackerman [1987:1–4] on Sir James Frazer). Third, I have attempted to choose anthropologists who are representative of basic trends within anthropology—unilineal evolution, Boasian historicism, functionalism, cultural materialism, structuralism, semiotics, feminism, and post-modernism. Fourth, I have limited myself to anthropologists from the United States, Great Britain, and France, and emphasize Anglo-American anthropology which I assume is of most interest to my audience. Finally, I have not discussed social thinkers in related fields who have made huge impacts on anthropology: Marx, Freud, Weber, Bourdieu, Giddens, and so on. That would involve writing a biographical encyclopedia of the social sciences, which is not my goal, intention, or desire.

The final selection of 21 anthropologists—Edward Tylor, Lewis Henry Morgan, Franz Boas, Emile Durkheim, Alfred Kroeber, Ruth Benedict, Edward Sapir, Margaret Mead, Marcel Mauss, Bronislaw Malinowski, A.R. Radcliffe-Brown, Leslie White, Julian Steward, Marvin Harris, Eleanor Burke Leacock, Edward Evans-Pritchard, Victor Turner, Mary Douglas, Claude Lévi-Strauss, Clifford Geertz, and James Fernandez—is not an exhaustive list, but a starting point for further research, classroom discussion, and student inquiry into the ideas and individuals who have shaped anthropology by contributing their particular and creative visions of culture. ✦

Bibliography

Ackerman, Robert
1987 James Frazer: A Life. Cambridge: Cambridge University Press.

Harris, Marvin
1968 The Rise of Anthropological Theory: A History of Theories of Culture. New York: Thomas Y. Crowell Company.

Hatch, Elvin
1973 Theories of Man and Culture. New York: Columbia University Press.

Kuper, Adam
1983 Anthropology and Anthropologists: The Modern British School. London: Routledge & Kegan Paul.

Peacock, James
1994 The AAA President's Report: Challenges Facing the Discipline. Anthropology Newsletter 35(9):1, 5.

Part One

Founders

Anthropology addresses a series of questions that humans have considered for millennia: What is the nature of society? Why do cultures change? What is the relationship between the person as an individual and the person as a member of a distinctive social group? What are the distinguishing characteristics of humanness? Why are cultures different?

The written record of such inquiries covers at least 2500 years. In 4th-century B.C. Athens, Aristotle pondered the organization of the state and used the organic analogy—the comparison of society to a living organism—which became a recurrent theme in 19th- and 20th-century anthropology. The 14th-century Arab geographer Ibn Khaldun explained the differences between cultures in terms of climate—passionate, expressive societies exist in warmer climates while restrained, impassive cultures exist in northern climates. In 1725, Giovanni Vico, a poor scholar in Italy, wrote *Scienza Nuova* and outlined a historical model of the evolution of human society. By the 1700s a wide range of moral philosophers were considering the nature of human cultures, drawing on ethnographic sources from Herodotus, Garcilaso de la Vega, Joseph Lafitau, and others.

So how can we call four men—Edward Tylor, Lewis Henry Morgan, Emile Durkheim, and Franz Boas—the "founders" of anthropology? First, because there are direct connections between modern anthropological issues and the ideas of these late-19th-century and early-20th-century scholars. A significant change occurred in the social sciences with the publication of Charles Darwin's (1858) *The Origin of Species*. The directness of Darwin's impact has been discussed by Stocking (1968, 1987), but it seems clear that the Darwinian theory of biological variation served as a model for inquiry into the nature of human cultural differences. The mid-19th century is a threshold: earlier writers may have thought about cultural differences and the nature of humanity, but their approaches to understanding are distinct from post-Darwinian science. It is not that earlier scholars were unaware of cultural differences, but rather that they lacked "the slightest clue as to how cultural differences might be scientifically explained" (Harris 1968:18). Morgan, Tylor, Durkheim and Boas stand on this side of that intellectual divide, and thus their ideas remain more immediate and direct.

Prior to 1860, according to the Oxford English Dictionary, "anthropology" meant the study of human nature encompassing physiology and psychology; after 1860, the word denotes a science of humankind "in its widest sense." This shift in usage marks a change in an intellectual field that the works of Morgan, Tylor, Boas and Durkheim partly created.

Second, each of these men were founders in a practical sense: they were instrumental in establishing anthropology as an academic discipline. Between 1860 and 1900, anthropology changed from a loose collection of shared interests into a formally defined science of humankind. Tylor, Morgan, Durkheim and Boas were directly involved in the creations of new anthropological institutions. Tylor held the first professorship of anthropology at Oxford, and he wrote the first anthropology text book. Morgan obtained support for anthropological research from the Smithsonian Institution and the U.S. government. Durkheim outlined a new curriculum of social inquiry, founded influential journals, and established a cadre of students and colleagues who in turn would shape French social science through the 1970s. Boas would supervise the first American Ph.D. in anthropology, establish new journals and associations, and literally set the broad investigative boundaries of American anthropology.

Finally, Tylor, Morgan, Durkheim and Boas—though drawing on existing conceptual frameworks and ideas—articulated new sets of anthropological problems and proposed methods for their scientific study. In so doing, they developed ways of thinking about human culture that continue to inform our inquiries, and which definitely shaped the course of 20th-century anthropology. Tylor's definition of culture, Morgan's examination of social evolution, Durkheim's creation of a science of society, and Boas' insistence on viewing cultures in specific historical contexts—these positions form the landscape of the emergent field of anthropology as it developed from the late-19th century to the present. These men were founders. ✦

Chapter 1

Edward Tylor

The Evolution of Culture

Edward Burnett Tylor (1832–1917) is considered the founding father of British anthropology. Tylor was the first professor of anthropology at Oxford, he was active in establishing anthropological associations and institutions, and his ideas contributed to the intellectual debates of the late-19th century sparked by Darwin's *The Origin of Species*. His friend A.C. Haddon wrote that Tylor's books, "while replete with vast erudition, are so suggestive and graced by such quiet humour that they have become 'classics,' and have profoundly influenced modern thought. From their first appearance it was recognized that a master-mind was guiding the destinies of the nascent science" (Haddon 1910:159). When a contemporary, the religious scholar Max Müller, dubbed anthropology "Mr. Tylor's science," it was a recognition of Tylor's impact on the definition of a scholarly field.

Central to Tylor's contribution was his definition of culture:

> Culture or Civilization, taken in its wide ethnographic sense, is that complex whole which includes knowledge, belief, art, morals, law, custom, and any other capabilities and habits acquired by man as a member of society. [1958 (1871):1]

In these opening lines of his major work, *Primitive Culture* (1871), Tylor first defined culture in "its modern technical or anthropological meaning" (Kroeber and Kluckhohn 1952:9; cf. Stocking 1963). It is a definition of culture which Bohannan and Glazer (1988:62) note, "is the only one most anthropologists can quote correctly, and the one they fall back on when others prove too cumbersome."

And yet one of his most careful modern readers, George W. Stocking, Jr., writes "To judge by current textbooks, Tylor has little to say to anthropology today" (Stocking 1968:176). Contending that many of his later readers simply misunderstood his concept of culture (Stocking 1963), Stocking concludes that Tylor was not "one of the major investors in the general intellectual capital of the modern human sciences," dwarfed by figures like Marx, Freud, Weber or Durkheim (Stocking 1987:301-302).

Ironically, Tylor's lasting influence was greater on American anthropology than on subsequent British social anthropology (see, for example, Evans-Pritchard's [1981:91–94] curiously curt discussion of his eminent predecessor at Oxford). In contrast, an American anthropologist like Robert Lowie (1939) lauded Tylor as a careful scholar with a "serene willingness to weigh evidence." Varying assessments of Tylor and his American contemporary, Lewis Henry Morgan, led Meyer Fortes (1969) to suggest that Morgan gave birth to British social anthropology, while the very British Tylor fathered American cultural anthropology.

How do we make sense of such contradictory assessments? Why was Tylor so influential in his time? What is the lasting value of his ideas?

Background

Born in 1832, Tylor's family were Quakers, then a religious minority, though one firmly part of the British middle class. Tylor's religion precluded education at Oxford or Cambridge, which only granted degrees to members of the Church of England. Tylor was educated in Quaker schools before joining the family foundry business at the age of 16. Tylor's Quaker upbringing also led to an agnosticism that tempered his studies of the origins of religion. Ackerman (1987:77) observes that Tylor's agnosticism led him to approach religions as intellectual systems rather than expressions of belief, noting that Tylor "cared more about creed than consolation."

In his early 20s, Tylor exhibited preliminary symptoms of tuberculosis, and "secure of a modest competency" in Marett's discreet phrase, Tylor left the family business and traveled to warmer latitudes to regain his health. In Cuba he met Henry Christy, a British businessman and avid archaeologist, and the two set off for a four-month journey through Mexico described in Tylor's first book, *Anahuac: Or Modern*

Mexico and Mexicans (Tylor 1861). *Anahuac* is a travelogue informed by wide reading and crafted with an eye for telling detail and an ear for dialogue.

From the port of Vera Cruz, Tylor and Christy traveled inland by stagecoach to Mexico City with frequent stops as the archaeologist Christy searched roadside gullies for obsidian arrowheads (1861:35). The travelers visited archaeological sites like Teotihuacan and Cholula, searched for potsherds in newly plowed fields, and compared the artifacts of Mexico with recent finds from Europe.

But most of *Anahuac* describes modern, not ancient, Mexico. Tylor and Christy toured sugar plantations, textile factories, *pulque* shops and haciendas. He describes Mexico's political instability and poverty. Tylor's anticlerical upbringing erupts in a rash of diatribes against the Catholic Church. His criticisms are so stinging that Tylor himself admits, "It seems hard to be always attacking the Roman Catholic clergy," but then proceeds to blame priests for the "doleful ignorance" and poverty of the population (1861:126). In *Anahuac* Tylor shows himself as an informed and observant, though not unprejudiced, writer.

Over the next four years, Tylor matured into a more serious student of human culture. In 1865 he published *Researches into the Early History of Mankind and the Development of Civilization*, which outlined the analytical themes that he developed the rest of his life. "The early Culture History of Mankind," Tylor (1964 [1865]:137) wrote, "is capable of being treated as an Inductive Science, by collecting and grouping facts."

Tylor sifted through missionaries' accounts, explorers' journals, ancient texts, and ethnological reports to search for similarities in human cultures. "When similar arts, customs, beliefs or legends are found in several distant regions, among peoples not known to be of the same stock," Tylor (1964 [1865]:3) asked, "how is this similarity to be accounted for?" Essentially there are two possible explanations: the similarity is either the result of parallel invention—"the like working of men's minds under like conditions"—or it is evidence of contacts, direct or indirect, contemporary or historical—between the societies and the consequent diffusion of cultural knowledge.

Tylor's consideration of diffusion marks his early work, yet Stocking (1963:788) notes that Tylor increasingly emphasized the importance of evolution over diffusion or parallel invention. Sixteen years later, the scholar would conceive of his textbook *Anthropology* as "a series of chapters demonstrating the fact and course of progression in various areas of life," almost exclusively emphasizing evolution.

Evolution and progress were important themes even in Tylor's first serious ethnological book. Nearly half of *Researches into the Early History of Mankind* . . . considers the evolution of language and symbols. Although admitting that there is "no evidence of man ever having lived in society without use of spoken language," Tylor describes certain societies with "a speech so imperfect that even if talking of ordinary matters they have to eke it out by gestures." Weighing alternate hypotheses, he suggests that such societies either are "the strongest case of degeneration known in the history of the human race or supply a telling argument that the gesture-language is part of the original utterance of mankind . . ." (Tylor 1964 [1865]:62–64). In his first serious anthropological book, Tylor sketches a handful of themes he will develop in later work: the interpretation of myth, native rationales of dreams, and the logic of sympathetic magic, among others. *Researches* also contains his initial methodological musings about how to document the evolution of human society (see, for example, Tylor 1964 [1865]:236–241).

Researches into the Early History of Mankind . . . was published by John Murray and Sons, publishers of the most important scientific writings of the 19th century, including Lyell's *Principles of Geology* and Darwin's *The Origin of Species*. It was a measure of Tylor's growing status in the scientific community. By the late 1860s Tylor "had climbed into the scientific establishment," Joan Leopold (1980:19) writes, becoming the friend of Alfred Russel Wallace, Thomas Henry Huxley, and other eminent Victorians, writing articles and reviews for major periodicals and giving public lectures. Tylor's achievement was marked by his election as a Fellow of the Royal Society in 1871, and the publication of *Primitive Culture*.

Primitive Culture

In *Primitive Culture* Tylor sets out to reconstruct the history of human culture and immediately faces a major problem: how can humanity's prehistoric, unwritten history be known? Tylor closely followed contemporary archaeological discoveries of stone tools and extinct mammals in Great Britain and France, but fragments of bone and stone were not enough to reconstruct the "complex whole" of Culture or

Civilization. And so Tylor crafted his reconstruction on two principles: uniformitarianism and the concept of survivals.

> The condition of culture among the various societies of mankind, insofar as it is capable of being investigated on general principles, is a subject apt for the study of laws of human thought and action. On the one hand, the uniformity which so largely pervades civilization may be ascribed, in great measure, to the uniform action of uniform causes: while on the other hand its various grades may be regarded as stages of development or evolution, each the outcome of previous history, and about to do its proper part in shaping the history of the future. [1958 (1871):1]

Uniformitarianism was derived from Charles Lyell's multi-volume *Principles of Geology* (1830–1833). Lyell argued that the geological processes observable today—erosion, sedimentation, and so on—were the processes that shaped the Earth rather than spectacular, unique catastrophes like Noah's Flood. Observations of modern processes allowed for reconstructing the history of the Earth because the same geological processes were at work then as now.

This was also true for culture, Tylor argued, because culture was created by universally similar human minds and governed by the same basic laws of cognition. "Surveyed in a broad view," Tylor wrote:

> . . . the character and habit of mankind at once display that similarity and consistency which led the Italian proverb-maker to declare "all the world is one country.". . . To general likeness in human nature on the one hand, and to general likeness in the circumstances of life on the other, this similarity and consistency may no doubt be traced, and they may be studied with especial fitness comparing races near the same grade of civilization. [Tylor 1958 (1871):6]

Setting aside for the moment the issue of "grade of civilization," Tylor's key point is that the processes of culture are similar for all people, regardless of where or when they lived, because human minds are similar (Tylor 1958 [1871]:159). This is the central logic of Tylor's uniformitarianism: culture or civilization consists of knowledge, beliefs, art, morals, customs and other mental constructs; since human mental processes are universal, human societies have developed culture along "nearly uniform channels," characterized by progress and expressed in the evolution of culture.

This has three implications. First, race does not explain cultural differences. Believing that it was "possible and desirable to eliminate considerations of hereditary varieties or races of man," Tylor contended

his study demonstrated "that stages of culture may be compared without taking into account how far tribes who use the same implement,
follow the same custom, or believe the same myth, may differ in their
bodily configuration and the colour of their skin and hair" (Tylor 1871
[1958]:7). Rather, if two societies have analogous cultural traits (pottery
or monotheism or stock markets), it is because either a) the trait has
diffused from one society to another, or b) because independent inventions have developed due to the similarly constructed human minds
encountering similar situations.

    Second, it means that societies with similar cultural traits may rep-
resent analogous stages in the development of human culture. Citing
Samuel Johnson's fairly predictable insult "one set of savages is like
another," Tylor surprisingly exclaims, "How true a generalization
this really is, any Ethnological Museum may show" (1958 [1871]:6).
Tylor quickly explains that these similarities are most pronounced in
the realm of technology—the tools for hunting, fishing, fire-making,
cooking, and so on—although cross-cultural similarities also exist in
mythology, kinship, and other aspects of social life. Such parallels
reflect similar stages of cultural development among existing societies
and also allow us to reconstruct prehistoric societies. Since the laws of
mind are uniform, the patterns of contemporary "primitive" societies
must be similar to those of extinct prehistoric peoples, a "hypothetical
primitive condition [that] corresponds in a considerable degree to that
of modern savage tribes, who in spite of their difference and distance,
have in common certain elements of civilization, which seem remains
of an early state of the human race at large" (Tylor 1958 [1871]:21).
Tylor essentially asserted, as Robert Ackerman (1987:78) states, that
"human nature and development being relatively homogeneous, one
might legitimately discover, in the behaviour of contemporary primitive peoples, living links in the evolutionary chain."

    Third, Tylor's uniformitarianism allowed him to reconstruct the
specific processes leading to a particular belief, moral, or set of cultural
knowledge. Since culture was a cognitive construction created by similar human minds solving the problems of existence in a rational
though often erroneous way, it was possible for Tylor to retrace the
logical steps which led to a superstition, folk belief, or "irrational"
practice.

    Tylor's reconstruction of the evolution of human culture relied on
the *comparative method* and the *doctrine of survivals*. The comparative
method is based on a straightforward logic: similar objects are historically related. Apes, monkeys and humans have five digits because

those animals are historically related. The words *no*, *non*, and *nein* are similar because English, French and German share historical roots. By Tylor's time the comparative method had produced major advances in different fields. The method was evident in Georges Cuvier's (1769–1832) comparative zoology and in the major advances in comparative linguistics, particularly the discovery of a proto-Indo-European language reconstructed from linguistic fragments found in Sanskrit (Hoeningswald 1963).

The comparative method forms the basis of a history of origins. Tylor presents his version of the comparative method as a natural history of human culture: "A first step in the study of civilization is to dissect it into details, and to classify these in their proper groups" (Tylor 1958 [1871]:7). For example, "myths" may be classified into myths about the sun, myths about eclipses or earthquakes, myths about the names of places, myths about the establishment of a tribe, and so on. Each of these, he argues, is a species of the genus "myth," and ethnography becomes natural history. Tylor states, "the ethnographer's business is to classify such details with a view of making out their distribution in geography and history, and the relations which exist among them" (Tylor 1958 [1871]:8).

Temporal and spatial distributions of cultural traits may reflect different processes. Some patterns could result from contacts between different cultures and the diffusion of cultural traits. Other patterns could represent parallel resolution of similar problems of existence: fishnets are similar worldwide because there are only certain ways you can catch fish. But also patterns could be reflections of earlier stages of human culture, traits which Tylor named "survivals."

For example, throughout the United States you see signs like "Ye Olde Steak House," or "Ye Olde Coffee Shoppe" or—my personal favorite—"Ye Olde Pizza Parlor." Most Americans will pronouce the word as "yee" and recognize it as an archaic English word, but not know that "Y" was a symbol for the "th" sound and, thus, that "Ye" is simply "The." The symbol has survived, although its meaning is not really understood. "Ye" is a survival.

Tylor (1958 [1871]:16) defines survivals as "processes, customs, opinions, and so forth, which have been carried by force of habit into a new state of society different from that in which they had their original home and they remain as proofs and examples of an older condition of culture out of which a newer has been evolved."

We say "God bless you" when someone sneezes because it is a survival, not because we still believe the soul is leaving the body. We celebrate Halloween because it is a survival, not because we are placating the wild spirits on the night before All Souls' Day. We shake hands as a form of greeting because it is a custom, not to show that we are unarmed. We frequently use words, gestures, sayings, and practices whose original meanings have been lost but in our daily encounters nonetheless survive.

Survivals, Tylor argues, are not merely quaint customs, but are the vestiges of previous culture. "Children's sports, popular sayings, absurd customs, may be practically unimportant, but are not philosophically insignificant bearing as they do on one of the most instructive phases of early culture" (Tylor 1958 [1871]:111). Such "relics of primitive barbarism" allow the ethnographer to reconstruct earlier cultural patterns and ultimately define the evolution of culture.

Human history, Tylor believed, was characterized by progress. In technology, the development of firearms showed a clear progression from matchlock to wheel lock to flintlock to percussion cap to automatic weapon. The order of technological change is obvious: one innovation leads to another. The crossbow is clearly derived from the longbow, and no one would doubt the relationship even without a written record (Tylor 1958 [1871]:15). Similarly, other dimensions of culture can be seen as having a progressive relationship, demonstrating "that the main tendency from primaeval up to modern times has been from savagery towards civilization" (Tylor 1958 [1871]:21).

At this point Tylor pursues a tenuous line of logic: just as specific cultural traits may be vestigial survivals of an earlier culture, *entire societies* may reflect earlier stages of human evolution. A society which in the late-19th century used stone tools was not simply a society without metal tools, but literally a vestige of prehistory, a "Stone Age" culture. The study of extant "primitive" societies is the investigation of "primaeval monuments of barbaric thought and life" leading to a reconstruction of the stages of evolution through which humans—at least some humans—have progressed.

At this point Tylor's cautious argument swerves into essentially unreflective assumption and prejudice. Civilization, Tylor writes,

> may be looked upon as the general improvement of mankind by higher organization of the individual and society, to the end of promoting at once man's goodness, power and happiness. This theoretical civilization does in no small measure correspond with actual civilization, as traced by comparing savagery with barbarism, and barbarism with modern educated life. So far as we take into account only material and intellectual culture, this is especially true. Acquaintance

with the physical laws of the world, and the accompanying power of adapting nature to man's own ends, are, on the whole, lowest among savages, mean among barbarians, and highest among modern educated nations. [1958 (1871):27]

Not surprisingly, Tylor's "physical laws" are the principles of Western science; alternative epistemologies are merely error-filled remnants of prescientific barbarism. Based on a society's mastery of "material and intellectual culture," one can assign a relative rank on an evolutionary scale:

> Thus, on the definite basis of compared facts, ethnographers are able to set up at least a rough scale of civilization. Few would dispute that the following races are arranged rightly in order of culture:—Australian, Tahitian, Aztec, Chinese, Italian. [1958 (1871):27]

Obviously many people would dispute this order, particularly Australians, Tahitians, Aztecs and Chinese. How can any ranking of societies be untainted by prejudice? The convulsions of the 20th century make it difficult to assume that "modern educated nations" successfully promote humanity's goodness, power, and happiness. Most modern readers stumble on the very ideas that Tylor took for granted.

Perhaps less obvious is the problem in considering entire societies as evolutionary survivals of earlier stages of human progress. The concept of a "survival" suggests that a cultural practice—"Ye" or "Gesundheit"—has been carried unchanged from the past into the present, and we can cite examples of such "survivals." But it is another matter to hold that an entire human group has been static, a fossilized representative of an earlier cultural stage. Tylor had no reason to think that the histories of the Australians or Tahitians were either brief or static and no basis to assume that such societies reflected earlier forms of human culture rather than just different, contemporary patterns. Simply, this was justified by Tylor's assumption of human progress.

Progress and *Anthropology*

Progress is the backbone of Tylor's *Anthropology* (1881), the first textbook on the subject. Written for a popular audience, Tylor deletes most of the references to nonevolutionary processes in this book, focusing instead on the developmental issues of "how mankind came to be as they are, and to live as they do" (1960 [1881]:1). He emphasizes the progress of cultural development: "History . . . shows arts, sciences, and political institutions beginning in ruder states, and becoming in the course of ages more intelligent, more systematic, more perfectly arranged or organized to answer their purposes" (1960 [1881]:11). In the balance of *Anthropology*, Tylor summarizes his discussions of language, technology and religion with a clarity and purpose rarely present in *Researches into the Early History of Mankind . . .* or *Primitive Culture*.

Tylor's evolution exhibits an uneven determinism. On the one hand, human history is framed by progress rather than degeneration, by transformation from the simple to complex, and by the trajectory from savagery to civilization. Progress, Tylor believed, did not end in the 19th century but was transformed from an unconscious tendency to a conscious tenet: "Acquainted with events and their consequences far and wide over the world, we are able to direct our own course with more confidence toward improvement" (1960 [1881]:275). Anthropology contributes to human progress; knowing the course of human history "from the remote past to the present, will not only help us to forecast the future, but may guide us in our duty of leaving the world better than we found it" (1960 [1881]:275). Tylor (1964 [1865]:539) writes "the science of culture is essentially a reformer's science." Perhaps Tylor's Quaker liberalism led him to embrace progress and reform (Stocking 1968).

Most of Tylor's adult life was spent in Oxford where he became Keeper of the University Museum in 1883. In 1884 Tylor was given a Readership in Anthropology and held that position until 1896 when he was named the first Professor of Anthropology. He lectured on the origins of human culture, myth and magic, and the distribution of cultural traits. After the publication of *Anthropology* Tylor spent his time teaching and developing academic institutions and anthropological associations rather than writing new works. But Tylor remained extremely influential on the development of British anthropology. He developed potential questions for researchers to ask in the field, he influenced scholars like James Frazer, A.C. Haddon, and W.R. Rivers, and gave numerous public lectures. *Primitive Culture* was reprinted ten times and was translated into Russian, German, French, and Polish during Tylor's lifetime.

Tylor retired from Oxford in 1909 as Professor Emeritus and his achievements were recognized by a knighthood in 1912. His final years were marked by decreasing mental clarity, and his friends lamented that Tylor never produced another work as great as *Primitive Culture* (Lang 1907; Stocking 1968).

Conclusion

Edward Burnett Tylor shaped the development of anthropology as a field of inquiry. Tylor's comparative method was emulated by many scholars and then fiercely attacked by Franz Boas and other American cultural anthropologists. Tylor's ideas about the origins of religion would lead others, like James Frazer, to investigate religions as systems of knowledge and Tylor's concept of animism would remain a key contribution in comparative studies of religion (Sharpe 1986:56–58).

But of his contributions, it was Tylor's definition of the concept of culture that is most enduring. By arguing for the nonbiological basis of social difference, Tylor stepped away from the racial explanations which characterized Western thought since the ancient Greeks (cf. Harris 1968:140–141). By outlining general principles of social life, Tylor gave new directions to comparative inquiry into human life. And finally, in defining the cultural dimension of human existence, Edward Tylor created anthropology, the study of humankind. ✦

Bibliography

Ackerman, Robert
1986 J.G. Frazer: His Life and Work. Cambridge: Cambridge University Press.

Evans-Prichard, Edward
1981 A History of Ethnological Thought. New York: Basic Books.

Fortes, Meyer
1969 Kinship and the Social Order: The Legacy of Lewis Henry Morgan. Chicago: Aldine Publishing Co.

Freire-Marreco, Barbara
1907 A Bibliography of Edward Burnett Tylor. In Anthropological Essays Presented to Edward Tylor in Honour of his 75th Birthday, October 2, 1907. W. Rivers, R. Marett, and N. Thomas, eds. Pp. 375–409. Oxford: Clarendon Press.

Haddon, A.C.
1910 A History of Anthropology. New York: G. P. Putnam's Sons.

Lang, Andrew
1907 Edward Burnett Tylor. In Anthropological Essays Presented to Edward Tylor in Honour of his 75th Birthday, October 2, 1907. W. Rivers, R. Marett, and N. Thomas, eds. Pp. 1–15. Oxford: Clarendon Press.

Lowie, Robert
1938 The History of Ethnological Thought. New York: Holt, Rinehart & Winston.

Marrett, R.
1936 Tylor. New York: Wiley and Sons.

Sharpe, Eric
1986 Comparative Religions: A History. La Salle, Illinois: Open Court Press.

Stocking Jr., George W.
1963 Matthew Arnold, E.B. Tylor and the Uses of Invention. American Anthropologist 65:783–799.
1968 Edward Tylor. International Encyclopedia of the Social Sciences/vol. 16:170–177.
1987 Victorian Anthropology. New York: The Free Press.

Tylor, Edward
1861 Anahuac or Mexico and the Mexicans, Ancient and Modern. London: Longman, Green, Loingman and Roberts.
1964 Researches into the Early History of Mankind and the Development of Civilization. Chicago: University of Chicago Press. [Originally published 1865.]
1958 Primitive Culture. New York: Harper & Row, Publishers. [Originally published 1871.]
1960 Anthropology. Ann Arbor: University of Michigan Press. [Originally published 1881.]

Chapter 2

Lewis Henry Morgan

The Evolution of Society

It is commonly alleged that the Victorian evolutionists based their conclusions solely on library research, sheltered from the vagaries of anthropological fieldwork or the complexities of interacting with real people. Bronislaw Malinowski, who revolutionized anthropological fieldwork in the 20th century (see Chapter 10), characterized the 19th-century evolutionists as "satisfied in reaching a rigid, self-contained entity" uncomplicated by the messy facts of cultural life (Malinowski 1944:31). Lewis Henry Morgan was the great exception.

Drawn to ethnography by his personal and professional ties to the Seneca Nation, a tribe of the Iroquois League, Morgan made extensive visits among various Iroquois groups. His notebooks and journals indicate "an acute and resourceful observer" (White 1958:4). Morgan also studied Native American groups in Kansas and Nebraska (1859–1860), the upper Missouri (1862), and the American Southwest (1878)—trips that involved intensive, if not prolonged, fieldwork. Robert Lowie (1930:169–170), an anthropologist and expert on the Crow, remarked that Morgan's description of the Crow kinship system, though based on a brief trip, "was vastly superior to my own original attempt in this direction." Lowie admitted, "my error seems the less pardonable because the essential facts had already been grasped by Morgan." Combining field observations with extensive cross-cultural data, Lewis Henry Morgan produced masterful compilations of anthropological information.

So is there any truth to Malinowski's criticism? Perhaps—but in Morgan's case it is misplaced. It is not that Morgan was unconcerned with ethnographic data, but that Morgan analyzed those data within a single evolutionary framework. Morgan's evolutionary approach was attacked by Boas, Kroeber, and others, but it also influenced the materialist approaches of Karl Marx, Friedrich Engels, and Leslie White. For example, Engels' 1884 *Origins of Family, Private Property and the State* is subtitled "which is based on the Findings of L. H. Morgan in his *Ancient Society*." Charles Darwin considered Morgan to be America's most eminent social scientist, and even a strict anti-evolutionist like Lowie (1936:181) could admire Morgan as "not a flashy intellect, but one of unusual honesty, depth, and tenacity. . . ." His career, one biographer suggested, "is one of the strangest in American intellectual history" (Resek 1960:vii).

Background

Born in 1818, Morgan was raised on the frontier of western New York, and lived his life against the backdrop of manifest destiny, economic expansion and collapse, and American civil war. Trained as a lawyer, a Whig in personality and politics, an ardent supporter of the market and the Republic, it is hard to imagine a less likely contributor to Marxist theory than Lewis Henry Morgan.

Educated at Union College in Schenectady, Morgan embodied progress as an inevitable social process and as a personal code. Admitted to the bar in 1842 but unable to find legal work because of a lingering economic depression, Morgan occupied himself by penning lectures and articles on temperance, parallels between ancient Greece and mid-19th-century America, and other topics. In late 1844 Morgan opened a legal practice in Rochester, New York. Like many men of his time and class, Morgan joined a social club, the Order of the Gordian Knot, which originally drew on Greco-Roman themes. Yet gradually the association changed to emphasize uniquely American qualities and was renamed the Grand Order of the Iroquois, a change proposed by Morgan.

Morgan became consumed with the study of Iroquois culture, incorporating ethnographic facts into the protocols of the club. More serious activities soon followed. In the late 1840s, Morgan immersed himself in Iroquois studies. As he devoted more time to ethnology, Morgan's legal practice suffered, and Morgan decided to summarize his Iroquois research and then turn back to law. In six months, Morgan completed *League of the Ho-dé-no-sau-nee or Iroquois*.

The *League . . . of the Iroquois* summarized Morgan's studies about Iroquois religion, domestic architecture, government and social organization, material culture, language, and place names. Richly illustrated with figures and maps, the monograph presented detailed ethnographic data, such as word lists, place names, and plans; it remains an invaluable source of information. Morgan's work received generally, but not universally, positive reviews. The American explorer and ethnologist John Wesley Powell (1880:114) described it as "the first scientific account of an Indian tribe given to the world." In contrast, the historian Francis Parkman argued that Morgan overemphasized the uniqueness of the Iroquois regarding "as the peculiar distinction of the Iroquois, that which is in fact common to many other tribes" (cited in Resek 1960:44). Parkman's criticism had merit: at this point, Morgan's anthropological knowledge was profound, but provincial.

During the next decade, Morgan attended to law and business, developing a modest fortune based on mining, land, and railroad interests. But in the late 1850s Morgan returned to ethnology, and specifically to studies of Iroquois kinship and social organizations.

Morgan discussed Iroquois kinship in the *League . . . of the Iroquois*, but in 1857 he read an expanded paper on "Laws of Descent of the Iroquois" to the American Association for the Advancement of Science. The Iroquois kinship system surprised Morgan. For example, collateral kin were classified as lineal kin—the same terms are used for "Father" and "Father's Brother," for "Mother" and "Mother's Sister," and for siblings and parallel cousins. Descent among the Seneca was reckoned through the mother's line, and thus a child is a member of her/his mother's lineage, not father's. Morgan further observed that Iroquois political organization was an extension of kinship. "In fact," Morgan wrote, "their celebrated League was but an elaboration of these relationships into a complex, and even stupendous system of civil polity" (Morgan 1858:132).

In 1859 Morgan discovered that similar kinship systems were used by the Ojibwa of upper Michigan and possibly among the Dakota and Creek (White 1960:6–7). This led Morgan to a new approach to ethnographic data. Rather than solely document the folklore and nobility of the Iroquois, Morgan began to explore the relationships between different societies as reflected in shared systems of kinship. Morgan's greatest discovery, as anthropologist Leslie White (1957:257) put it, was "the fact that customs of designating relatives have scientific significance." That discovery was documented in Morgan's magnum opus, *Systems of Consanguinity and Affinity of the Human Family*.

Kinship and Evolution

Morgan began a global inquiry about kinship systems. Supported by the Smithsonian Institution and the State Department, Morgan sent a printed questionnaire requesting information about kinship terms to consular officials, missionaries, and scientists around the world. This cross-cultural survey combined with Morgan's own field research resulted in kinship data from 139 different groups in North America, Asia, Oceania, and ancient and modern Europe. (Africa, South America, and Australia remained essentially unknown.)

Morgan's goal was to trace the connections between systems of kinship and to explore their "progressive changes" as man developed through "the ages of barbarism" (Morgan 1871:vi). At this point, Morgan had not outlined the evolutionary scheme that forms the explanatory structure of his *Ancient Society*. Rather, Morgan approached kinship systems as if they were languages and models his analysis on the comparative method (see pp. 22–23). Just as scholars had demonstrated the development and historical relationships between different language families based on linguistic similarities, Morgan argued that, "In the systems of relationship of the great families of mankind some of the oldest memorials of human thought and experience are deposited and preserved" (Morgan 1871:vi).

Morgan argued that all kinship systems could be divided into two large groups—descriptive systems and classificatory systems. Descriptive systems—like that used in English—keep lineal relatives distinct from collateral kin; "Father" and "Father's Brother" are *not* given the same term. In descriptive systems there are fewer special kin terms and these terms are applied to kin who are relatively close to the speaker, referred to as "Ego" (Morgan 1871:468–469).

In contrast, classificatory systems treat lineal and collateral kin as if they were the same, distinguishing generation (Ego's Father vs. Ego's Father's Father) and gender (Ego's male cousins vs. Ego's female cousins), but using the same term for "Father" and "Father's Brother," for "Mother" and "Mother's Sister," etc., similar to the pattern Morgan first identified among the Iroquois.

In his survey, Morgan identified six families of kinship systems, three descriptive ones (Semitic, Aryan, and Uralian) and three classificatory ones (Malayan, Turanian, and Ganowanian). *Semitic* kin systems were found among Arabs, Hebrews and Armenians; *Aryan* systems were used by speakers of Persian, Sanskrit and all the European language groups, modern and ancient; whereas *Uralian* kin systems were found among Turk, Magyar, Finn and Estonian populations. Of the classificatory systems, *Ganowanian* was a term Morgan invented (after the Seneca words for "bow and arrow"!) to cover all native North Americans; *Turanian* included Chinese, Japanese, Hindu and other groups of the Indian subcontinent; while *Malayan* subsumed Hawaiians, Maoris and all the other Oceanic groups in the sample.

These six families of kinship systems may be divided, Morgan wrote

> . . . into two great divisions. Upon one side are the Aryan, Semitic, and Uralian, and upon the other the Ganowanian, the Turanian, and Malayan, *which gives nearly the line of demarcation between civilized and uncivilized nations* (emphasis added). [Morgan 1871:469]

This is a startling conclusion: the difference between classificatory and descriptive kinship systems marks the distinction between uncivilized and civilized. How could Morgan conclude this? How could he link differences in kinship systems to the levels of cultural advancement?

Morgan's logic was subtle, but flawed. First, Morgan argued that kinship systems were based on "natural suggestions," primitive ruminations "which arise spontaneously in the mind with the exercise of normal intelligence" (Morgan 1871:472), a point similar to Tylor's emphasis on the mental construction of culture (see pp. 20–22). Descriptive systems were natural inferences about descent when marriage was based on monogamy. Kinfolk, Morgan argued, would attempt to explain their relationships by referring to a series of married ancestors (Morgan 1871:472). Like Tylor, Morgan viewed culture as rationalizations about reality made by "savage philosophers," rationales which could be reconstructed by the ethnographer.

But then how do classificatory systems develop? Classificatory systems, Morgan argued, are also inferences from social relationships, but those where marriage is either polygamous, communal, or promiscuous. For example, Morgan discussed the Hawaiian kin classification in which Ego uses the same kin term for "Father," "Father's Brother," and "Mother's Brother" and another term for "Mother," "Mother's Sister," and "Father's Sister." Morgan interpreted Hawaiian kinship as reflecting

> promiscuous intercourse within prescribed limits. The existence of this custom necessarily implies an antecedent condition of promiscuous intercourse, involving the cohabitation of brothers and sisters, and perhaps of parents and child; thus finding mankind in a condition akin to that of the inferior animals, and more intensely barbarous

than we have been accustomed to regard as a possible state of man.
[Morgan 1970:481]

The classification systems are reasonable inferences based on promiscuous sex and indeterminate parentage (Morgan 1871:482–483). (I refer
to my brothers' children as my children because I have intercourse
with my brothers' wives, and how can I tell whose kid is whose? We're
just one big happy family.)

Morgan inferred different social relations from distinct kinship systems, and then arranged them on a continuum from "most primitive"
to "most civilized," from promiscuous intercourse to monogamy. But
given the "natural stability of domestic institutions" (Morgan
1871:15), why would one system give rise to another? Why would classificatory systems evolve into descriptive ones? Why would kinship
ever change?

Morgan offers a mix of explanations, each envisioning the "reform"
of a previous state of society. When communal husbands defend their
communal wives from other men, promiscuous society is partially
"reformed." This begins a process which ultimately leads to "the family
as it now exists" (Morgan 1871:481), i.e., the independent nuclear family based on monogamous marriage.

But the real change follows the invention of private property; at
this point, Morgan dramatically expands the implications of his study.

> There is one powerful motive which might under certain circum-
> stances tend to the overthrow of the classificatory form and the sub-
> stitution of the descriptive, but it would arise after the attainment of
> civilization. This is the inheritance of estates. [And] Hence the growth
> of property and the settlement of its distribution might be expected
> to lead to a more precise discrimination of consanguinity. . . . [Mor-
> gan 1871:14]

With the "rise of property, . . . the settlement of its rights, and above
all, with the established certainty of its transmission to lineal descendants . . ." descriptive kin systems evolve and the nuclear family eventually develops. The family "became organized and individualized by
property rights and privileges" (Morgan 1871:492). Social structure and
economy are thus linked.

The British social anthropologist Meyer Fortes (1969:32) has written
of Morgan's "combination of insight and confusion," arguing that Morgan's appeal to the role of private property was "pure guesswork—a projection of his private values as an American of his day in a society
undergoing rapid economic expansion." Rife with assumption and reliant

on conjectural history, Morgan had no evidence that Hawaiian kin terms were remnants of a promiscuous horde or that "barbarous nations" were ignorant of inherited property (Morgan 1871:492).

Yet, Morgan was among the first to explore the importance of kin systems and their relationship to other aspects of human life, such as economy and politics. What began as a method for understanding the historical connections between societies was transformed into a scheme for understanding the development of all human society, the framework he elaborated in *Ancient Society*.

Ancient Society

The central tenets of Morgan's classic are stated in the opening paragraph:

> The latest investigations respecting the early condition of the human race are tending to the conclusion that mankind commenced their career at the bottom of the scale and worked their way up from savagery to civilization through the slow accumulation of experimental knowledge.

> As it is undeniable that portions of the human family have existed in a state of savagery, other portions in a state of barbarism, and still other portions in a state of civilization, it seems equally so that these three distinct conditions are connected with each other in a natural as well as necessary sequence of progress. [Morgan 1877:3]

Thus the different portions of humanity—whether in Asia, Europe, Africa, Australia or the Americas—represented different points along a common line of progress. "The history of the human race," Morgan (1877:vi) observed, "is one in source, one in experience, and one in progress." Savagery in one culture, barbarism in another, and civilization in a third were not the result of different races being genetically condemned to backwardness or development; they were simply societies perched at different stages on a common progression of cultural evolution. Morgan writes:

> It may be remarked finally that the experience of mankind has run in nearly uniform channels; that human necessities in similar condition have been substantially the same; and that the operations of the mental principle have been uniform in virtue of the specific identity of the brain of all the races of mankind. [Morgan 1978:8]

For Morgan the terms "savagery," "barbarism" and "civilization" represented well-defined stages of progress measured by four sets of cultural achievements: 1) inventions and discoveries, 2) the idea of government, 3) the organization of the family, and 4) the concept of property. The lines of progress were clearest in the field of inventions and discoveries because certain inventions necessarily preceded others (fire before pottery, hunting before pastoralism). Therefore Morgan chose technological developments as the primary but not sole "test of progress" marking the different stages of cultural evolution.

Morgan divided the earliest stage or "ethnical period" into *Lower Status of Savagery* which began with the earliest humans and ended with knowledge of fire and fishing, *Middle Status of Savagery* which began with fire and fishing and lasted until the invention of the bow and arrow, and *Upper Status of Savagery* which began with the bow and arrow but ended with the development of pottery.

The invention of pottery marked the divide between Savagery and Barbarism. *Lower Status of Barbarism* began with pottery and ended with the domestication of animals in the Old World and the irrigated agriculture and substantial architecture in the New World. Those developments marked the *Middle Status of Barbarism,* which lasted until the invention of smelting iron ore. The *Upper Status of Barbarism* began with iron smelting and continued until the development of a phonetic alphabet which marks the development of *Civilization*, a stage which continues, without additional subdivisions, to this day.

Morgan argued that the "successive arts of subsistence" were the foundation on which "human supremacy on the earth depended," suggesting that "the great epochs of human progress have been identified, more or less directly, with the enlargement of the sources of subsistence" (Morgan 1877:19). This materialist basis of cultural evolution has been considered Morgan's principal legacy by subsequent evolutionists like Marx, Engels, Leslie White (Chapter 13), Marvin Harris (Chapter 15), and Eleanor Leacock (Chapter 16). And yet, *Ancient Society* is not a coherently materialist theory, since it incorporates mentalistic explanations for changes in other arenas such as government, family, and property (see Service 1985:48–53).

Morgan's discussion of "Growth of the Idea of Government" comprises 60 percent of *Ancient Society*. By "government" Morgan referred to what modern anthropologists call social organization *and* political organization. Morgan explicitly distinguished social order based on kin ties (*societas*) from social order based on political ties (*civitas*):

The experience of mankind . . . has developed but two plans of government, using plan in its scientific sense. Both were definite and systematic organizations of society. The first and most ancient was social organization, founded upon gentes, phratries and tribes. The second and latest in time was a political organization founded upon territory and upon property. Under the first a gentile society was created, in which the government dealt with persons through their relation to a gens and tribe. These relations were purely personal. Under the second a political society was created, in which the government dealt with persons through their relations to territory, e.g. the township, the county, and the state. These relations were purely territorial. The two plans were fundamentally different. One belongs to ancient society, the other to modern. [Morgan 1877:62]

Morgan briefly describes the organization of society based on sex, reprising his reconstruction of the communal and brother-sister families, then proceeds to his principal concern, the nature of the gens or, in modern anthropological terms, the lineage. In Morgan's terms the gens is a named social group of consanguineal kin (i.e. kin related by "blood," not marriage) descended from a common ancestor (Morgan 1877:63).

Whether matrilineal or patrilineal, the gens was the "fundamental basis of ancient society" found in cultures around the world and spanning the ethnical periods from Savagery to Civilization (Morgan 1877:64). When bound together into groups of two or more gens—which Morgan called "phratries," but today are known as "clans"—such kin-based social institutions provided the structure for the distribution of rights, property, and political offices. When a group of gens or phratries also had a single name for the entire group, spoke a single dialect, had a supreme government and an identified territory, then social order had reached the level of the tribe (Morgan 1877:102–103). In turn, when tribes coalesced into a single entity, a nation existed. Thus, Morgan argued that government evolved from promiscuous horde to brother-sister group families, from group families to gens, and then progressively through stages of phratry, tribe, and nation.

Morgan's scheme for the evolution of the family is largely derived from his discussions in *Systems of Consanguinity and Affinity of the Human Family*, but his treatment of property is more developed in *Ancient Society*. Arguing that the growth of property would "keep pace with the progress of inventions and discoveries" and that the possession and inheritance of property was regulated by progressive forms of social organization, Morgan directly linked concepts of property with technological and social evolution (Morgan 1877:525–526). During the stage of Savagery, property was minimal and not inherited since it was buried as grave goods when the owner died. In the Lower Status of Barbarism, property increased in quantity but was distributed among the gens on a member's death without specific inheritance by spouses (Morgan 1877:530–531). By the Middle Status of Barbarism and with the development of agriculture, property increased in quantity and variety. New relationships developed between people and land, different forms of communal land ownership with individual rights to farm and use but not to sell (Morgan 1877:535–536). By the end of the Upper Status of Barbarism, two forms of land tenure evolved, state ownership and individual ownership, which became well-established by the ethnical period of Civilization (Morgan 1877:552).

But how did Morgan determine the relationship between ethnical periods, essentially defined by technological inventions, and forms of government and property? Basically in two ways. First, he proposed a plausible, but conjectural history, arguing that different forms of social organization or of property were necessarily based on earlier, simpler forms in the same way that metallurgy presumed the prior invention of fire.

Second, Morgan assumed that primitive societies were representative of earlier stages of social evolution, producing a relative ordering of social and property forms. With the exception of the Lower Status of Savagery, for which "No exemplification of tribes of mankind in this condition remained to the historical period," primitive, non-Western societies represented the stages in cultural evolution, a point Tylor also made (see pp. 22–26) and that was later echoed by the French social theorist, Emile Durkheim (see Chapter 4). Morgan held that:

> the domestic institutions of the barbarous, and even of the savage ancestors of mankind, are still exemplified in portions of the human family with such completeness that, with the exception of the strictly primitive period [i.e. Lower Savagery], the several stages of this progress are tolerably well preserved. They are seen in the organization of society upon the basis of sex, then upon the basis of kin, and finally upon the basis of territory; through the successive forms of marriage and of the family with the systems of consanguinity thereby created; and through house life and architecture; and through progress in usages with respect to the ownership and inheritance of property. [Morgan 1978:7]

Thus, an ethnographic study of the Australian aborigines or the Iroquois or ancient Romans was not a study of different cultures, but of representatives of specific stages of cultural evolution. Civilized nations had progressed through similar stages, and profited by the "heroic exertions and the patient toil" of barbarian and savage ancestors, which was "part of the plan of the Supreme Intelligence to develop a barbarian out of a savage, and a civilized man out of this barbarian" (Morgan 1877:554).

Conclusion

In many ways *Ancient Society* was Morgan's most important work and least convincing; it was influential and enraging. As noted above, Morgan's statements about the relationships between property relationships and social order were developed by Engels, and through Engel's work Morgan's ideas were spread world-wide. In response, Franz Boas would mount a severe critique of Morgan's and Tylor's "comparative method," attacking the idea that humanity had passed through unilineal, progressive stages (see pp. 48–49).

In the 1940s Morgan's emphasis on the technological realm was recast by Leslie White (see Chapter 13) into a theory of cultural evolution; in fact, Morgan never seemed certain that "the arts of subsistence" were the causal determinants that White proposed, nor does White's work contain the mentalist elements found throughout *Ancient Society* suggesting that cultural developments were produced by individual will and rational choice (Colson 1974:10–11).

Though not without flaws, Morgan's contributions to anthropology remain essential and permanent. First, Morgan outlined the importance of the study of kinship systems, recognizing the significance of classificatory systems, the role of lineal descent groups in social organization, and the complementary patterns of kin-based political orders and those based on non-kin relationships. Second, Morgan conducted research that attempted to be systematic and global, anticipating by a century large-scale cross-cultural studies like the Human Relations Area Files. And finally, Morgan attempted to organize anthropological data in terms of an explicit framework of cultural evolution rather than simply treat cultural differences as ethnographic curios.

Lewis Henry Morgan died on December 17, 1881; he was 63 years old. His long-time friend, the Reverend Joshua McIlvaine (to whom *Systems of Consanguinity and Affinity of the Human Family* is dedicated), delivered the benediction, but only after first presenting an analysis of the classificatory kinship system. It was a fitting tribute to Morgan's lifework, a body of work in which his confidence in reason's ability to discover the laws of nature is present on every page. ✦

Bibliography

Colson, Elizabeth
1974 Tradition and Contract: The Problem of Order. Chicago: Aldine Publishing Co.

Fortes, Meyer
1969 Kinship and the Social Order: The Legacy of Lewis Henry Morgan. Chicago: Aldine Publishing Co.

Lowie, Robert
1936 Lewis H. Morgan in Historical Perspective. *In* Essays in Anthropology Presented to A. L. Kroeber in Celebration of His Sixtieth Birthday. R. Lowie, ed. Pp. 169–181. Berkeley: University of California Press.

Malinowski, Bronislaw
1944 A Scientific Theory of Culture and Other Essays. Chapel Hill: University of North Carolina Press.

Morgan, Lewis H.
1858 Laws of Descent Among the Iroquois. Proceedings of the American Association for the Advancement of Science for August 1857 11:132–148. Cambridge, MA.
1901 League of the Ho-dé-no-sau-nee or Iroquois. Edited and annotated by H. Lloyd. New York: Dodd, Mead & Co. [Originally published 1851; facsimile reprint 1966. New York: Burt Franklin.]
1871 Systems of Consanguinity and Affinity of the Human Family. Smithsonian Contributions to Knowledge, Vol. XVII. Washington, D.C. [Facsimile reprint 1970. Oosterhout N.B., The Netherlands: Anthropological Publications.]
1877 Ancient Society or Researches in the Lines of Human Progress from Savagery, through Barbarism to Civilization. New York: Henry Holt and Company. [Facsimile reprint 1978. Palo Alto: New York Labor News.]
1959 The Indian Journals, 1859–1862. Edited and with an introduction by Leslie White. Ann Arbor: The University of Michigan Press.
1965 Houses and House-Life of the American Aborigines. Chicago: University of Chicago Press. [Originally published in Contributions to North American Ethnology 4, Washington, DC, 1881.]

Powell, John Wesley
1880 Sketch of Lewis Henry Morgan. Popular Science Monthly 18:114–121.

Resek, Carl
1960 Lewis Henry Morgan: American Scholar. Chicago: University of Chicago Press.

Service, Elman
1985 A Century of Controversy: Ethnological Issues from 1860 to 1960. New
York: Academic Press.

White, Leslie
1937 Extracts from the European Travel Journal of Lewis H. Morgan. Rochester
Historical Society Publications XVI:221–390.
1942 Lewis H. Morgan's Journal of A Trip to Southwestern Colorado and New
Mexico, 1878. American Antiquity 8:1–26.
1944 Morgan's Attitude Toward Religion and Science. American Anthropologist 46:218–230.
1951 Lewis H. Morgan's Western Field Trips. American Anthropologist 53:11–18.
1957 How Morgan Came to Write Systems of Consanguinity and Affinity.
Papers of the Michigan Academy of Science, Arts, and Lettters XLII.
1959 Lewis Henry Morgan: His Life and Researches. In The Indian Journals,
1859–1862. L. White, ed. Pp. 3–12. Ann Arbor: The University of Michigan Press.

Chapter 3

Franz Boas
Culture in Context

Franz Boas (1858–1942) shaped the direction of 20th-century American anthropology. His former student, Alfred Kroeber, wrote only months after Boas' death that "the world lost its greatest anthropologist and America one of its most colorful intellectual figures" (1943:5). Echoing this assessment thirty years later, George Stocking Jr. (1974:1) wrote, "there is no real question that [Boas] was the most important single force in shaping American anthropology in the first half of the 20th century."

Boas' influence was institutional, intellectual, and personal. Like Tylor and Durkheim, Boas played a pivotal role in moving anthropology into academia, in establishing associations and journals, and by creating essential networks of institutional support from the public, policy makers, and other scientists.

Boas defined the principal fields of inquiry that American anthropologists would pursue. His wide interests—spanning from biological anthropology to linguistics—gave American anthropology a topical breadth which is not really present in Great Britain or France, where anthropology is pre-eminently social anthropology, and archaeology and biological anthropology are separate fields. The fact that American anthropology has included socio-cultural anthropology, linguistics, physical anthropology, and archaeology—the so-called four fields approach—is partly a reflection of Boas' broad interests.

Boas created an anthropology very different from those of Morgan, Tylor, or Durkheim. Rather than assuming that cultural practices were explicable only in reference to broad evolutionary stages, Boas argued that they were understandable only in specific cultural contexts.

For example, Boas and the anthropologist O.T. Mason engaged in a spirited debate about the organization of ethnographic materials in museum displays: it is an unlikely subject for a fierce debate, but it produced an illuminating exchange. Mason, an evolutionist, proposed organizing ethnographic displays in the Smithsonian Institution by artifact classes—pottery, stone tools, musical instruments—regardless of their place of origin, displaying what Mason called "similarities in the products of industry." Mason wanted to illustrate the evolutionary parallels in human nature, arguing that cultural products stemmed from similar, universal causes.

Boas' response was quick and telling. Boas contended that cultural traits first must be explained in terms of specific cultural contexts rather than by broad reference to general evolutionary trends. "In the collections of the national museum," Boas (1887:486) wrote, "the marked character of the North-West American tribes is almost lost, because the objects are scattered in different parts of the building and are exhibited among those from other tribes." Instead of being presented in technological "stages," ethnographic collections should be "arranged according to tribes, in order to teach the peculiar style of each group. The art and characteristic style of a people can be understood only by studying its productions as a whole."

Over the next decade, Boas expanded this critique into a larger-scale attack on the theories of Morgan, Tylor, and other evolutionists. Boas' basic approach—culture was to be understood from detailed studies of specific cultures—was passed onto the first cohort of professional American anthropologists, individuals who would literally shape the field of anthropological inquiry: Alfred Kroeber (Chapter 5), Ruth Benedict (Chapter 6), Edward Sapir (Chapter 7), Margaret Mead (Chapter 8), and many others. In turn, Boas' students, as anthropologist Marvin Harris (1968:251) writes, "set forth the main lines of development of anthropological research and instruction at crucial institutions around the country." Thus Boas' personal contacts with his students extended his intellectual influence and shaped the institutions of American anthropology.

And yet, as Kroeber (1943:24) noted, ". . . It has long been notoriously difficult to convey the essence of Boas' contribution in anthropology to non-anthropologists" (a task at which Kroeber also failed). This difficulty, and the fact that Boas played a pivotal role in the establishment of American anthropology, make even a brief explanation of Boas' contribution of essential value.

Background

The founder of American anthropology was born in northwestern Germany into a prosperous Jewish family that was committed to progressive education and politics. He wrote that he was raised "in a German home in which the ideals of the Revolution of 1848 were a living force," referring to the European revolutions that fought for universal suffrage, freedoms of press and assembly, and other liberal democratic reforms—revolts ultimately repressed by the military and monarchy. Of his parents' Judaism Boas (1939:19) wrote, "My father had retained an emotional affection for the ceremonial of his parental home, without allowing it to influence his intellectual freedom," and concluded, "my parents had broken through the shackles of dogma." By his own account, these influences shaped Boas' anthropology and his social activism.

Boas was educated in his hometown and then went off to study physics, mathematics, and geography in a string of universities. "My university studies were a compromise," Boas (1939:20) recalled, between an "emotional interest in the phenomena of the world," which led to geography, and an "intellectual interest" in the formal analyses of mathematics and physics. His doctoral dissertation was on the color of water, a topic emphasizing physics over geography; he received his doctorate in 1881 at the age of 23. Kroeber contended that Boas' education "as a physicist heavily determined his whole intellectual career," creating his "gifts for dealing with abstract form or structure and of intellectual precision and rigor" (Kroeber 1943:7).

After a year of military service, Boas was at loose ends; he wanted to study human societies, but lacked financial support. After a string of setbacks, in June 1883 Boas joined a German expedition to the Arctic to pursue research on the Inuit in order "to discover how far one can get, by studying a very special and not simple case, in determining the relationship between the life of a people and environment" (Boas 1974 [1882]:44). Supported by writing freelance articles for a Berlin newspaper, Boas spent a year on Baffin Island in Canada's Northwest Territories. Traveling by dog-sled during the Arctic winter in -50 degree temperatures, Boas charted the Baffinland coastline, collected Inuit legends, and observed rites and ceremonies. Ultimately, Boas was unsatisfied with his ethnographic research, calling it "shallow" and a "disappointment"; nevertheless, he recognized that the year in the Arctic "had a profound influence upon the development of my views . . . because it led me away from my former interests and toward the desire to understand what determines the behavior of human beings" (Boas 1939:20–21).

Boas returned from the Arctic to uncertain prospects, unsuccessfully applying for jobs and fellowships in the United States, then working in Germany for 18 months before returning to America. In the fall of 1886 he worked for the Canadian Geological Survey in southern British Columbia conducting a brief ethnographic survey in the vicinity of Vancouver Island (Rohner and Rohner 1969). Returning to New York in 1887, Boas accepted a job as assistant editor of *Science*, and with some financial security, married and became an American citizen.

From his position at *Science* Boas extended his influence almost immediately. In 1888 the British Association for the Advancement of Science asked Boas to collect ethnographic data on the Northwest Coast. After a successful trip, the BAAS supported a second field trip to the Northwest Coast in 1889 in which Boas studied native languages, made anthropometric measurements, and investigated social organizations of the Kwakiutl and Tsimshian (Boas 1974a [1898]). In 1889 Boas obtained a teaching position at the newly founded Clark University in Worcester, Massachusetts, where the first American Ph.D. in anthropology was granted under his leadership in 1892 (Kroeber 1943:12). In 1892 financial turmoil at Clark University led to a massive faculty resignation. Boas also left to join the anthropological staff at the Chicago World Columbian Exposition who were working on displaying Native American materials. A short-term position at the newly established Field Museum of Natural History in Chicago was followed by part-time work for the Smithsonian, another field trip to the Northwest Coast sponsored by the British Association, and unfulfilled hopes of a position at the American Museum of Natural History in New York. This professional turmoil was deepened by the death of his child (Hyatt 1990:33).

It was a dark and difficult time. Boas' letters from the field oscillate from quick descriptions of research accomplished to depressed accounts of financial insecurities, underscored by a deep longing for his wife and surviving children.

But in 1895 things began to change. John Wesley Powell offered Boas an editorial position at the Smithsonian's Bureau of American Ethnology, which galvanized the American Museum of Natural History into making a counter-proposal that Boas accepted. Appointed to the AMNH in December 1895, Boas finally obtained a permanent position. "No longer concerned with economic survival," Hyatt (1990:35) writes, "he began to concentrate on the science of anthropology and its many applications."

From his base in New York, Boas began to influence American anthropology. In May 1896 he was hired as lecturer in physical anthropology at Columbia College and was appointed professor in 1899. He maintained his position at the American Museum of Natural History throughout this period and became Curator of Anthropology in 1901, weaving close ties between the AMNH and Columbia. Boas seized his opportunity with extraordinary energy and expertise. Harris (1968:252), a prolific scholar in his own right (see Chapter 15), writes:

> Boas' accomplishments as a teacher, administrator, researcher, founder and president of societies, editor, lecturer, and traveler are exhausting to behold. To anyone who has ever worried about publishing or perishing, the fact that all this activity was accompanied by the publication of a torrent of books and articles is well nigh terrifying.

From 1895 till his death in 1942, Boas' resume becomes a blur of publications and accomplishments, almost as if he wanted to compensate for the frustrations of his early career. Boas became full professor at Columbia University in 1899 and was elected to the National Academy of Sciences in 1900. He helped establish the American Anthropological Association and revived the journal *American Anthropologist*. Boas founded the *International Journal of American Linguistics* in 1917, which continues to be published; helped establish an archaeological field school in Mexico; presided over a series of field research projects, particularly in the Northwest Coast, while continuing to publish constantly.

Boas authored six books and more than 700 articles; his bibliography records his diverse research (Andrews 1943). Most numerous are his articles and reports on his investigations in the Arctic and Northwest Coast; Boas' publications on the Kwakiutl, Tsimshian and other Northwest Coast societies total over 10,000 printed pages (Codere 1959). Boas made major contributions in the study of language. For four decades Boas taught two seminars at Columbia University: one on statistical methods, the other on North American Indian languages. Boas published extensively on Northwest Coast Indian languages and established a research agenda for recording Native American languages (Boas 1966c).

Third, Boas' work in anthropometry was a major field of endeavor with significant implications for public policy. In Boas' time, race was considered a fixed biological category; individual races were thought to have specific properties—physical, mental, and cultural. Many formal studies defined racial variation based on cranial measurements rather than "obvious" characteristics like skin color. Skull form, it was thought, was a more stable property and thus a better basis for defining racial categories, yet the stability of cranial form had been assumed, never demonstrated. In 1911 Boas published the results of a massive study of the head form of 17,821 immigrants and conducted sophisticated statistical analyses of the data (remember, this was done without computers). Boas showed that cranial form was anything but stable, with significant differences between immigrant parents and their American-born children (Boas 1966a). Boas demonstrated that traits thought to be fixed, genetically inherited traits were actually modified by environment. And if such a stable racial trait as cranial form was influenced by environment, then *all* other racial classifications and characterizations became suspect.

In 1931 Boas gave his presidential address, entitled "Race and Progress," to the American Association for the Advancement of Science (1966b). Boas summarized four decades of research, applying it to America's most cancerous social problem, racism. Throughout his career, Boas attacked racist pseudoscientific studies linking race and intelligence. Arguing that variations among individuals were greater than those between races, Boas concluded that "biological differences between races are small. There is no reason to believe that one race is by nature so much more intelligent, endowed with great will power, or emotionally more stable than another . . ." (1966b:13–14). Not only was Boas offended by bad science, but he drew on his personal experience of anti-Semitism; these factors produced an informed and fervent rejection of racism. Boas was involved in the establishment of the NAACP and wrote about race in popular magazines as well as in scientific journals (Hyatt 1990:83–99).

His 1931 speech was a central statement about a long battle against racism. Boas argued that because of intermarriage and mating there were no biologically "pure" races, and that, contrary to a then-common view, the "mixture" of races had no harmful consequences. Further, variations between individuals within races were greater than differences between races. Boas questioned the significance of IQ tests and discounted studies showing racial variations in intelligence. In addition to attacking the biological concept of race, he attacked the social concept. "Among us race antagonism is a fact," Boas stated. He then argued that America's great problem is a social stratification based on racial characteristics which lead to divisive conflict (Boas 1966b:13–15). Boas concluded his AAAS address with this essential challenge:

> As long as we insist on [socio-economic] stratification in racial layers, we shall pay the penalty in the form of interracial struggle. Will it be better for us to continue as we have been doing, or shall we try to recognize the conditions that lead to the fundamental antagonisms that trouble us? [1966b:17]

Boas continued to speak out against racism and by 1933 he was an early critic of Nazism. Boas attacked their racist policies, argued that Hitler and his leading supporters should be confined to an insane asylum, and wrote anti-Nazi polemics that the Allied underground smuggled into Germany (Herskovits 1943:45–46). Boas was a committed, public intellectual. (For more detailed discussions of Boas' diverse accomplishments in academic and public life, see Herskovits 1953; Hyatt 1990; Spier 1959; and Stocking 1974.)

The Integration of Cultures

Like any developing scholar, Boas' opinions evolved over the course of his career, but his most consistently held position was that cultures were integrated wholes produced by specific historical processes rather than reflections of universal evolutionary stages. In his earliest works Boas wrote passages which could have been penned by Edward Tylor: "The frequent occurrence of similar phenomena in cultural areas that have no historical contact . . . shows that the human mind develops everywhere according to the same laws" (Boas 1966d [1888]:637). By the late 1890s, however, Boas had developed his critique of evolutionary frameworks and the comparative method. Boas argued that the comparative approaches of Morgan and Tylor were undercut by three flaws: 1) the assumption of unilineal evolution, 2) the notion of modern societies as evolutionary survivals, and 3) the classification of societies based on weak data and inappropriate criteria. These flaws were the targets of the Boasian attack.

Boas dismissed the evolutionary frameworks of Morgan, Tylor and others as untested and untestable. In his "The Methods of Ethnology" Boas summarizes the evolutionary position, which

> presupposes that the course of historical changes in the cultural life of mankind follows definite laws which are applicable everywhere, and which bring it about that cultural development, in its main lines, is the same among all races and all peoples. [And] *As soon as we admit*

that the hypothesis of a uniform evolution has to be proved before it can be accepted the whole structure loses its foundation. [Boas 1966f (1920):281; emphasis added]

Boas undercut the entire basis of 19th-century cultural evolution. We might agree with Tylor and Morgan that certain technological processes have an inherent evolutionary order—fire must precede pottery making, flintlocks were invented before automatic rifles—but there is no ethnographic evidence indicating that matrilineal kin systems preceded patrilineal kin systems or that religions based on animism developed before polytheistic religions. Boas argued that this unilineal ordering is a simple assumption; there is no proven historical relationship nor any way to prove such a relationship. Therefore, evolutionary frameworks were unproven assumptions imposed on the data, not theories derived from ethnographic data.

Further, Boas argued, the unilineal classification of different societies assumed that different societies with similar cultural patterns (e.g., they used Hawaiian kinship classifications [see p. 33] or the bow and arrow) were at similar evolutionary levels.

On the contrary, he believed that very similar cultural practices may arise from different causes. Anthropology's primary task, according to Boas, was to provide "a penetrating analysis of a unique culture describing its form, the dynamic reactions of the individual to the culture and of the culture to the individual" (Boas 1966g [1936]:310–311). Boas did not assume (as some of his students did) that general laws of human behavior did not exist, but rather that those laws could be derived only from an understanding of specific historical processes.

We agree that certain laws exist which govern the growth of human culture, and it is our endeavor to discover these laws. The object of our investigation is to find the processes by which certain stages of culture have developed. The customs and beliefs themselves are not the ultimate objects of research. We desire to learn the reasons why such customs and beliefs exist—in other words, we wish to discover the history of their development.

. . . A detailed study of customs in their bearings to the total culture of the tribe practicing them, and in connection with an investigation of their geographical distribution among neighboring tribes, affords us almost always a means of determining with considerable accuracy the historical causes that led to the formation of the customs in question and to the psychological processes that were at work in their development. The results of inquiries may be three-fold. They may reveal the environmental conditions which have created or modified elements; they may clear up psychological factors which are at work in shaping culture; or they may bring before our eyes the effects that historical connections have had upon the growth of the culture. [Boas 1966e (1896):276]

Thus Boas suggests that law-like generalizations can be based on adaptational, psychological, or historical factors, but only if documented by well-established ethnographic cases:

The comparative method and the historical method, if I may use these terms, have been struggling for supremacy for a long time, but we may hope that each will soon find its appropriate place and function. The historical method has reached a sounder basis by abandoning the misleading principle of assuming connection wherever similarities of culture are found. The comparative method, notwithstanding all that has been said and written in its praise, has been remarkably barren of definite results, and I believe it will not become fruitful until we renounce the vain endeavor to construct a uniform systematic history of the evolution of culture, and until we begin to make our comparisons on the broader and sounder basis which I venture to outline. Up to this time we have too much reveled in more or less ingenious vagaries. The solid work is still all before us. [Boas 1966e (1896):280]

Conclusion

Franz Boas argued that detailed studies of particular societies had to consider the entire range of cultural behavior, and thus the concepts of anthropological holism and cultural particularism became twin tenets of American anthropology. In later years Boas grew even more skeptical about the possibility of deriving cultural laws. Writing in 1932, Boas concludes:

Cultural phenomena are of such complexity that it seems to me doubtful whether valid cultural laws can be found. The causal conditions of cultural happenings lie always in the interaction between individual and society, and no classificatory study of societies will solve this problem. The morphological classification of societies may call to our attention some problems. It will not solve them. In every case it is reducible to the same source, the interaction between the individual and society. [1966b:257]

Unfortunately, Boas did not articulate the relationship between cultural elements and cultural wholes. Stocking poses the unresolved paradox:

> On the one hand, culture was simply an accidental accretion of individual elements. On the other, culture—despite Boas' renunciation of organic growth—was at the same time an integrated spiritual totality that somehow conditioned the form of its elements. [Stocking 1974:5–6]

Boas demolished the evolutionary framework, provided methodologies for the investigation of specific cultures and hinted at the relationship between individuals and society, cultural elements and cultural wholes—but never really answered *how* cultures become integrated wholes.

Due to Boas' enormous influence on the practice of anthropology in America, anthropological research took a decidedly anti-theoretical turn in the early 20th century, much research focusing on the differences rather than the similarities between societies. When cultural elements were held in common, they were interpreted as evidence of historical contact and diffusion and not unilineal evolution. The anti-evolutionary position would dominate American anthropology until the 1940s, when an evolutionary approach would be reformulated in the work of Leslie White (Chapter 13) and Julian Steward (Chapter 14).

Until his death in 1942, Boas continued his remarkably detailed, stunningly diverse studies of humanity, and his influence was felt for decades later as many of his students turned their attention to what Boas saw as the key nexus, the relationship between the individual and society. ✦

Bibliography

Boas, Franz

1966a Changes in Bodily Form of Descendants of Immigrants. *In* Race, Language and Culture. Pp. 60–75. New York: Free Press.

1966b The Aims of Anthropological Research. *In* Race, Language and Culture. Pp. 243–259. New York: Free Press. [Originally published 1932.]

1966c Introduction: International Journal of American Linguistics. *In* Race, Language and Culture. Pp. 199–210. New York: Free Press. [Originally published 1917.]

1966d The Aims of Ethnology. *In* Race, Language and Culture. Pp. 626–638. New York: Free Press. [Originally published in 1888.]

1966e The Limitations of the Comparative Method of Anthropology. *In* Race, Language and Culture. Pp. 270–280. New York: Fress Press [Originally published 1896.]

1966f The Methods of Ethnology. *In* Race, Language and Culture. Pp. 281–289. [Originally published 1920.]

1966g History and Science in Anthropology: A Reply. *In* Race, Language and Culture. Pp. 305–311. [Originally published 1936.]

1974a Fieldwork for the British Association, 1888–1897. *In* The Shaping of American Anthropology 1883–1911, A Franz Boas Reader. G. Stocking Jr., ed. Pp. 88–197. New York: Basic Books. [Originally published 1898.]

Harris, Marvin

1968 The Rise of Anthropological Theory: A History of Theories of Culture. New York: Thomas Y. Crowell.

Hyatt, Marshall

1990 Franz Boas, Social Activist: The Dynamics of Ethnicity. New York: Greenwood Press.

Kroeber, Alfred

1943 Franz Boas: The Man. In Franz Boas, 1858–1942. American Anthropological Association, Memoir 61. New York: Krauss Reprint.

Rohner, Ronald and Evelyn C. Rohner

1969 Introduction. The Ethnography of Franz Boas: Letters and Diaries of Franz Boas Written on the Northwest Coast from 1886 to 1931. Compiled and edited by R. Rohner. Pp. xiii–xxx. Chicago: University of Chicago Press.

Spier, Leslie

1959 Some Central Elements in the Legacy. *In* The Anthropology of Franz Boas: Essays on the Centennial of His Birth. W. Goldschmidt, ed. Pp. 146–155. Memoir 89, American Anthropological Association.

Stocking, George, Jr.

1974 Introduction: The Basic Assumptions of Boasian Anthropology. *In* The Shaping of American Anthropology 1883–1911, A Franz Boas Reader. G. Stocking Jr., ed. Pp. 1–20. New York: Basic Books.

Chapter 4

Emile Durkheim

The Organic Society

The tradition of anthropological inquiry concerned with the character of social integration descends from the works of the French sociologist and educator Emile Durkheim (1858–1917). This line passes from Durkheim to his students, particularly Marcel Mauss (Chapter 9), and through them to the British school of social anthropology exemplified by A. R. Radcliffe-Brown (see Chapter 11), Evans-Pritchard (Chapter 12), and more recently Mary Douglas (Chapter 20), and many others. These scholars share a concern with the arrangement and articulation of basic social segments: How are different kin groups, classes, and political and religious units structured such that a given, coherent society exists? With his analytical focus on social integration, Durkheim's influence permeates a wide range of anthropological endeavor, including British social anthropology, anthropological approaches to religion, and questions about the origins of the state and the evolution of social complexity.

Given the influence of Durkheim's ideas, it is hard to understand how little impact Durkheim had on early American anthropology. As one historian has noted, ". . . the American school of anthropologists (Ruth Benedict, Clyde Kluckhohn, Margaret Mead) owed a good deal to him, even, or chiefly, when they contradicted several of his conclusions" (Peyre 1960:23). The anthropologist Paul Bohannan (1960:77) wrote, "A few cultural anthropologists have roundly rejected Durkheim; others have rephrased him to their own ends; most have simply ignored him."

Why this lack of appreciation and indifference? Partly it was due to the barriers of language; only one of Durkheim's books, *The Elementary*

Forms of the Religious Life, was translated into English during his life-time (in 1915), and his other classic, *The Division of Labor in Society*, originally written in 1893, was not translated into English until 1933. Some American anthropologists dismissed Durkheim for his lack of fieldwork, his assumption that certain societies (like the Arunta of Australia) were archetypally primitive, and for his apparent lack of concern with the details of ethnographic data. Yet, the more fundamental barrier which existed between American anthropologists and Durkheim and the scholars he influenced was a basic distinction between culture and society.

As discussed in Chapter 1, Tylor's definition of culture emphasized the intellectual, ideational aspects of culture—culture was shared, learned, patterned "knowledge." For much of the 20th century, American anthropology has approached "culture" in this manner, distinguishing "culture" from "society." For example, Alfred Kroeber (1952a:118–119) cited the "existence of cultureless or essentially cultureless subhuman societies" like those of ants or bees as evidence for the difference between society and culture (see pp. 73–74). Durkheim, intent on creating "a science of society," was viewed as somewhat irrelevant by American cultural anthropologists. In an address to the 1950 American Anthropological Association, Kroeber dealt with Durkheim in a surprisingly casual manner:

> Durkheim, to sum him up, may be rated a positivist; an empiricist in
> principle, but with only mild urge toward the use of wide context;
> like most of his countrymen [Kroeber engages in anti-French slurs]
> more interested in sharp principles than in variety of comparative
> data; not ethnocentric but yet little given to relativistic and pluralistic
> recognitions; and continuing to the end to believe that cultural phe-
> nomena can be adequately subsumed under purely social concepts.
> Durkheim left a school, but his actual constructive influence outside
> France has been slight, except on and through Radcliffe-Brown. [Kroe-
> ber 1952b:146]

From a current perspective, Kroeber's assessment of Durkheim is not only insulting but incorrect. Clearly this misappreciation involved more than language barriers; Kroeber, Lowie, and many other American anthropologists were cosmopolitan scholars comfortable in French. So either Durkheim's current status is misplaced or Kroeber and his colleagues were unable to understand the lasting value of Durkheim's ideas.

Background

Emile Durkheim was born in 1858 to a Jewish family in the Alsace region of eastern France. Much of Durkheim's life was framed by conflicts between Germany and France, first in the Franco-Prussian War 1870–1871—in which France was crushed, Napoleon III captured, and Alsace ceded to the Germans—and later World War I. The destruction experienced by France and the Allies was severe, and like so many others, Durkheim lost many loved ones, including his son, André, and every one of his students except for Marcel Mauss. By all accounts, the war aged him before his time; he died at the age of 59. But this was all in the future.

As a youth, Durkheim was recognized for his brilliance and began to advance through the centralized hierarchy of the French educational system. Durkheim spent his adult life within this system, as an instructor at several lycées teaching philosophy to 17-year-old boys, and after a year's sabbatical in Germany, as a professor of social science at the University of Bordeaux. He was "called" to the University of Paris in 1902 and became a full professor there in 1906, teaching courses in education, philosophy, and sociology.

For Durkheim (1960:325), sociology was "the science of societies"; Durkheim's sociology lacked the emphasis on Western, industrialized society typical of American sociology. In the French university, sociology was taught as a dimension of philosophy, but the implications of Durkheim's teaching were felt in a number of other disciplines. Peyre (1960:15) writes that "sociology became a catalyst that transformed a number of other disciplines," such as law, economics, geography, and anthropology and ethnology, exemplified by the works of Mauss (see Chapter 9) and Claude Lévi-Strauss (Chapter 17) and several generations of French social scientists.

And so the paradox reemerges: how could such an influential scholar have so little impact on the early years of American anthropology? The answer relates, in part, to the interpretation of two of Durkheim's central themes: the ideas of mechanic solidarity versus organic solidarity, and the *conscience collective*.

Mechanic and Organic Solidarity

In the preface to his first classic, *The Division of Labor in Society*, Durkheim (1964:33) begins with an acute phrase, "We do not wish to extract ethics from science, but to establish the science of ethics, which is quite different. Moral facts are phenomena like others; they consist of rules of action recognizable by certain distinctive characteristics." When we understand that for Durkheim "moral" implies not only value (as in the *moral* of a story) but also outlook (as in *morale*), then it becomes clear that he is describing the study of values, world view, and beliefs and proposing that they are amenable to scientific inquiry (cf. Bohannan and Glazer 1972:232). The specific focus of Durkheim's work was, in his words,

> . . . the question of the relations of the individual to social solidarity. Why does the individual, while becoming more autonomous, depend more upon society? How can he be at once more individual and more solidary. Certainly these two movements, contradictory as they appear, develop in parallel fashion. This is the problem we are raising. [Durkheim 1964:37]

A moment's reflection shows that Durkheim is on to something. A hunter and gatherer, living as an integral part of a band, can also survive on his own; his social identity is as a member of a group even though he has all the skills necessary for individual survival. We, members of industrialized societies, living independently and often in isolation, rely on others to raise our food, fix our cars, determine the value of our labors, and so on; we are socially independent, but we cannot survive without others. *The Division of Labor in Society* is not about the *sexual* division of labor, but rather about how society can be alternately segmented or unitary and characterized by homogeneity or heterogeneity and yet, somehow, stay together.

In Durkheim's era, the division of labor was not an esoteric subject; it characterized the transformation of European life during the Industrial Revolution. It was at the heart of Adam Smith's analysis of the *Wealth of Nations*, it was central to Marx's critique of capitalism, and it was relevant to issues that touched off massive social upheavals, like the revolt of the Paris Commune in 1871, which was bloodily suppressed. The division of labor and the emergence of new social classes were themes for social analysis with real impacts, much like academic discussions of race and ethnic relations are immediately relevant to people in the United States today. And so Durkheim was attempting to understand, at least partially, how his own society had come into being.

To explore this question, Durkheim chose a comparative method, but it is a comparative method different in logic and intent than the comparative method employed by Tylor and Morgan (see pp. 22–23,

35), which involved identifying similarities in cultural traits to reconstruct historical connections. For Durkheim, the comparative method consisted of contrasting entire societies in order to identify dimensions of social integration.

Durkheim proposed that societies have different configurations of social integration or "solidarity." He argued that different societies could have distinct types of solidarity as the basis of social existence, and he called these "mechanical solidarity" and "organic solidarity." Mechanical solidarity "comes from a certain number of states of conscience which are common to all the members of the same society" (1964:109). Mechanical solidarity applies to societies in which all members have a common, shared, social experience, but who do not necessarily depend on each other to survive. This form of solidarity is called mechanical, Durkheim writes, not because ". . . it is produced by mechanical or artificial means. We call it that only by analogy to the cohesion which unites the elements of an inanimate body, as opposed to that which makes a unity out of the elements of a living body" (1964:130). In mechanical solidarity societies, Durkheim believed, the individual was directly and equally attached to society, normative values were shared and more important than individual ones, and special subdivisions within a society were either absent or weak.

This contrasts with societies in which diverse, interdependent subdivisions are linked by formal institutions into a single society. This form of solidarity Durkheim called "organic," in the sense of a complex biological organism:

> This solidarity resembles that which we observe among the higher animals. Each organ, in effect, has its special physiognomy, its autonomy. And moreover, *the unity of the organism is as great as the individuation of the parts is more marked.* Because of this analogy we propose to call the solidarity which is due to the division of labor, organic. [1964:131; emphasis added]

Thus Durkheim outlined two models of social integration that characterized two contrasting societal structures. A mechanical solidarity society was "an absolutely homogeneous mass whose parts were not distinguished from one another, and which consequently had no structure" (in Giddens 1972:141). Organic solidarity societies, on the other hand,

> are formed not by the repetition of similar, homogeneous segments, but by a system of different organs each of which has a special role, and which are themselves formed of differentiated parts. Not only are

social elements not of the same nature, but they are not distributed in the same way. They are . . . coordinated and subordinated one to another around the same central organ which exercises a moderating action over the rest of the organism. [Giddens 1972:143]

For example, a wide range of institutions in American society are in some sense dependent on the legal system: corporations, marriages and families, nonprofit organizations, political offices, and so on. Each of these institutions is separate and different, but subordinate to the rule of law which thus exercises its "moderating influence" over the different organs of American society.

The differences between mechanical solidarity and organic solidarity were so marked that the development of one form could only be at the expense of the other, and historically that meant the evolution of organic solidarity as mechanical solidarity declined.

Durkheim culled his examples of traditional, non-Western societies from the Bible, classical texts, and primitive ethnographies to show that such different groups as the Australian aborigines, the unspecified tribes of native America and Africa, and the tribes of Israel all exhibit mechanical solidarity (1964:176–178). In contrast, such different societies as the Franks and the early Roman republic exhibit organic solidarity (1964:183–185). On such slender empirical grounds, Durkheim deduced a set of historical expectations, a set of developmental hypotheses.

First, Durkheim proposed that, "Whereas lower societies are spread over immense areas relative to the size of their populations, among more advanced peoples population tends to become more and more concentrated" (in Giddens 1972:152). This process begins with the development of agriculture, "since it necessitates a life in a fixed territory . . .", and intensifies with industrialization. Second, the development of towns marks a threshold between mechanical and organic solidarity. Towns, Durkheim writes, "always result from the need of individuals to put themselves constantly in the closest possible contact with each other," presumably because their diverse tasks, parceled out by the division of labor, must be exchanged to be of value. In contrast, "As long as society is essentially segmental [and solidarity is mechanical], towns do not exist" (Durkheim (1972:152). Concurrently, the shift from mechanical to organic solidarity is marked by the "number and rapidity of the means of communication and transportation" (1972:153), the network that binds together the disparate organs of society.

Thus Durkheim outlined a model that not only categorized existing and historically known societies, but provided a theory about the evolution of different social forms. The shift from mechanical to organic solidarity resulted from the greater division of labor; with greater numbers of separate tasks, the need for integrating structures increased. In turn, the division of labor became more marked as greater concentrations of people lived in one place; that is because, as Durkheim hypothesizes, "If work becomes progressively divided as societies become more voluminous and dense, it is not because external circumstances are more varied, but because struggle for existence is more acute" (1972:153). Borrowing directly from Darwin, Durkheim argued that as more people live together, competition over resources intensifies and, in response, people pursue different economic niches, evolving into different social groups. Once the trend to greater concentration of population begins, a series of social consequences follow that are expressed by differences in the fundamental organization of society.

But apart from the laws and contracts and markets that bind a society together, what is it that gives a society a distinctive, common identity? Durkheim analyzed that question with a concept that is one of the more misunderstood ideas in the social sciences, the *conscience collective*.

The Conscience Collective

The anthropologist Paul Bohannan (1960:77–78) wrote that "Durkheim, like all original thinkers, had to stretch the language he used for the exposition of his ideas to the limits, and perhaps beyond." The difficulty in understanding the notion of the *conscience collective* stems from the inherent ambiguity of the term compounded by the definitional nuances lost in the translation of the phrase from French to English. The French *conscience* combines both the sense of awareness associated in English with "consciousness" and the sense of a regulating function associated with "conscience." But in addition, *conscience* implies "that of which someone is (or many persons are) aware." Paul Bohannan writes, "the only suitable English word for this notion is the anthropologist's term 'culture.' Thus the French term *conscience* means three things: internalized sanctions, awareness, and perceived culture."

This combination of two concepts—being aware of something and the object of awareness—makes the term *conscience* so slippery for English speakers, and yet so important to Durkheim's work. "This ambiguous assimilation of the knowing instrument and the known thing—of consciousness and culture—into a single concept was vital to Durkheim's thought," Bohannan writes (1960:79). "Encompassing what are for English-speaking thinkers, at least those in social science, two substantives, the knower and the known, Durkheim focused his attention on the verbal connection between them: the 'knowing,' or, as he called, it the process of representation" (Bohannan 1960:79).

The subtleties of *conscience collective* may have contributed to Durkheim's neglect in early American anthropology. For Boas (pp. 66–67) and Kroeber (pp. 73–74), culture consisted of learned and shared knowledge and behavior, expressed in such different ways as technology, social organization, or language. Further, cultural knowledge was both separate from the process by which it was obtained and distinct from the society which held that knowledge. Finally, few American anthropologists were interested in the process of cultural acquisition (enculturation) until the 1930s. And so not only did Durkheim's *conscience collective* combine two terms that English speakers would distinguish, but it also drew attention to the process of cultural knowing that early American anthropologists did not often consider. No wonder the idea seemed confusing or useless.

Yet *conscience collective* was pivotal in Durkheim's work because it connected the different patterns of social solidarity to the processes of enculturation within a particular society. *Conscience collective* has different properties in societies based on mechanical solidarity versus those based on organic solidarity. First, in mechanical solidarity the individual tends to have values or views which are shared with all other members of society; in that sense, as Giddens (1972:5) writes, "individual 'consciousness' is simply a microcosm of *conscience collective*," which is not the case under organic solidarity. Second, in societies characterized by mechanical solidarity, the *conscience collective* has a greater intellectual and emotional hold over the individual. Third, in societies characterized by mechanical solidarity the *conscience collective* has greater rigidity; certain behaviors are required or prohibited and everyone knows what they are, whereas in organic societies—like our own—there may be constant debates about acceptable behaviors or appropriate values. And finally, there is a difference in content. In societies associated with mechanical solidarity the *conscience collective* is broadly associated with religion; the sanctions for social norms come from the supernatural. In societies characterized by organic solidarity, the role of religion is diminished. Durkheim writes:

> But, if there is one truth that history teaches us beyond doubt, it is
> that religion tends to embrace a smaller and smaller portion of social

life. Originally, it pervades everything; everything social is religious; the two words are synonymous. Then, little by little, political, economic, scientific functions free themselves from the religious function, constitute themselves apart and take on a more and more acknowledged temporal character. God, who was at first present in all human relations, progressively withdraws from them; he abandons the world to men and their disputes. [Durkheim 1964:169]

In this dramatic manner, Durkheim highlights the pervasive importance of religion in society, something that had not been studied systematically by social scientists to that point. Durkheim (1964:168) bemoaned the lack of "any scientific notion of what religion is," and set out to change that situation in his classic, *The Elementary Forms of the Religious Life*.

The Elementary Forms of the Religious Life

In this work, Durkheim set out to describe the basic elements of religious life by studying the most primitive social organization he knew of, the native peoples of central Australia. He outlined his method in the opening paragraph of the book:

[We] propose to study the most primitive and simple religion which is actually known, to make an analysis of it, and to attempt an explanation of it. A religious system may be said to be the most primitive which one can observe when it fulfills the two following conditions: in the first place, when it is found in a society whose organization is surpassed by no others in simplicity; and secondly, when it is possible to explain it without making use of any element borrowed from a previous religion. [1968:13]

Durkheim thus attempted to identify not only the elemental constituents of religion, but the origins of religion. Previously, two basic ideas had been advanced about the origins of religion. First was animism, an idea developed by Tylor that characterized religion as originating with an individual's explanation of misunderstood phenomena. Animism is the idea that spirits occupy all sorts of objects. Just as humans have different states of being—asleep and awake, living and dead—that imply the existence of an animating force, objects also have *anima*, and primitive religious activities revolve around avoiding, propitiating, or placating those spirits. An alternative concept, naturism, saw religion as an expression of natural forces and objects— weather, fire, the sea, lightning, and so on. Durkheim quotes a major proponent of naturism, Max Müller, as writing, "at first sight, nothing seemed less natural than nature. Nature was the greatest surprise, a terror, a marvel, a standing miracle . . . " (Durkheim 1968:92). Religion, Müller held, arose from attempts to understand these phenomena. Thus animism and naturism similarly view religion as originating with individuals' explanations of natural phenomena.

Durkheim's approach was fundamentally different:

> [R]eligion is something eminently social. Religious representations are collective representations which express collective realities; the rites are a manner of acting which take rise in the midst of assembled groups and which are destined to excite, maintain or recreate certain mental states in these groups. So if the categories are of religious origins they ought to participate in this nature common to all religious facts; they too should be social affairs and the product of collective thought. [1968:22]

For that reason, Durkheim was interested in the totem as expressed by native peoples of central Australia. Totem refers to a category of things—animals, plants, celestial bodies, ancestral mythic beings—associated with a social group. The name of the totem, for example, "red kangaroo," refers to the clan associated with that totem. The totem is the name and emblem of the clan and is incorporated into the liturgy of religious practices. The totem is, Durkheim writes (1968:140), "the very type of sacred thing." Its sacredness is imparted to those things associated with it, its loss is the greatest imaginable disaster, and specific taboos transform the animal or object into embodiments of sacredness. Yet, a specific totem is only sacred to a particular clan and not to any other. Such a brief synopsis hardly does justice to Durkheim's analysis of totemism or the vast literature subsequent to his work, but it illustrates how Durkheim perceived the social nature of religion.

Durkheim emphasized the elemental properties of religion:

> A religion is a unified system of beliefs and practices relative to sacred things, that is to say, things set apart and forbidden—beliefs and practices which unite into one single moral community, called a Church, all those who adhere to them. [1968:62]

What makes religion distinctive is its focus on the sacred, which is itself a social construction. There is nothing inherently sacred or profane in the world. A place, a symbol, or a personality becomes sacred because it is socially classified as sacred. It is impossible to separate the object of worship from the process of socially defining the sacred: in other words, the knower and the known (to use Bohannan's phrase) are indivisible, mutually created by the process of knowing.

What was true of sacredness was equally true of other shared cognitive categories, what Durkheim called "collective representations." Collective representations include such systems of knowledge as cardinal directions, temporal divisions, color categories, and social distinctions—classifications unique to different societies. The arbitrary yet very systematic nature of collective representations (e.g., all Americans agree that South is opposite of North and there are sixty minutes in an hour) indicate they are not simply products of individual musings about the nature of existence. The collective representations of religion are not derived from individual psychology because, Durkheim writes,

> between these two sorts of representations there is all the difference which exists between the individual and the social, and one can no more derive the second from the first than he can deduce society from the individual, the whole from the part, the complex from the simple. Society is a reality *sui generis*; it has its own peculiar characteristics, which are not found elsewhere and which are not met with again in the same form in all the rest of the universe. [1968:29]

Collective representations exist because there are two different spheres of human knowledge, the individual and the social, and Emile Durkheim developed a theory of the social basis of cultural knowledge.

Conclusion

The early American anthropologists criticized Durkheim's lack of field-work experience, his over-reliance on a few ethnographies, and his simplistic classification of very different societies into the category "primitive." But many American anthropologists also seem to have misunderstood what Durkheim was trying to do—attempting to build a theory of society.

Among Durkheim's many contributions to social science, this may be his most profound: the idea that there is a distinct realm of human existence, society, which is not derived from any other source. Society has characteristic structures that allow us to distinguish social forms, those based on mechanical solidarity versus those based on organic solidarity. We can perceive the origins of organic solidarity in those pure examples of mechanical solidarity that Durkheim called (1964:174) "the veritable social protoplasm, the germ out of which all social types would develop." Change occurred systematically, caused by innovations in the economy that affected human population densities which then led to the increasing division of labor. Such developments are paralleled by changes in the *conscience collective*: in the degree to which an individual's belief represents everybody's belief, in the controlling power of belief, in the diminishing importance of religious institutions and the domination of secular ones. That issue Durkheim explores by showing that religion is eminently social, and not the extrapolation of individual musings to a larger audience. Along with other categories, the boundaries between sacred and profane are collective—social—representations. Therefore, understanding the different currents of human existence requires focusing on the social dimensions because it is there that the differences are created, defined, expressed, and transmitted. These are some of the key notions in the science of society created by Emile Durkheim. ✦

Bibliography

Bohannan, Paul
1960 Conscience Collective and Culture. *In* Emile Durkheim, 1858–1917. K. Wolff, ed. Pp. 77–96. Columbus: Ohio State University Press.

Durkheim, Emile
1965 The Division of Labor in Society. G. Simpson, tran. New York: The Free Press of Glencoe.
1968 The Elementary Forms of the Religious Life. J. Swain, tran. New York: The Free Press.
1972 Selected Writings. Edited, translated and introduced by A. Giddens. Cambridge: Cambridge University Press.

Kroeber, Alfred
1952a Introduction. *In* The Nature of Culture. Pp. 3–11. Chicago: University of Chicago Press.
1952b The Concept of Culture in Science. *In* The Nature of Culture. Pp. 118–135. Chicago: University of Chicago Press.

Peyre, Henri
1960 Durkheim: the Man, his Time, and his Intellectual Background. *In* Emile Durkheim, 1858–1917. K. Wolff, ed. Pp. 3–31. Columbus: Ohio State University Press.

Wolff, Kurt
1960 An Introductory Durkheim Bibliography. *In* Emile Durkheim, 1858–1917. K. Wolff, ed. Pp. 437–445. Columbus: Ohio State University Press.

Part Two

The Nature of Culture

The Boasian critique of the comparative method and evolutionary schemes created an analytical vacuum. If cultural patterns are not the reflections of earlier stages of human development that has run "in nearly uniform channels" in Tylor's phrase, then what do cultural patterns reflect? If cultures are essentially the accidental accumulations of diverse traits and values brought together by specific historical circumstances of innovation, diffusion, and migration, how is it that cultures are integrated wholes? If, as Boas had written, "the causal conditions of cultural happenings lie always in the interaction between individual and society," what is the nature of that interaction? What holds cultures together? What gives cultures their distinctive essences?

These questions plagued Boas' students like Alfred Kroeber, Ruth Benedict, Edward Sapir, and Margaret Mead. And although the answers they arrived at were different, their respective explorations were framed by three concepts: the causal priority of culture, the concept of the microcosm, and the recognition that cultural knowledge was rapidly vanishing.

Boas' specific critiques of unilineal evolution and racial explanations of behavior led to the general conclusion that culture could only be explained in reference to specific cultural patterns, that culture explains culture, a position known as *cultural determinism* (Hatch 1973:49). Thus, the idea of *cultural relativism* holds that one can only understand a specific society's practices within its specific cultural context (Hatch 1983). Similarly, explanation requires understanding how historical processes of diffusion, migration, and invention produced a particular cultural pattern, the idea of *historical particularism* (Harris

1968:250–289). More broadly, the above implies that culture cannot be explained by reference to human biology, individual psychology, or any factors other than cultural ones.

But how can such factors be identified? Boas and his students believed that the laws governing culture, if they existed, could be discovered only through the study of small-scale societies in which culture could be examined in microcosm. During the early-20th century there is a general assumption that small-scale societies—the isolated camp, the primitive village—provided a discrete analytical unit where the patterns of culture could be observed in microcosm. In such "simple societies" it would be possible for the anthropologist to observe clearly dimensions of culture obscured in larger, more complex societies.

But those small, traditional cultures were disappearing rapidly. In American and British anthropology there was a broad recognition that traditional cultural knowledge was being lost in the face of Western colonization and globalization. Anthropologists responded by going into the field to "salvage" the last vestiges of traditional culture. Anthropologists George Marcus and Michael Fischer (1986:24) observe that "the main motif that ethnography as a science developed was that of salvaging cultural diversity. The ethnographer would capture in writing the authenticity of changing cultures, so they could be entered into the record for the great comparative project of anthropology. . . ."

From that comparative project would emerge the general laws of culture, laws inferred from specific studies of small-scale traditional societies. Working from this common set of assumptions, Kroeber, Benedict, Sapir, and Mead each attempted to understand the patterning of culture from different analytical angles.

For Kroeber, culture is a phenomenon distinct from that of society, the individual, or the organism. Culture exists on its own analytical level, irreducible to other levels of phenomena and explicable in terms of its own particular characteristics. Culture is learned and shared— as Tylor had said—but it is also variable, plastic, value-laden, superpersonal, and anonymous. Cultural innovations are not the products of lone genius, but expressions of "regularities of form and style and significance." Changes in some dimensions of culture, most notably in matters of style, may actually be governed by a superorganic oscillation that occurs unbeknownst to the individual members of a culture. And thus culture is distinct from, and dominant over, the individual.

For Benedict, cultures are more than the sum of their parts; they are configurations based on fundamental values of existence that differ between cultures. Cultures have a distinctive essence because key values are learned by individuals as members of particular cultures. American society has its outline—dynamic, constantly changing, fragmentary—because we value individualism, innovation, and success. The connection between the individual and society is based on values; individuals who through temperament and training share the values of their society are successful; those who don't are deviants. And yet those core values are not the same for all societies, and thus the successful person in one culture is the deviant in another.

Mead took a very similar approach. Like Benedict, Mead saw the relation between individual and society as based on values, but they are very specific values transmitted during childrearing. Rather than concerning herself with overall configurations, Mead was much concerned with rather specific sets of cultural values: is adolescent sex traumatic or easy, is a baby breastfed on demand or rudely weaned, is food shared or hoarded? In these and other cases the way children are raised determines the adults they become and that process gives societies their distinctiveness and shape.

Sapir's explanation was very different. Sapir contended that culture is a constantly edited document created by individuals engaged in public discourse. Far from being the passive creations of culture, individuals build cultures in their actions and words. Rather than collective expressions of fundamental, timeless values, Sapir argued that even the most basic contentions of culture are fodder for debate and disagreement. There are limits to points of disagreement, however, and the boundaries are set by language. The categories of different languages express basic ideas about how the universe is perceived, how causality is explained, about how time, mass, space, number, and so on are conceptualized. Speakers of the same language will tend to use similar linguistic categories. For example, if we set a time for a meeting, we may argue about whether I am late, but not about the number of minutes in an hour. Such linguistic categories are instilled unthinkingly as a child learns a language, becoming so ingrained that we don't argue about them. And thus the use of language and symbols allows humans to actively create new cultural forms, but the linguistic categories inherent in language give an overall shape to cultural experience.

It is often said that Boas cast an enormous influence over American anthropology, but perhaps nowhere is that more evident than in his students' efforts to understand the nature of culture. ✦

Bibliography

Harris, Marvin
1968 The Rise of Anthropological Theory: A History of Theories of Culture. New York: Thomas Y. Crowell Company.

Hatch, Elvin
1973 Theories of Man and Culture. New York: Columbia University Press.
1983 Culture and Morality. New York: Columbia University Press.

Marcus, George E. and Michael M.J. Fischer
1986 Anthropology as Cultural Critique: An Experimental Moment in the Human Sciences. Chicago: University of Chicago Press.

Chapter 5

Alfred Kroeber

Configurations of Culture

It is tempting to call Alfred Kroeber (1876–1960) the last Renaissance man of anthropology. During his 85-year lifetime, Kroeber lived through and shaped major changes in anthropology, which changed from merely documenting the exotic to concerning itself with the different arenas of human life and developed a holistic view of humans within our cultural and biological contexts. Alfred Kroeber ranged across all those fields; he was the last anthropological generalist.

Since Kroeber's time, the number of anthropologists and the quantity of anthropological research has grown so enormously that it is difficult to keep up with the literature in one field, let alone another. Between 1892 and 1901 a total of *six Ph.Ds* in anthropology were granted by American universities, Kroeber's among them; in 1995, *484 Ph.Ds* in anthropology were awarded (Givens and Jablonski 1996). Although anthropology as a whole, as a communal effort, maintains a holistic, multidimensional perspective, few anthropologists pursue more than a single field; we are social anthropologists or archaeologists or physical anthropologists or linguists. Within such fields we are even further specialized as California archaeologists or Andean archaeologists or linguists specializing in Mayan, Romance or Austronesian languages.

The lack of generalists since Kroeber's time both mirrors an information explosion and the growing emphasis on specialization of all academic disciplines. But Kroeber's breadth was exceptional even for his time and reflects a deeply original, creative mind at work at a time when almost everything in American anthropology was new.

Background

Alfred Kroeber was born in New Jersey in 1876, the year of Custer's defeat at Little Big Horn; much of his research on Native American life and language occurred during the twilight of American Indian independence. Kroeber's family were upper-middle-class German-Americans who insisted on a challenging educational regime of tutors, private schools, and hard work. He entered Columbia College at the age of 16 and majored in English, later receiving an M.A. with a thesis on British plays. Kroeber's early education directly led to his more "humanistic" approach to anthropology. Kroeber drifted into anthropology when he took a seminar in American Indian languages from Franz Boas, a seminar which met around Boas' dining room table (Steward 1973:6). Boas supervised Kroeber's doctoral dissertation on the art of the Arapaho (Kroeber 1901); it was only 28 pages long.

Kroeber's dissertation may have been brief, but he was an extremely prolific writer. In 1936 when he was honored on his 60th birthday, a bibliography of his writings included 175 entries (this seems to have been an underestimate and a subsequent list shows 306 works). In the following 25 years of his life—at a time when most people slow down—Kroeber's writings grew to 532 publications: articles, monographs, reviews, book introductions, essays, and so on (Gibson and Rowe 1961).

A review of these titles indicates Alfred Kroeber's major research interests. First is his work on the native peoples of California (e.g., Kroeber 1904, 1906, 1907a, 1907b, 1909, 1910, 1911, 1925, 1929, 1932). Kroeber was one of the first members of the anthropology department at UC Berkeley. He was hired to study the Indians of California, essentially doing "salvage ethnography" to recover the vestiges of precontact language and society before it was completely wiped out by Euro-American society. Kroeber published some 70 writings on the ethnology of native California, but his magnum opus was the *Handbook of California Indians* (Kroeber 1925). This 1000-page tome summarized Kroeber's investigations of every native group in California. It is a remarkable compendium, including aboriginal population estimates, lists of native toponyms, details of subsistence, cosmology, kinship, and social organization. Kroeber made numerous field trips, interviewed dozens of informants, summarized published sources, and scoured mission registers. It remains an important source of information, in many cases the only source.

Kroeber shared this desire to preserve rapidly disappearing cultural knowledge with other American anthropologists like Boas and Mead and also with British anthropologists (Kuper 1983:5–6). As anthropologists began to conduct fieldwork it quickly became apparent that traditional societies were being destroyed. The Cambridge anthropologist and psychologist W.H.R. Rivers wrote in 1913, "In many parts of the world the death of an old man brings with it the loss of knowledge never to be replaced." In the United States and Great Britain there was a shared sense that major theoretical issues could be addressed only with information that was disappearing daily, and this sparked a concerted effort to gather the available empirical data.

Kroeber's salvage ethnography led to a basic approach of ethnographic analysis: the culture element distribution list (Aginsky 1943; Driver 1937, 1939; Drucker 1950; Stewart 1939; Klimek 1935; Kroeber 1935, 1939; Voeglin 1938; for discussion, see Heizer 1963). He faced a basic set of problems (Kroeber 1939:4–6): 1) How are cultures to be defined? 2) How are their precontact practices to be reconstructed from current knowledge? and 3) How are the interactions between cultures to be measured? In native North America there were some obvious differences in the geographical distribution of cultural practices: Indians in the American Southwest and east of the Mississippi grew maize; Indians of the Plains and Great Basin did not. But such rough classifications failed to capture more subtle variations within particular cultural areas, nor did they account for the blurred edges of all such areas, and they assumed that certain aspects of culture—for example, agriculture—were more important than others. As Kroeber worked within California, it became obvious that there were significant differences among California Indians; for example, native Californians had the highest linguistic diversity of any region in North America, leading one scholar to call it "the Babel of ancient America" (Moratto 1984:530). Such cultural diversity had to be measured and explained, and Kroeber designed the cultural element lists to deal with this problem. Kroeber often approached the analysis of cultures as a natural historian, specifically like a Linnean taxonomist interested in classifying species rather than a modern evolutionary taxonomist concerned with variations in a population. The cultural element survey reflects this approach.

Kroeber divided culture into minimal units which could be characterized qualitatively. For example, did a specific group practice "polyandry" or "cremation," did they use a "sinew-backed bow" or "beaver-teeth dice," "eat acorn mush" or did their young men drink a dangerous hallucinogenic made from jimson weed? These lists were prepared and graduate students were sent out to interview native informants and check off the elements; the results were tabulated and published. Julian Steward (1961:1057), one of Kroeber's graduate students, wrote:

> Kroeber obtained funds for an ambitious four-year field project of element list surveys which was carried out by 13 field workers and included 254 tribes and tribal subdivisions west of the Rocky Mountains. The lists ranged from 3,000 to more than 6,000 elements, the presence and absence of which were recorded for each local group.

The element surveys were plotted in space in an attempt to understand the boundaries of particular cultures, and that led to the issue of interaction between cultures. Steward (1961:1057) continues:

> The territorial plotting of element distributions raised questions about the mechanism of diffusion of each element, which had usually been conceived of as a fairly simple process through which one society transmitted cultural features to another merely because of contiguity. Kroeber modified this concept . . . by showing that cultural products may be imitated by peoples who had no direct contact with their originators.

In hindsight, the element survey approach has a number of flaws. First, it atomizes culture into bits and pieces, and considers each element to be of equal significance (certainly the use of beaver teeth dice and the practice of polyandry have different levels of importance). Second, the approach assumes that the presence of that cultural element in one society is equivalent to the presence of that cultural element in another. For example, the swastika was used in native North America, India, Nazi Germany, and is used in the United States today. Even though the swastika is found in all these places, it clearly has several different meanings. Third, the cultural element survey created a static, synchronic view of a society, implying that the only mechanisms of cultural change were invention (an individual's creation of a new cultural trait), migration (the movement of a society with new cultural traits into a new area), and diffusion (the spread of cultural traits without migration). But for all its flaws, the cultural elements survey met one important goal: it produced systematic information on societies which were being destroyed.

Culture and Configurations

Kroeber was not interested in mere minutiae; he was also concerned with the broad patterns of culture that characterized entire societies or what he referred to as major styles that marked particular cultural configurations. Analogous to Benedict's concept discussed in Chapter 6, Kroeber states that "Patterns are those arrangements or systems of internal relationship which give to any culture its coherence or plan, and keep it from being a mere accumulation of random bits" (Kroeber 1948:131). Such patterns ". . . or configurations or Gestalts," Kroeber (1952a:5) wrote, "are what seem to me to be most productive to distinguish or formulate in culture."

Kroeber drew a sharp definitional boundary between culture and society. Society occurs whenever there is group life—including among social insects like bees and ants—but culture consists of learned and shared elements of custom and belief (Kroeber 1952b:118–19). Further, Kroeber believed that such customs and beliefs existed independently of the individuals who held such beliefs. In a brief after-dinner talk in 1946 to a group of anthropologists, Kroeber outlined his position. Culture is transmitted by human interactions, "not by the genetic mechanism of heredity but by the interconditioning of zygotes." Regardless of its origins, "culture quickly tends to become supra-personal and anonymous," falling "into patterns, or regularities of form and style and significance." And finally, Kroeber (1952c:104) argued that culture "embodies values, which may be formulated (overtly as mores) or felt (implicitly, as in folkways) by the society carrying the culture, and which it is part of the business of the anthropologist to characterize and define." Thus Kroeber's basic definition of culture is that it is learned, shared, patterned, and meaningful.

Kroeber tried to steer his analysis between two extremes that dominated early-20th-century ways of thinking about humans: racial determinism and the Great Man Theory. Very early in his career (1917)—and clearly showing Boas' influence (see pp. 47–48)—Kroeber attacked the notion that different races have different innate properties. He questioned a number of assumptions linking genetic background to behavior such as that the Eskimo innately desires blubber or the French are inherently facile with language, and also the tendency to equate "race" and "civilization."

At the time, Kroeber argued against the Great Man Theory, contending that even geniuses did not so much shape their cultures as represent them. Kroeber found repeated examples of multiple geniuses—like the independent invention of calculus by Leibnitz in 1684 and Newton in 1687, the development of the theory of natural selection by Charles Darwin and Alfred Russel Wallace, and the invention of the steamboat by Robert Fulton and at least four other contemporary inventors. "The history of inventions," Kroeber (1952d:45) wrote, "is a chain of parallel instances." The co-occurrence of such inventions, he concluded, was evidence that something larger was at work, some force greater than either genetic inheritance or genius. That force was greater than the organism—it was *superorganic*:

> The reason why mental heredity has so little if anything to do with civilization, is that civilization is not mental action but a body or stream of products of mental exercise. [And] The social or cultural . . . is in its essence non-individual. Civilization as such begins only where the individual ends; and whoever does not in some measure perceive this fact . . . can find no meaning in civilization, and history for him must be only a wearying jumble, or an opportunity for the exercise of art [i.e., making things up]. [Kroeber 1952d:40]

For Kroeber, that organizing force was culture—nongenetic, shared, anonymous, and patterned knowledge.

The configurations of culture are produced by the history of a particular set of cultural values. Kroeber noted (1952a:4) ". . . that it is of the nature of culture to be heavily conditioned by its own cumulative past, so that the most fruitful approach to its understanding is a historical one." The historical approach showed broader and broader connections between cultural elements as they were expressed in space and time (Kroeber 1952a:5). Placing these elements in this manner, one could identify configurations and their development, prominence, decline and replacement. That, Kroeber felt, was the nature of explanation.

Kroeber turned his attention to scores of topics—Peruvian archaeology, American Indian linguistics, and so on—but arguably his most intriguing analysis was of a subject that might seem strange: changes in women's dress. It was a topic that Kroeber wrote about at least twice, first in 1919 and then again in 1940. Kroeber was drawn to study women's fashion because it reflected "pure" style and because changes in fashion could be dated by studying historic Parisian fashion magazines. By the time of the second study, Kroeber had data ranging from 1787 to 1936. Kroeber measured a range of variables, such as dress length and dress width, and then conducted a statistical and time series analysis. What he found was that certain major fluctuations had different periodicities; i.e., dress length was greatest in the 18th century and the mid- and late-19th century with shorter dresses most common at about 1815 and 1931. Further, Kroeber found some interesting style variation patterns. Most years, variation from the central trend was minor, whether the tendency was for long dresses or short dresses, but in some periods there was a great degree of variation before the central tendency was reasserted. Kroeber considered a variety of historical causes—e.g., did periods of political instability cause greater variation in hem length?—and failed to find any causes for such patterns other than the simple, superorganic fluctuation of style.

> The primary factor [for such fashion changes] would seem to be adherence to or departure from an ideal though unconscious pattern for formal clothing in women. The consistent conformity of variability to certain magnitudes of proportion—mostly a conformity of low variabilities to high magnitudes [i.e. when skirts are shortest, everyone's skirts are short]—leaves little room for any other conclusion. [Richardson and Kroeber 1952:368]

In sum, Kroeber studied women's fashion because it exemplified his conception of what culture was. Clearly nongenetic, fashion was obviously free of the influences of heredity. Obviously shared, fashion was more than the idiosyncratic exercise of genius. Reducible to elements, fashion traits could be plotted in time; in this case space was held constant by considering only *Parisian* fashion. Clearly patterned, fashion underwent long-term systematic fluctuations. And finally, his explanation was historical because changes in fashion could not be understood by appeal to outside factors but only explained within their specific cultural configuration. And thus Kroeber's analysis of this unlikely topic captured the basic characteristics of his approach to culture.

Kroeber attempted to repeat his microcosmic analysis in the narrow field of Parisian fashion in a parallel, enormous study of world civilization, *Configurations of Culture Growth* (1944). During his cultural element distribution studies, Kroeber had developed the notion of culture climax. A culture climax is when "historically known cultural growths . . . show a virtual coincidence of florescence in the several faces of culture" (Kroeber 1939:5). Since Kroeber had long argued that cultural innovations were not the products of "Great Men" but rather of "parallel instances," then a study of superior inventions documents "the frequent habit of societies to develop their cultures to their highest levels spasmodically: especially in their intellectual and aesthetic aspects, but also in more material and practical aspects" (Kroeber 1944:5). If genius were simply the result of genetics, then superior innovations should occur randomly; that they do not indicates "the causal participation of a cultural factor, the intervention of a superpersonal element in the personal activity of genius" (Kroeber 1944:13). And yet Kroeber (1944:761) found "no evidence of any true law in the phenomena dealt with; nothing cyclical, regularly repetitive, or necessary." If anything, this simply strengthened Kroeber's idea of the irreducibility of culture.

For Kroeber, culture was a mental construct completely distinct from other phenomena. Culture, he wrote (1948:254), "is superorganic and superindividual in that, although carried, participated in and produced by organic individuals, it is acquired; and it is acquired by learning." Culture cannot be explained by organic individual needs as Malinowski claimed (Kroeber 1948:309–310; on Malinowski, see pp. 132–135), and it cannot be treated as equivalent to "society" (Kroeber 1948:847–849). Cultural patterns can be understood only within a historical approach which emphasizes change through time, the cultural antecedents of new cultural patterns, and the importance of understanding cultural phenomena within particular configurations (Kroeber 1957, 1963a, 1963b; see Hatch 1973:94–95 for discussion).

Conclusion

Kroeber's broad contributions to anthropology make any brief summary of his career nearly impossible, but Steward's (1961) obituary captures many of Kroeber's basic ideas. Kroeber believed "that culture derived from culture" and that psychological, adaptational, or organic explanations were indefensible. His historical approach was "superorganic and supra-individual" and two-fold, first characterizing cultures "by the minutiae of their content" while also seeking "major styles, philosophies, and values" (Steward 1961:1050).

Kroeber's contribution to American anthropology has a mixed legacy. There is little question of his substantive contributions to ethnology, ethnography, linguistics, and archaeology, but in contrast there is little current enthusiasm for Kroeber's concerns with the superorganic, the style and patterns of civilization, or the anonymity of culture. As a theoretician, Kroeber's position is more frequently argued against than embraced (Benedict 1934:231; Harris 1968:320–337). And yet, Kroeber's attempt to find the unifying basis of culture was a central problem faced by many of his contemporaries, including Benedict, Sapir, and Mead. ✦

Bibliography

Aginsky, Bernard
1943 Culture Element Distributions XXIV: Central Sierra. Anthropological Records 8(4). Berkeley: University of California Press.

Driver, Harold
1937 Culture Element Distributions VI: Southern Sierra Nevada. Anthropological Records 1:53–154. Berkeley: University of California Press.
1939 Culture Element Distributions X: Northwest California. Anthropological Records, 1(6):297–433. Berkeley: University of California Press.

Drucker, Philip
1950 Culture Element Distributions XXVI: Northwest Coast. Anthropological Records 9(3). Berkeley: University of California Press.

Gibson, Anne and John Rowe
1961 A Bibliography of the Publications of Alfred Louis Kroeber. American Anthropologist 63:1060–1087.

Givens, Douglas and Timothy Jablonski
1996 Degrees, FYI. Anthropology Newsletter 37(5):7.

Hatch, Elvin
1973 Theories of Man and Culture. New York: Columbia University Press.

Heizer, Robert
1963 Foreword. In Cultural and Natural Areas of Native North America, 4th ed. A. L. Kroeber. Berkeley: University of California Press. [Originally published 1939.]

Klimek, Stanislaw
1935 Culture Element Distributions I: The Structure of California Indian Culture. University of California Publications in American Archaeology and Ethnology 37:12–70.

Kroeber, Alfred
1901 Decorative Symbolism of the Arapaho. American Anthropologist 3:308–336.
1904 The Languages of the Coast of California South of San Francisco. University of California Publications in American Archaeology and Ethnology 2(2):29–80.
1906 The Dialect Divisions of the Moquelumnan Family in Relation to the Internal Differentiation of other Linguistic Families of California. American Anthropologist 8:652–663.
1907a The Washo Language of East Central California and Nevada. University of California Publications in American Archaeology and Ethnology 4(5):251–317.
1907b The Yokuts Language of South Central California. University of California Publications in American Archaeology and Ethnology 2(5):163–377.
1909 Some Notes on the Shoshonean Dialects of Southern California. University of California Publications in American Archaeology and Ethnology 8(5):235–269.
1910 The Chumash and Costanoan Languages. University of California Publications in American Archaeology and Ethnology 9:237–271.

1911 The Languages of the Coast of California North of San Francisco. University of California Publications in American Archaeology and Ethnology 9(3):37–271.

1920 California Culture Provinces. University of California Publications in American Archaeology and Ethnology 17(2):151–170.

1925 Handbook of the Indians of California. Bureau of American Ethnology, Bulletin 78. Washington, D.C.: Smithsonian Institution.

1929 The Valley Nisenan. University of California Publications in American Archaeology and Ethnology 24(4):253–290.

1932 The Patwin and their Neighbors. University of California Publications in American Archaeology and Ethnology 29 (4):253–423.

1935 Preface. In Culture Element Distributions I: The Structure of California Indian Culture. By S. Klimek. University of California Publications in American Archaeology and Ethnology 37:1–11.

1939 Cultural and Natural Areas of Native North America. University of California Publications in American Archaeology and Ethnology 38:1–240.

1944 Configurations of Culture Growth. Berkeley: University of California Press.

1948 Anthropology: Race, Language, Culture, Psychology, Prehistory. New York: Harcourt, Brace & World.

1952a Introduction. In The Nature of Culture. Pp. 3–11. Chicago: University of Chicago Press.

1952b The Concept of Culture in Science. In The Nature of Culture. Pp. 118–135. Chicago: University of Chicago Press.

1952c Culture, Events, and Individuals. In The Nature of Culture. Pp. 104–106. Chicago: University of Chicago Press.

1952d The Superorganic. In The Nature of Culture. Pp. 22–51. Chicago: University of Chicago Press. [Originally published 1917.]

1957 Style and Civilizations. Ithaca: Cornell University.

1963a History and Anthropology in the Study of Civilizations. In An Anthropologist Looks at History. Theodora Kroeber, ed. Pp. 160–171. Berkeley: University of California Press.

1963b An Anthropologist Looks at History. In An Anthropologist Looks at History, Theodora Kroeber, ed. Pp. 152–159. Berkeley: University of California Press.

Kuper, Adam
1983 Anthropology and Anthropologists: The Modern British School. London: Routledge & Kegan Paul.

Moratto, Michael
1984 California Archaeology. New York: Academic Press.

Steward, Julian
1961 Alfred Louis Kroeber 1876–1960. American Anthropologist 63:1038–1087.

1973 Alfred Kroeber. New York: Columbia University Press.

Chapter 6

Ruth Benedict

Patterns of Culture

Ironically, interest in Ruth Benedict's life story overshadows her ideas as an anthropologist, which focused on the relationship between the individual and society. Benedict is the subject of three biographies (Caffrey 1989; Mead 1974; Modell 1983). Benedict is a captivating subject for biographers because she was not only a brilliant anthropologist, but a brilliant woman who was an anthropologist. Benedict was one of the first women to attain prominence as a social scientist, and her life exemplifies the difficult, often conflicting choices that women face in American society. The trajectories of her life and career in anthropology were shaped by that fact.

Background

Ruth Benedict (née Fulton) was educated at Vassar College, which was established in the 1880s with the goal of educating women on an equal plane with men. Although women's university education had existed for 20 years when Ruth Benedict enrolled in 1905, it was still sufficiently new that *Ladies Home Journal* in October 1905 published an article titled, "Madcap Frolics of College Girls," followed in the November issue by the riveting article, "What College Girls Eat" (Caffrey 1989:43). Ruth Benedict studied literature and poetry and later in her life she published poems in poetry magazines and journals. But her exposure to critical analysis, even more than to poetry, was to impact on her anthropology. At Vassar she was exposed to a wide range of Progressive political issues and Modernist artistic trends, and to a challenging body of English and German literature, particularly the works of Friedrich Nietzsche.

Nietzsche's works are not read by most Americans today, but many of us know the opening notes of *2001: A Space Odyssey*, actually a tone poem composed by Richard Strauss based on Nietzsche's *Thus Spake Zarathustra*. Nietzsche chose to write a collection of philosophical statements as if they were spoken by the Persian philosopher Zarathustra (Zoroaster); in fact, they were Nietzsche's own recipes calling for creativity, revolt against conformity, and vigorous engagement with life. Caffrey writes:

> Nietzsche advocated creative iconoclasm. The Self desires to create beyond itself, he wrote: "Creating—that is the great salvation from suffering, and life's alleviation." The creativity he advocated was the creativity of new values. "Not around the inventors of new noise, but around the inventors of new values, doth the world revolve; *inaudibly* it revolveth." [Note the biblical tone of the archaic forms chosen in this translation.] But changing values involved destroying of the old as well as replacement with the new. "False shores and false securities did the good teach you," he wrote for the "good" [i.e., the proper people of society] could not create; instead they crucified the true creators. . . . [Nietzsche] advocated the destruction of conventional morality and conformity because they suffocated creativity. He affirmed physical joy. He called for a renunciation of materialism and for his readers to develop God within themselves. All of these were qualities Ruth believed most important. . . . *Thus Spake Zarathustra* gave her a sense of freedom from that restrictive past and a purpose for living out her future. [1989:54–55]

In 1914 Benedict married Stanley Benedict, but over the years their marriage unraveled. After stints of unsatisfying participation in social work and repressing her own interests for the sake of her marriage, she went back to school at the age of 31 at the New School for Social Research. After a year she was encouraged to take graduate courses at Columbia University where she began an association with Franz Boas that lasted from 1921 until Boas' death in 1942.

Boas supervised Benedict's dissertation—"The Concept of the Guardian Spirit in North America"—which was later published by the American Anthropological Association (Benedict 1923). The dissertation was based on library research rather than field work, but the fact that she obtained her Ph.D. in three semesters is still remarkable. Except for a brief 1922 study of the Serrano in southern California (Benedict 1924), all of Benedict's early writings were based on library research (e.g. Benedict 1922). Beginning in the mid-1920s, however, Benedict went to the American Southwest for summer field research projects among the Zuni (1924), Zuni and Cochiti (1925), O'otam (Pima 1927), and Mescalero Apache (1931). Benedict's Zuni research would become central to her 1934 book *Patterns of Culture*.

During this period Benedict was developing her interests in personality and culture, editing the *Journal of American Folklore*, and teaching at Columbia, where the relationship between Boas and Benedict continued to evolve. After serving as her mentor, Boas became her professional colleague when he got her a position in the Department of Anthropology, which he chaired. Gradually, Benedict was made a full-fledged faculty member, and at her death in 1948 she was one of Columbia University's most eminent professors.

Patterns of Culture

Patterns of Culture was an extremely popular book from the time it was published in 1934. Translated into a dozen languages, issued in 1946 as a paperback that sold for a twenty-five cents, as of 1974 *Patterns of Culture* had sold 1.6 million copies (Mead 1974:1). It is still in print. The ideas of the book spread outside of academia into the American society in general. Because the ideas have permeated modern American culture, we now take them as commonplace. *Patterns of Culture* was written for the non-anthropologist and as Caffrey (1989:209) observes, "it acted as a signal of and a catalyst for the final acceptance of a profound paradigm change in the social sciences and in American society . . . ." Benedict found alleviation from suffering, in Nietzsche's phrase, in the creativity of intellect; *Patterns of Culture* is clear evidence of that intellect at work.

First, it emphasized the importance of culture versus biology; by contrasting the starkly different patterns of life among the Zuni, Dobu, and Kwakiutl, Benedict demonstrated the causal primacy of culture in understanding differences between modern humans. By extension, the profiles of these three societies so different from American society further weakened the grip of Victorian mores on American life.

Second, Benedict's emphasis on *patterns* of culture was a new twist on a fairly twisted idea. The concept of patterns was similar in some ways to the culture-element complexes that Kroeber and others had discussed (see pp. 65–66): patterned co-occurrences of cultural traits that marked different cultural groups. For example, anthropologist

Clark Wissler described the horse-complex among Plains Indians, a constellation of cultural practices including the tipi, travois, buffalo hunting, raiding, and the Sun Dance—all of which revolved around the horse. Similarly, we could define an American car culture in which a wide range of cultural elements—billboards, cellular phones, commuter schools, etc.—are all linked by the presence of automobiles.

But Benedict and other anthropologists were searching for something more subtle and profound, the relationship not only between a set of things and behaviors, but between the underlying ideas, values, and mores that characterize a particular society. The notion of the "Gestalt" configuration was influential at this time. Coming from the German word for the outline of a physical shape, psychologists had applied the notion to experiments in learning behavior that suggested people learn in response to underlying patterns called forth by a specific event rather than by direct stimulus response. Thus we learn that boisterous behavior is inappropriate in a church, but then extend that knowledge to cathedrals and synagogues, certain public monuments (Lincoln Memorial), backyard weddings, and so on. Even in new situations we follow previously learned instructions because the new situation calls forth a basic learned pattern. "The Gestalt idea of configuration," Margaret Caffrey writes, "fell on open minds in America. A configuration was a form of pattern that linked facts and events with the attitudes and beliefs underlying them" (1989:154). Ruth Benedict made this notion of the Gestalt/configuration/pattern central to her work:

> Gestalt (configuration) psychology has done some of the most strik-
> ing work in justifying the importance of this point of departure from
> the whole rather than from the parts. Gestalt psychologists have
> shown that in the simplest sense-perception no analysis of the sepa-
> rate precepts can account for the total experience. It is not enough to
> divide perceptions up into objective fragments. The subjective frame-
> work, the forms provided by past experience, are crucial and cannot
> be omitted. [Benedict 1959:51]

When Benedict contrasts "objective" and "subjective," she is not using subjective as a synonym for "mere opinion" or an ethnocentric projection; she is attempting to characterize the subjective values that explain why members of a particular society behave in certain ways. Benedict used the concept of pattern to refer to a society's underlying "values of existence." She wrote, "Cultures . . . are more than the sum of their traits. We may know all about the distribution of a tribe's form of marriage, ritual dances, and puberty initiations and yet understand nothing of the culture as a whole which has used these elements to its own purpose" (1959:47).

Benedict exposed the differences in cultural patterns by contrasting three relatively well-studied and markedly different societies: the "Pueblo" Indians (Zuni and Hopi); the Dobu, who live on an island off the south shore of eastern New Guinea; and the Northwest Coast Indians (Tsimshian, Kwakiutl, Coast Salish) who live between Puget Sound and southwestern Alaska. The three groups were chosen because they had been studied by anthropologists whose work Benedict trusted: Reo Fortune had studied the Dobu (he was married to Margaret Mead at the time, see p. 103), Boas had worked on the Northwest Coast, and Benedict herself had conducted research at Zuni pueblo. They were also completely different societies with fundamentally different cultural configurations. Marshaling extensive ethnographic detail, Benedict sifted out the fundamental elements of the cultural pattern. For example, she wrote of the Dobu:

> The Dobuan . . . is dour, prudish, and passionate, consumed with jealousy and suspicion and resentment. Every moment of prosperity he conceives himself to have wrung from a malicious world by a conflict in which he has worsted his opponent. The good man is the one who has many such conflicts to his credit, as anyone can see from the fact that he has survived with a measure of prosperity. It is taken for granted that he has thieved, killed children and his close associates by sorcery, cheated whenever he dared. [1959:168–169]

Contrast this with the Zuni ideal of the good man:

> The ideal man in Zuni is a person of dignity and affability who has never tried to lead, and who has never called forth comment from his neighbours. Any conflict, even though right is on his side, is held against him. The highest praise, describing an impeccable townsman, runs: "He is a nice polite man. No one ever hears anything from him. He never gets into trouble. He's Badger clan and Muhekwe kiva and he always dances in the summer dances." He should "talk lots," as they say—this is, he should always set people at their ease—and he should without fail co-operate easily with others either in the field or in ritual, never betraying a suspicion of arrogance or a strong emotion. [Benedict 1959:99]

Benedict was not just reciting her own prejudices about people; she was proposing ethnographically informed generalizations about the distinct values of different societies. Such societies were so fundamentally different that Benedict turned to Nietzsche's work to borrow two concepts, the Apollonian and Dionysian approaches to existence. Benedict contrasted the configuration of the Zuni and other Puebloan Indians with that of the Kwakiutl and many other North American groups:

> The basic contrast between the Pueblos and the other cultures of North American is the contrast that is named and described by Nietzsche in his studies of Greek tragedy. He discusses two diametrically opposed ways of arriving at the values of existence. The Dionysian pursues them through "the annihilation of the ordinary bounds and limits of existence"; he seeks to attain in his most valued moments escape from the boundaries imposed upon him by his five senses, to break through into another order of existence. The desire of the Dionysian, in personal experience or in ritual, is to press through it toward a certain psychological state, to achieve excess. The closest analogy to the emotions he seeks is drunkenness, and he values the illuminations of frenzy. With Blake, he believes "the path of excess leads to the palace of wisdom." The Apollonian distrusts all this, and often has little idea of the nature of such experiences. He finds means to outlaw them from his conscious life. He knows but one law, measure in the Hellenic sense. He keeps within the middle of the road, stays within the known map, does not meddle with disruptive psychological states. In Nietzsche's fine phrase, even in the exaltation of the dance he "remains what he is, and retains his civic name." [Benedict 1959:78–79]

"The Southwest Pueblos are Apollonian," Benedict wrote, and in contrast to many North American groups:

> Zuni ideals and institutions . . . are rigorous on this point. The known map, the middle of the road to any Apollonian, is embodied in the common tradition of his people. To stay within it is to commit himself to precedent, to tradition. Therefore those influences that are powerful against tradition are uncongenial and minimized in their institutions, and the greatest of these is individualism." [Benedict 1959:80]

Outside of the Pueblos:

> American Indians as a whole, and including those of Mexico [i.e., the Aztec], were passionately Dionysian. They valued all violent experience, all means by which human beings may break through the usual sensory routine, and to all such experiences they attributed the highest value. [Benedict 1959:80]

In spite of the many differences in Native American language and culture, Benedict saw a common emphasis on Dionysian behavior. The most conspicuous evidence was the vision quest, in which an individual—through fasting, drugs (tobacco), and self-mutilation—attempts to break through commonplace existence and obtain a personal vision through direct contact with the supernatural. Such a set of core values shaped larger cultural practices, resulting in distinctive patterns of culture.

And yet not all individuals comfortably fit into the accepted patterns of cultural life. Ruth Benedict knew this from her own experience. She had, as a person, reached a point when she could no longer conform to the normal values for American women in the 1920s; she had not accepted all the core values of her own culture. Benedict saw the potential for conflict between the individual and culture in her own life, and assumed that this would occur in other societies.

And so the final part of *Patterns of Culture* addresses this problem. "We have seen that any society selects some segment of the arc of possible human behavior," Benedict wrote (1959:254), "and in so far as it achieves integration its institutions tend to further the expression of its selected segment and inhibit opposite expressions." Human nature is so malleable, the lessons of one's culture are so explicit, and the sanctions for disobedience so severe, that the vast majority of people not only accept the core values but assume that "their particular institutions reflect an ultimate and universal sanity" (Benedict 1959:254). And yet not everyone finds the institutions of a given culture "equally congenial . . . favored are those . . . whose potentialities most nearly coincide with the type of behavior selected by their society" (Benedict 1959:255). Benedict argues that "deviation" is essentially a conflict between individual personality and a given culture's values and not a singular dimension true for all humans. The deviant in Dobu society is "the man who was naturally friendly," (Benedict 1959:258); the honored man in a Dionysian society is the despised pariah in an Apollonian culture.

So *Patterns of Culture* poses an interesting conflict between the individual and culture: on the one hand, culture is an expression of core values which most people learn and absorb; on the other hand, there are individual personalities that lie outside the particular segment of the arc of possibilities that defines that culture. Therefore, not only are cultural values relative, but the very definition of deviance as well. Benedict's book is one of the founding anthropological texts on the relationship between culture and personality.

Conclusion

Benedict wrote more than just *Patterns of Culture*, of course. During World War II Benedict worked for the Office of War Information by sifting through published materials about other cultures in support of the American war effort, and conducting studies of "cultures at a distance." The best-known study, *The Chrysanthemum and the Sword* (1949), was an examination of the core values of Japanese society and how such values influenced Japanese behavior during the war and the post-war American occupation. Less well-known is Benedict's earlier study of the people and culture of Thailand (1952; written in 1943), which anticipates the methods of *The Chrysanthemum and the Sword*.

Benedict contributed to the war effort in another, very different way: she and Gene Weltfish (1943) wrote a ten-cent anti-racist pamphlet entitled *The Races of Mankind*. In the face of Nazi racial policies and racial conflicts within the United States, and as American troops fought around the globe, issues of race were paramount. Benedict and Weltfish summarized the current scientific views on race and argued that racial differences were minimal when compared to cultural differences. This argument was also advanced in *Patterns of Culture* and echoed Boas' discussion of race (see pp. 46–48). When the U.S. Army decided to distribute the pamphlet, conservative congressmen attacked it as "Communist propaganda." This patently absurd charge attracted publicity and helped sell over 750,000 copies of the pamphlet, which was translated into seven languages (Edwards 1968).

Other successes notwithstanding, none of Benedict's works surpassed *Patterns of Culture*, in terms of theoretical impact. Its clear argument exposing the basic patterns of a society, the set of basic values which make a cultural chord was fundamental. As the shift from major to minor keys in the opening notes of *Thus Spake Zarathustra* conveys a sense of the universe's majesty and mystery, the Apollonian and Dionysian archetypes evoke certain fundamentals of a society. Note, Benedict was not trying to create a classification system for cultures, although it may seem so. "Categories become a liability," she (1959:238) wrote, "when they are taken as inevitable and applicable alike to all civilizations and events." Cultures were not ragtag assortments of elements tossed together by historical accident; rather, Benedict showed that cultural differences were multifaceted expressions of a society's most basic core values. The goal of anthropology was to document these different patterns.

Benedict wrote about the social outcome of that process in the last lines of her *Patterns of Culture*:

> We shall arrive then at a more realistic social faith, accepting as grounds of hope and as new bases for tolerance the coexisting and equally valid patterns of life which mankind has created for itself from the raw materials of existence. [Benedict 1959:278] ✦

Bibliography

Benedict, Ruth
1922 The Vision in Plains Culture. American Anthropologist 24:1–23. [Reprinted 1959. *In* An Anthropologist at Work: Writings of Ruth Benedict, Margaret Mead, ed. New York: Houghton Mifflin Company.]
1923 The Concept of the Guardian Spirit in North America. American Anthropological Association, Memoir 29. [Reprinted 1974. Millwood, New Jersey: Kraus Reprint Company.]
1924 A Brief Sketch of Serrano Culture. American Anthropologist 26:366–392. [Reprinted 1959. *In* An Anthropologist at Work: Writings of Ruth Benedict, Margaret Mead, ed. New York: Houghton Mifflin Company.]
1931 Tales of the Cochiti Indians. Bureau of American Ethnology, Bulletin 98. Washington, D.C.: Smithsonian Institution.
1932 Configurations of Culture in North America. American Anthropologist 34:1–27. [Reprinted 1974. *In* Ruth Benedict by Margaret Mead. New York: Columbia University Press.]
1946 The Chrysanthemum and the Sword: Patterns of Japanese Culture. New York: Houghton Mifflin Company.
1952 Thai Culture and Behavior: An Unpublished War Time Study. September 1943. Southeast Asia Program, Data Paper No. 4. Department of Far Eastern Studies. Ithaca: Cornell University.
1959 Patterns of Culture. New York: Houghton Mifflin Co. [Originally published 1934.]
1968 Race: Science and Politics. [Originally published 1940.] *Including* The Races of Mankind by Ruth Benedict and Gene Weltfish. New York: Viking Press. [Originally published 1940.]

Caffrey, Margaret
1989 Ruth Benedict: Stranger in the Land. Austin: University of Texas Press.

Edwards, Violet
1968 Note on The Races of Mankind. *In* Race: Science and Politics by Ruth Benedict. Pp. 167–168. New York: Viking Press.

Mead, Margaret
1966 An Anthropologist at Work: The Writings of Ruth Benedict. New York: Atherton Press.
1974 Ruth Benedict. New York: Columbia University Press.

Modell, Julia
1983 Ruth Benedict: Patterns of a Life. Philadelphia: University of Pennsylvania Press.

Chapter 7

Edward Sapir

Culture, Language and the Individual

Edward Sapir (1884–1939), a former student wrote, "was one of those rare men among scientists and scholars who are spoken of by their colleagues in terms of genius" (Mandelbaum 1968:v). In her obituary of Sapir in *American Anthropologist*, Ruth Benedict (1939:465) wrote, "Few men in academic life have been so brilliantly endowed as Professor Sapir, and the loss which linguistics and anthropology have sustained cannot be measured. To those of us who have been his friends, his death leaves a vacancy which can never be filled" (Benedict 1939:468).

Sapir was recognized as the most brilliant linguist of his era, a "genius" to many (Darnell 1990:x), who revolutionized the study of American Indian languages. He also shaped interdisciplinary studies of human relations and institutions and the field later known as "culture and personality." But the central anthropological theories which Sapir proposed regard the relationship between the individual and culture as dynamically shaped by language.

Sapir's name is linked with that of his student, Benjamin Whorf (1897–1941), in the famous Sapir-Whorf hypothesis, which posits a relationship between the categories of meaning found within a language and the mental categories speakers of that language use to describe and classify the world. The implications of this simple hypothesis are profound. It suggests that understanding meaning—in all its different dimensions—is as important as understanding phonetics, syntax, and grammar, the most common dimensions of linguistic analysis prior to Sapir's work. The Sapir-Whorf hypothesis implies that different languages mark different systems of perception and the differences between societies' cultural behavior are communicated by and codified in the structure of linguistic meaning. The study of another culture's language is more than an investigation into how they speak; it's an inquiry into how cultural existence is created.

Sapir's contributions occurred in the context of an anthropological linguistics with long antecedents, but most immediately shaped through the work of Franz Boas. At a time when much ethnographic work was focused on elements of culture which did not require language mastery—e.g., trait studies of material culture or studies conducted through interpreters—Boas' emphasis on the importance of learning non-Western languages was innovative. In 1911 Boas wrote in his *Handbook of American Indian Languages*:

> A command of the language [of a tribe] is an indispensable means of obtaining accurate and thorough [ethnological] knowledge, because much information can be gained by listening to conversations of the natives and by taking part in their daily life, which, to the observer who has no command of the language, will remain entirely inaccessible. [1911:60]

This notion of language as a research tool was less important than the idea that language provided insights into other dimensions of culture, however. Boas particularly emphasized the importance of recording extended native language texts dictated by speakers. These texts could then be wrung of every drop of available information and correlated with other sources of information. The linguist Roman Jakobson describes the impact of Boas' idea:

> Language was considered by Boas not only as part of ethnological phenomena in general but even as "one of the most instructive fields of inquiry" and his motivation is thoroughly remarkable: "The great advantage that linguistics offers in this respect," Boas tells in his magnificent introduction to the *Handbook of American Indian Languages* (1911), "is the fact that, on the whole, the categories which are formed always remain unconscious and that for this reason the processes which lead to their formation can be followed without the misleading and disturbing factors of secondary explanations, which are so common in ethnology." [Jakobson 1966:129]

This "fertile and pathbreaking" idea, Jakobson (1966:130) continues, implies that:

> Among the various ethnological phenomena the linguistic processes (or rather operations) exemplify most strikingly and plainly the logic of the unconscious. For this reason—Boas insists—"the very fact of the unconsciousness of the linguistic processes helps us to gain a clear

understanding of the ethnological phenomena, a point the importance of which cannot be underrated." The place of language with
regard to the other social systems and the meaning of linguistics for a
thorough insight into the diverse ethnological patterns had never
been stated so precisely.

And thus the fact that cross-cousins and parallel cousins are linguistically distinguished in Crow and not in English is not simply
because the languages use different words, but because the classification of relatives differs due to the social roles (i.e., potential spouses)
such kin have in relationship to the speaker, Ego. Literally, language
reflects and shapes the world as it is perceived by humans, and understanding the organization of linguistic meaning illuminates the basic
structures of culture. That basic concept, with its roots in Boas' approach
to linguistics, was elaborated and refined in the works of Edward Sapir.

Background

Sapir, a Jew born in Prussia, arrived in New York with his parents when
he was five years old, part of the great emigration from Europe that
was funneled through Ellis Island. Growing up poor on the East Side of
New York, Sapir's intellectual gifts became obvious at an early age. He
won scholarships to Columbia College, where he graduated in 1904 at
the age of 20, completing his undergraduate education in just three
years (Darnell 1990:5). He immediately continued graduate studies at
Columbia under Boas, and in 1905 did fieldwork with the Wishram of
the lower Columbia River valley; the resulting study was published in
1909. Sapir went to Oregon to study the Takelma language in 1906,
research that formed the basis of his doctoral dissertation. The difficulties of the Takelma language make his dissertation quite remarkable;
Benedict noted, "There was no period of apprenticeship in Sapir's linguistic work; his phonetic and morphological gifts are as apparent in
this boyhood work as in that of a student of long and arduous experience." The same year Sapir finished his dissertation (1907) he also
published two articles on Takelma ethnology in the *American Anthropologist* and in the *Journal of American Folklore* (Sapir 1907a, 1907b).

Sapir was a research assistant at Berkeley in 1907–1908, working on
the native Californian language, Yana. Next he went to the University
of Pennsylvania, which supported his research on the Southern Paiute,
the first scientific study of a Shoshonean language. Working with Toni
Tillohash, a Southern Paiute man employed by the University of

Pennsylvania Museum, Sapir created a grammar of Southern Paiute which set new standards in its sensitivity to the native speaker's intuitive use of language (Darnell 1990:34–35).

In 1910 Sapir obtained his first permanent position as the chief of the Division of Anthropology, Geological Survey of Canada, based in Ottawa (Darnell 1990:65–79). From this post Sapir conducted research on the Nootka of British Columbia and a variety of Athabaskan languages; this work led to the definition of Na-Dene, a linguistic stock consisting of Northwest Coast languages like Haida, Tlingit, and other Athabaskan languages, including Navaho.

During his 15 years in Ottawa, Sapir turned his attention to problems of historical linguistics. "Certain resemblances in vocabulary and phonetics are undoubtedly due to borrowing of one language from another," Sapir wrote in the 1929 *Enyclopedia Britannica*, "but the more deeplying resemblances, such as can be demonstrated, for instance, for Shoshonean, Piman, and Nahuatl or for Athabaskan and Tlingit, must be due to a common origin now greatly obscured by the operation of phonetic laws, grammatical developments and losses, analogical disturbances, and borrowing of elements from sources" (1968a:171). To understand these historical connections, Sapir proposed a reclassification of American Indian languages. The classification proposed by Major John Wesley Powell—the great explorer, geologist and ethnologist—posited some 55 different linguistic stocks for North America, treating each as fundamentally distinct. Sapir saw greater connections between American Indian languages and replaced Powell's scheme with a mere six linguistic stocks for North America: 1) Eskimo-Aleut, 2) Algonkin, 3) Dene, 4) Penutian, 5) Hokan, and 6) Aztec-Tanoan (today called Uto-Aztecan). Languages within such stocks might be mutually unintelligible but exhibit clear affinities and shared ancestry, as do English, German, Danish, Swedish, and Norwegian, for example. Sapir's six-unit classification of American Indian languages dominated American linguistics into the 1960s, and it remains an essential framework for organizing Native American languages (Darnell 1990:110).

Sapir's Ottawa period was a time of intellectual isolation. Ottawa was far from the centers of anthropology in New York, Berkeley, and Chicago. Sapir's position in the Geological Survey did not involve teaching, so he lacked the stimulation of exchanges with students. The letters exchanged during this time between Sapir and Ruth Benedict make his sense of isolation clear.

But the time in Ottawa was also marked by extreme creativity (Darnell 1990:87–88). Sapir had a wide-ranging intellect, seemingly captivated by everything to do with words, and his publications from the Ottawa period indicate an extraordinary productivity. In addition to his writings in ethnology and linguistics, Sapir also published poetry, book reviews and essays on nonanthropological subjects. His 26 publications from 1922 include "The Fundamental Elements of Northern Yana" and "Athabaskan Tone"; as well as reviews of poetry and novels which were published in *The New Republic*, *The Dial*, and *Canadian Bookman*; 16 original poems, and translations of three French Canadian folksongs. Such versatile virtuosity is very rare.

In 1925 Sapir eagerly accepted a position at the University of Chicago where he could teach a group of appreciative graduate students, and where he could develop his interests in the area of semantics—the study of meaning—and in personality and culture. This latter arena of interest led him to give central importance to the role of the individual in culture and marked a break with contemporary thinkers about the nature of culture.

Culture and the Individual

A recurrent aspect of early-20th-century definitions of culture is their emphasis on the superorganic, supraindividual nature of culture. The notion of the superorganic is best developed in Kroeber's work (see pp. 73–76), in which he argued that culture had a superorganic property that varied independently of the individuals who composed it, and also that culture, society, and the individual were discrete, irreducible phenomena. Sapir's position was very different: he believed that broad generalizations about society were misplaced and that "There are as many cultures as there are individuals in a population" (quoted by Benedict 1939:407).

This idea forms the background of an article Sapir wrote in 1938, entitled "Why Cultural Anthropology Needs the Psychiatrist" (1968b:569–577). Sapir opens with a discussion of J. O. Dorsey's study of the Omaha Indians and the fact that after making several anthropological generalizations ("The Omaha believe . . .") Dorsey said at various points, "Two Crows denies this." Sapir admits to being shocked when he read this as a student, assuming that Dorsey had not fulfilled his anthropological responsibility of providing the reader with a seamless view of a different society; instead the responsibility of weighing how Two Crows' different opinions fit into the general patterns of Omaha culture had been passed on to the reader. But in retrospective, Sapir wrote:

> We see now that Dorsey was ahead of his age. Living as he did in close touch with the Omaha Indians [Dorsey was a missionary], he knew he was dealing, not with a society or with a specimen of primitive man nor with a cross section of the history of primitive culture, but with a finite, though indefinite, number of human beings, who gave themselves the privilege of differing from each other not only in matters generally considered as "one's own business" but even on questions which clearly transcended the private individual's concern and were, by the anthropologist's definition, implied in the conception of a definitely delimited society with a definitely discoverable culture. [1968b:570–571]

Sapir was tantalized by Two Crows' "contrariness" because he saw the implications for our understanding of other cultures. First, as a matter of method, the inquiry into variation can be extremely fruitful even in matters that may seem to be objective. For example, if all the other Omaha say there are eight clans, but Two Crows states there are seven clans, Sapir (1968b:573–574) wonders "How could this be?" Well, it might be that one clan no longer exists in a practical sense, but that it's remembered by everyone (because a well-remembered elderly man formed a part of it) except Two Crows. Perhaps the clan had a particular social or ceremonial function that makes its "existence" hard to overlook. Maybe Two Crows comes from a clan that detested the now extinct clan, making it easy for him to forget it and giving him "the perfectly honest conviction that one need speak of only seven clans in the tribe." Two Crows "had a special kind of rightness, which was partly factual, and partly personal." But more important than this is the fundamental implication of Two Crows' opinion:

> The truth of the matter is that if we think long enough about Two Crows and his persistent denials, we shall have to admit that in some sense Two Crows is never wrong. It may not be a very useful sense for social science but in a strict methodology of science in general it dare not be completely ignored. The fact that this rebel, Two Crows, can in turn bend others to his own view of fact or theory or to his own preference in action shows that his divergence from custom had, from the very beginning, the essential possibility of culturalized behavior. [1968b:572]

Thus we arrive at a paradox, almost Zen-like in its counter-intuitive simplicity, that normative and deviant behaviors are equally cultural behaviors, that "the world of socialized behavior is nothing more than consensus of opinion" (1968b:572). Sapir's answer about the relationship between the individual and society is to simply point out that society consists of individuals, that culture is consensus, and that generalizations about cultural behavior are counterbalanced with individual, divergent behaviors. This is different from Benedict's approach, which presented the individual and culture as dichotomous; those individuals who through experience and personality fit easily into their culture were successes, those who did not were deviants (see pp. 83–85). Sapir denied this implicit opposition between individual and culture:

> There is no real opposition, at last analysis, between the concept of the culture of the group and the concept of individual culture. The two are interdependent. A healthy national culture is never a passively accepted heritage from the past, but implies the creative participation of the members of the community. . . . It is just as true, however, that the individual is helpless without a cultural heritage to work on. [Sapir 1968e:321]

Not surprisingly, Sapir extended this view of cultural behavior to that pure example of cultural practice, language:

> It is obvious that for the building up of society, its units and subdivisions, and the understandings which prevail between its members some processes of communication are needed. While we often speak of society as though it were a static structure defined by tradition, it is, in the more intimate sense, nothing of the kind, but a highly intricate network of partial or complete understandings between the members of organizational units of every degree of size and complexity. . . . It is only apparently a static sum of social institutions; actually it is being reanimated or creatively reaffirmed from day to day by particular acts of a communicative nature which obtain among individuals participating in it. [1968c:104]

On *Language*

In 1921 Sapir published *Language: An Introduction to the Study of Speech*, his only book for a general audience. Sapir's biographer, Regna Darnell (1990) writes that *Language* was directed to a broad readership lacking in his own foundations in ethnology and linguistics. "Anthropologists knew about fieldwork but not about linguistic methods," Darnell (1990:96) observes. "Linguists knew about the methods but not about their application to a full range of human languages. The educated public knew neither." The literary origins and Indo-European focus of traditional linguistics and the methodological weakness and non-Western emphasis of anthropology meant that neither discipline agreed on a common ground. Darnell (1990:96) writes that "disciplinary boundaries had cut off recognition of the actual creativity of language, which was, in all cultures, a rich and precise vehicle for the expression of thought. Sapir set himself the challenge of producing a book that could be understood by any educated person with an open mind. . . ."

First, Sapir described the dynamic artificiality of human communication: "Language is a purely human and noninstinctive method of communicating ideas, emotions, and desires by means of a system of voluntarily produced symbols" (1921:8). Sapir then shows that words are not symbols of specific perceptions or even specific objects but always refer to concepts of objects, "a convenient capsule of thought that embraces thousands of distinct experiences and that is ready to take in thousands more" (Sapir 1921:13). These capsules of thought not only express our thoughts, but in the process of learning language our thoughts are shaped by the concepts used to organize the perception of experience. That is true of even the most simple descriptive terms about the environment:

> The mere existence, for instance, of a certain type of animal in the physical environment of a people does not suffice to give rise to a linguistic symbol referring to it. It is necessary that the animal be known by the members of the group in common and that they have some interest, however slight, in it before the language of the community is called upon to make reference to this particular element of the physical environment. In other words, so far as language is concerned, all environmental influence reduces at last analysis to the influence of social environment. [1968d:90]

Sapir cites numerous examples of the ways that language reflects the socially significant aspects of the environment; he lists, for example, eighteen topographic features used by the Shoshone Paiute to describe the landscape of their desert homeland, including canyon with creek, canyon without water, slope of mountain or canyon wall receiving sunlight, shaded mountain slope or canyon wall, and so on (1968d:91). In passing, Sapir points out that virtually any Native American hunter and gatherer would be shocked by the range of plants we would simply refer to as "weeds." But note, our linguistic impression does not merely reflect our lack of social interest in seed collecting—the words we employ and the conceptual categories they imply *shape* the way we perceive the world. We look into a vacant lot and all we *see* are weeds. That basic truth is at the core of the Sapir-Whorf hypothesis, which links the categories of language and the cultural perception of the world.

The Sapir-Whorf Hypothesis

Benjamin Whorf was an amazing man who made significant contributions to linguistics in a scant dozen years before his early death in 1941 at the age of 44. Whorf was a peculiarly American type of genius (Chase 1956). He worked as a fire prevention engineer for the Hartford Fire Insurance Company for 22 years; his linguistic studies were done after work and during extended leaves from his company. Whorf's introduction to linguistics was circuitous, sparked by an interest in Aztec culture which led to an interest in Nahuatl, the Aztec language. His linguistic research was sufficiently impressive that he was awarded a grant to study Nahuatl in Mexico in 1930. Whorf's contributions and achievements, all self-tutored, were very impressive.

But Whorf's linguistic career took a major change when he met Sapir. In the fall of 1931 Sapir left the University of Chicago for Yale and Whorf immediately enrolled in Sapir's seminar. At Yale Whorf's study on American Indian languages intensified and he became a central member of a group of Yale graduate students—including Morris Swadesh, Charles Hockett, and Carl Voeglin—who made major contributions to American linguistics. Sapir was instrumental in directing Whorf towards a study of the Uto-Aztecan languages and particularly, Hopi, and the two men's interaction led to a basic concept, the Sapir-Whorf hypothesis.

As discussed above (pp. 88–89), the Sapir-Whorf hypothesis proposes that linguistic categories structure and transmit culturally learned perceptions of existence. It is difficult to determine each man's contribution to the hypothesis about the relationship between language, culture, and perception. Whorf's ideas are clearly based on Sapir's writings and teachings, although Sapir died before most of Whorf's writings were published and thus never commented directly on the Sapir-Whorf hypothesis (Darnell 1990:375).

In a paper titled "Linguistic Factors in the Terminology of Hopi Architecture," written in 1940 but not published until 1952, Whorf outlined the range of building terms and concepts associated with the

Hopi's pueblo constructions and, more generally, their concepts of space. Whorf notes that the Hopi terms "all denote three-dimensional solids in the geometrical sense, solid and rigid masses, or definitely bounded areas on or penetrations through such solids"; these words included *té'kwa* for a section of wall, unfinished wall, or walls of a ruin; *kí.?àmi* for roof; or *poksö* for a vent hole, unglazed window or chimney (1956:200). What Whorf did not find was a diversity of words for three-dimensional spaces—corridor, hall, passage, cellar, loft, attic, storeroom, chamber, and room—like we have in English. It is not that Hopi is linguistically impoverished in its description of architecture, but that the spaces are described not in functional or nominative terms but in locational terms. Whorf writes:

> This is in line with the way Hopi and, in fact, most or all Uto-Aztecan languages represent location in space, or regions in space. They are not set up as entities that can function in a sentence like terms for people, animals, or masses of matter having characteristic form, or, again, human groups and human relations, but are treated as *purely relations concepts*, of an adverbial type. Thus hollow spaces like room, chamber, hall, are not really *named* as objects are, but are rather *located*; i.e. positions of other things are specified so as to show their location in such hollow spaces. [1956:202]

According to Whorf, the Hopi emphasize solid and constructional elements rather than enclosed spaces and describe the spaces in spatial reference to each other. This is a fundamentally different way of thinking about architectural space than we have in English, in which some architectural locators even incorporate functional elements *(Where is it? Upstairs)*.

The differences between the Hopi and English treatment of interior architectural spaces is paralleled in the terms applied to buildings as a whole. Whorf points out that in English we have a large vocabulary for buildings with different functions—as in *church, chapel, cathedral, synagogue, meeting house, temple, shrine,* just to cite some religious structures—that does not exist in Hopi. Hopi has three words for structures, two of them minor—the word for shrine (*té*tèska*) and the word for tent (*mecávki*), an introduced item—and then *ki*he*, building. Even though the Hopi have different "types" of buildings—residences, storehouses, piki-houses (used only for baking corn wafers [*piki*]), and the semisubterranean circular kivas used only for ceremonies)—the language does not fuse structure and activity into functional sets. "They do not have . . . the pattern which is so natural to us," Whorf (1956:204) observes, "in which 'a church,' i.e. an institution, is a term that merges quite imperceptibly into 'a church' meaning a type of building used as a meeting place for this institution, with the distinction hardly felt until attention is drawn to it. . . ."

Such fundamental differences in the description of architectural space are paralleled by differences in basic classifications of the external world: colors, directions, weather phenomena, plant and animal classifications, kin relations, social obligations, and so on. These classifications reflect more than just different words applied to the same objects and concepts, but objects and concepts which are perceived and conceived of in fundamentally different ways. This basic realization, the central tenet of the Sapir-Whorf hypothesis, reverberated through anthropology and the other social sciences and focused attention on the issue of meaning.

Conclusion

Sapir and Whorf died within a few years of each other at the relatively young ages of 54 (Sapir) and 44 (Whorf). It is impossible to know what more these men would have achieved had they lived as long as Alfred Kroeber. Apart from his linguistic analyses and polymathic accomplishments, elements in Sapir's work have great importance for current anthropological thinking. The issue of meaning is central. Sapir's work shifted the focus of linguistic analysis from the word to its meaning, which immediately led to ideas about the cultural creation of meaning. If, as Two Crows seemed to demonstrate, the world of socialized behavior is simply, but significantly, nothing more than public consensus of opinion, then it follows that such a consensus is hammered out in argument, debate, gossip, rituals, and a whole array of symbolic interactions that anthropologists like Clifford Geertz (see Chapter 19) would refer to as "discourse" (Geertz 1973:9–10).

Culture is not a chaotic tangle of individual opinions, however, in the views of Sapir and Whorf, because language itself imposes certain structures on perception. As members of a culture and speakers of a language we learn certain implicit classifications and consider those classifications to be accurate renderings of the world. And since those linguistic categories vary, different cultures, though comprised of individuals who have the ability to disagree, also exhibit distinctive consensuses about the nature of existence. ✦

Bibliography

Benedict, Ruth
1939 Edward Sapir. American Anthropologist 41:465–477.

Carroll, John
1966 Benjamin Lee Whorf. *In* Portraits of Linguists: A Biographical Source Book for the History of Western Linguistics, 1746-1963. Vol 2. T. Sebeok, ed. Pp. 563–585. Bloomington: Indiana University Press.

Chase, Stuart
1956 Foreword. *In* Language, Thought, and Reality: Selected Writings of Benjamin Lee Whorf. J. Carroll, ed. Pp. v-x. Cambridge, MA: MIT Press.

Darnell, Regna
1990 Edward Sapir: Linguist, Anthropologist, Humanist. Berkeley: University of California Press.

Emmeneau, Murray
1966 Franz Boas as Linguist. *In* Portraits of Linguists: A Biographical Source Book for the History of Western Linguistics, 1746–1963. Vol 2. T. Sebeok, ed. Pp. 122–127. Bloomington: Indiana University Press.

Jakobson, Roman
1966 Franz Boas' Approach to Language. *In* Portraits of Linguists: A Biographical Source Book for the History of Western Linguistics, 1746–1963. Vol 2. T. Sebeok, ed. Pp. 127–139. Bloomington: Indiana University Press.

Mandelbaum, D.
1968 Editor's Introduction. *In* Selected Writings of Edward Sapir in Language, Culture and Personality. Pp. v–xii. Berkeley: University of California Press.

Sapir, Edward
1907a Notes on the Takelma Indians of Southwestern Oregon. American Anthropologist 9:251–275.
1907b Religious Ideas of the Takelma Indians of Southwestern Oregon. Journal of American Folklore 20:33–49.
1909 Takelma Texts. Anthropological Publications 2(1):1–263. University of Pennsylvannia.
1921 Language: An Introduction to the Study of Speech. New York: Harcourt, Brace & World.
1968a Central and North American Languages. *In* Selected Writings of Edward Sapir in Language, Culture and Personality. D. Mandelbaum, ed. Pp. 169–178. Berkeley: University of California Press.
1968b Why Cultural Anthropology Needs the Psychiatrist. *In* Selected Writings of Edward Sapir in Language, Culture and Personality. D. Mandelbaum, ed. Pp. 569–577. Berkeley: University of California Press.
1968c Communication. *In* Selected Writings of Edward Sapir in Language, Culture and Personality. D. Mandelbaum, ed. Pp. 104–109. Berkeley: University of California Press.
1968d Language and Environment. *In* Selected Writings of Edward Sapir in Language, Culture and Personality. D. Mandelbaum, ed. Pp. 89–103. Berkeley: University of California Press.

1968e Culture, Genuine and Spurious. *In* Selected Writings of Edward Sapir in Language, Culture and Personality. D. Mandelbaum, ed. Pp. 308–331. Berkeley: University of California Press.

Voeglin, Carl
1966 Edward Sapir. *In* Portraits of Linguists: A Biographical Source Book for the History of Western Linguistics, 1746–1963. Vol 2. T. Sebeok, ed. Pp. 489–492. Bloomington: Indiana University Press.

Whorf, Benjamin
1956 Linguistic Factors in the Terminology of Hopi Architecture. *In* Language, Thought, and Reality: Selected Writings of Benjamin Lee Whorf. J. Carroll, ed. Pp. 199–206. Cambridge, MA: MIT Press.

Chapter 8

Margaret Mead
The Individual and Culture

When she died in November 1978, Margaret Mead was the most widely read anthropologist in America; she probably still is. Her first book, *Coming of Age in Samoa,* was published in 1928, became an instant classic, and remains the best selling of all anthropological books (Freeman 1983:xii). The book's vast popularity stemmed from its central question, a question humans find fascinating: Why are we the way we are? Mead found the answer in three experiences that most people share—childhood, parenthood and sex—and thus her work was immediately relevant to literally millions of people. The wide interest in Mead's work and ideas is reflected by her numerous, diverse publications, and availability in a variety of media, including records, tapes, films, and videos. As of 1976 her bibliography listed over 1400 printed works: books, articles in scientific journals, book reviews, newspaper articles, statements entered as congressional testimony, conference reports, and a continuous stream of magazine articles (Gordon 1976). The magazine articles are interesting in their titles and venues: "South Sea Hints on Bringing Up Children" appeared in the September 1929 issue of *Parents Magazine*; the July 1948 *Mademoiselle* featured "Are Children Savages?"; and beginning in the 1960s Mead wrote a monthly column in *Redbook Magazine* in which she would answer readers' questions: "Margaret Mead Answers: Questions About School Prayers, Happiness, Telepathy, etc." (February 1963), "Margaret Mead Answers: Is Housework Easier than It Was 50 Years Ago? Was Shakespeare Really Shakespeare? What is the Fatal Fascination of Baseball?" (November 1964), and "Margaret Mead Answers: Questions about Jean-Paul Sartre, School Busing, Why People Like to Have Their Hair

Stand on End, etc." (March 1965). This shows a certain daredevil flair, a bold willingness to write about almost anything. "Anthropology had attracted Mead in the first place because its borders were so flexible," Jane Howard (1984:13) writes, "but even it could not contain her."

Mead's motive was advocacy, her desire to speak to central issues about society and to reform social conditions based on comparative anthropological data. The fact that another society did not, for example, feed infants on a rigid schedule implied that to do so involved learned behavior, behavior which could be identified and changed if desired. The impacts of different child-rearing practices on adult personality could be assessed, different practices could be advocated and adopted, and society could be improved. "The process of inquiry," her daughter Mary Catherine Bateson writes about Mead's experimentation with her own child, "involving the life of a child, could have been pursued only in a context of advocacy, and advocacy, for Margaret, was never far behind" (Bateson 1984:30).

Mead's insights into child-rearing were widely felt in American society. Mead chose Dr. Benjamin Spock as her daughter's pediatrician because he had been psychoanalyzed (Bateson 1984:31), and Mary Catherine Bateson was the first breast-fed and demand-fed infant he had encountered. As an anthropologist, Mead recorded her infant's feeding demands, found patterns in the times, and then scheduled her teaching and writing commitments around those times. This had some influence on Dr. Spock's writings on infant care, and consequently for the rearing of the post-World War II baby boomers. For better or worse, many of us were raised or raise our children in a manner indirectly influenced by Margaret Mead. As her daughter writes, "The innovations that Margaret made as a parent were actually greater than they seem now because so many have been incorporated into patterns of society" (Bateson 1984:33).

In spite of her prolific writings, or maybe because of them, Margaret Mead's influence on anthropology is diffuse. Unlike theoreticians like Sapir or Benedict whose core concepts can be neatly summarized and their implications derived, Margaret Mead's central idea—that differences between peoples are usually cultural differences imparted in childhood—does not lead to specific expectations but instead to a general shift in view, to a concern with how a human infant is transformed into an adult member of a particular society. And Mead's very public role as an advocate has raised questions about the accuracy of her anthropological research (Freeman 1983; Holmes 1987; Leacock 1993). Margaret Mead lived long, worked hard, and argued for combining social innovation and a respect for tradition in an effort to improve the human situation. The consequences of her life and work are deep and continuing.

Background

Margaret Mead was born in 1901 into an upper-middle-class, educated, and socially solid family. Her father was an economics professor, and her mother a college-educated woman active in a variety of social causes—civil rights, women's sufffrage, anti-fur—who imparted her sense of advocacy to her daughter. After a year at DePauw University, Mead transferred to Barnard College, the women's university associated with Columbia University in the heart of New York City. She thoroughly enjoyed herself at Barnard, forming lifelong friendships with other students and becoming swept up in the major theories, political issues, and controversies that flowed through academic circles with the development of modernism (Mead 1972).

As an English and psychology major, Mead took a course from Franz Boas in her senior year. She was captivated by Boas' lectures and after the first term attended every course and seminar he offered at Columbia. Mead was also fascinated by Boas' teaching assistant, Ruth Benedict, who convinced Mead to pursue anthropology as a graduate student. By the end of her senior year at Barnard, Mead was prepared to begin her studies in anthropology—and her first marriage to Luther Cressman, who went on to become a well-known archaeologist. She later married the anthropologist Reo Fortune, whose work *Sorcerers of Dobu* is a classic ethnography discussed by Benedict in *Patterns of Culture* (see pp. 82–83), and finally Gregory Bateson, one of the most creative and iconoclastic social scientists of the 20th century (Lipset 1980). Mead conducted fieldwork with Fortune and Bateson, and she and Bateson had a daughter, the anthropologist and writer Mary Catherine Bateson. Mead's anthropological research and her personal life were parallel explorations of the relationships between gender, childhood, and society.

Gender, Child-rearing and Culture: Fieldwork and Theory

Mead's theoretical ideas evolved directly from her field investigations. Between 1925 and 1939 Mead participated in five field trips and studied eight different societies. Oddly, her own dissertation was not based on fieldwork but on library research about the material culture of

Polynesia—a topic Boas assigned—and is described as detailed and competent by some (Thomas 1980) and lackluster by others (McDowell 1980:278). Mead's first field research was in Samoa where she spent eight months in the field in 1925. Her book, *Coming of Age in Samoa*, was the extremely popular outcome, and her results remain controversial (see discussion below, pp. 106–107). On the return voyage from Samoa Mead and Fortune worked on two field projects: a brief investigation of the Omaha during the summer of 1930 (her only work on a Native American group), and a much longer research project in New Guinea (1931–1933), a cross-cultural comparison described in her *Sex and Temperament in Three Primitive Societies* (1935). Later she conducted field research with Gregory Bateson in Bali in 1936–1938 and again in 1939 and among the Iatmul of New Guinea in 1938. The Balinese research is notable for its use of photography as a research tool, and it resulted in *Balinese Character* (Bateson and Mead 1942).

These three phases of fieldwork capture the ethnographic bases of Mead's central contribution: that specific child-rearing practices shape personalities that in turn give specific societies their essential natures. In the introduction to *Coming of Age in Samoa*, Mead wrote:

> [T]his tale of another way of life is mainly concerned with education, with the process by which the baby, arrived cultureless upon the human scene, becomes a full-fledged adult member of his or her society. The strongest light will fall upon the ways in which Samoan education, in its broadest sense, differs from our own. And from this contrast we may be able to turn, made newly and vividly self-conscious and self-critical, to judge anew and perhaps fashion differently the education we give our children. [Mead 1928:13]

Mead's profile of Samoan upbringing was based on a detailed study of 68 girls between the ages of 8 and 20 in three near contiguous villages on the island of Ta'u, the largest of the three islands which make up the Manu'a group of easternmost islands in American Samoa. A sample record sheet (Mead 1928:284) indicates that Mead collected a variety of personal and family data on the ways Samoans evaluated each other (the most beautiful girl, the wisest man, the worst boy), and administered a set of basic psychological tests such as rote memory for numbers. "But," Mead admitted,

> [T]his quantitative data represents the barest skeleton of the material which was gathered through months of observation of the individuals and of groups, alone, in their households, and at play. From these observations, the bulk of the conclusions are drawn concerning the attitudes of the children towards their families and towards each

other, their religious interests or the lack of them, and the details of their sex lives. This information cannot be reduced to tables or statistical statements. [1928:264]

The basic conclusion was that adolescence in Samoa was not a stressful period for girls, because in general Samoan society lacked stresses:

> The Samoan background which makes growing up so easy, so simple a matter, is the general casualness of the whole society. For Samoa is a place where no one plays for very high stakes, no one pays very heavy prices, no one suffers for his convictions or fights to the death for special ends. Disagreements between parent and child are settled by the child's moving across the street, between a man and his village by the man's removal to the next village, between a husband and wife's seducer by a few fine mats. . . . And in personal relations, caring is slight. Love and hate, jealousy and revenge, sorrow and bereavement, are all matters of weeks. From the first months of its life, when a child is handed carelessly from one woman's hands to another's, the lesson is learned of not caring for one person greatly, not setting high hopes on any one relationship. [Mead 1928:199]

Mead cited a number of observations to support her conclusion. Samoan babies are nursed on demand until two or three, but other foods like mashed papaya and coconut milk are given to the infant during the first week. After weaning, toddlers are turned over to a girl who is six or seven years old; these older children watch over and are held responsible for their charges' misbehavior. The Samoan household is bilateral and often extended; household composition varies from nuclear families to households of 15 to 20 people who may be related by marriage, blood, adoption or friendship. This flexibility of residence allows a Samoan child to take up residence with another set of relatives when there are conflicts at home.

Mead described sexual relations as frequent and usually without consequence. Of the 30 postpubescent girls Mead studied, 17 had heterosexual relations and 22 homosexual relations; most of the female virgins lived in the house of the Christian pastor. Liaisons occurred on the beach or when an intrepid lover crawled into the house; rape was infrequent (p. 93; cf. Freeman 1983) in contrast to the "*moetotolo*, in which a man stealthily appropriates the favours which are meant for another." Abortions may end pregnancies, although there is no great fuss made over "illegitimate" children who are incorporated into the household.

This ease of transitions, the fluidity of status changes, Mead argued, characterized childhood and society in Samoa. It was not simply a matter of childhood shaping society or vice-versa, but both. The implications of this research, and the discovery that adolescent turmoil was not an innate characteristic of the human condition, gave Mead's work great significance.

It is also a source of controversy 55 years later. In 1983 Derek Freeman published *Margaret Mead and Samoa: The Making and Unmasking of an Anthropological Myth* in which he argued that Mead systematically distorted Samoan society. Freeman, also a specialist on Samoa, contended that Mead "greatly underestimated the complexity of the culture, society, history, and psychology" of Samoans, assuming them to be "very simple" (Freeman 1983:285). That simplicity, Freeman held, merely reflected Mead's lack of command of Samoan language, her ignorance of the complexities of Samoan status and political systems, and a naive euphoria over Samoa as a tropical Eden. But most damning, in Freeman's critique, was that Mead went to Samoa with the preconceived intention of showing that culture, not biology, determined human responses to life's transitions, like adolescence. Freeman writes:

> It is thus evident that her writings from this period, about Samoa as about other South Seas cultures, had the explicit aim of confuting biological explanations of human behavior and vindicating the doctrines of the Boasian school. . . . [T]here can be no doubt that Mead's fervent desire to demonstrate the validity of the doctrines she held in common with Benedict and Boas led her, in Samoa, to overlook evidence running counter to her beliefs. . . . [Freeman 1983:282]

Freeman's accusations touched off a howl of controversy, quite separate from the evaluation of the evidence, since he had had evidence contradicting Mead since the 1960s, but only published it after her death. The debate, which was featured in the media, grew particularly vitriolic, because it touched a real nerve: the debasement of the best-known work of the best-known American anthropologist (see, for example, Holmes 1987; Leacock 1993).

But long before the controversy, Mead's work in Samoa set the pattern for a series of detailed ethnographic studies elsewhere in Oceania and Melanesia. *Sex and Temperament in Three Primitive Societies* presents the results of Mead's 1931–33 work among three New

Guinea societies. Her research examined a basic question about "the conditioning of the social personalities of the two sexes. " She wrote:

> This study is not concerned with whether there are or are not actual and universal differences between the sexes, either quantitative or qualitative. It is not concerned whether women are more variable than men, which was claimed before the doctrine of evolution exalted variability or less variable, which was claimed afterwards. It is not a treatise on the rights of women, nor an inquiry into the basis of feminism. It is, very simply, an account of how three primitive societies have grouped their social attitudes towards temperament about the very obvious facts of sex-difference. I studied this problem in simple societies because here we have the drama of civilization writ small, a social microcosm alike in kind, but different in size and magnitude, from the complex social structures. . . . Among the gentle mountain-dwelling Arapesh, the fierce cannibalistic Mundugumor, and the graceful headhunters of Tchambuli, I studied this question. Each of these tribes had, as has every human society, the point of sex-difference to use as one theme in the plot of social life, and each of these peoples has developed that theme differently. [Mead 1963:viii–ix]

These three groups lived within a 100-mile radius of each other on the northern shore of Papua New Guinea, and yet their personalities were completely distinct. Of the Arapesh, Mead wrote:

> [T]hey lack the conception of human nature as evil and in need of strong checks and curbs. . . . they regard both men and women as inherently gentle, responsive, and cooperative, able and willing to subordinate the self to the needs of those who are younger or weaker and to derive a major satisfaction from doing so. They have surrounded with delight that part of parenthood which we consider to be specially maternal, the minute, loving care for the little child and the selfless delight in that child's progress towards maturity. [1963:134]

Arapesh child-rearing responsibilities were so evenly divided between mother and father that, "if one comments upon a middle-aged man as good-looking, the people answer, 'Good-looking? Y-e-s? But you should have seen him before he bore all those children'" (Mead 1963:39).

The Mundugumor could not be more different. Living in a society "based upon a theory of a natural hostility that exists between all members of the same sex . . .," Mundugumor fathers and sons, and mothers and daughters were adversaries. "The Mundugumor man-child is born into a hostile world," Mead (1963: 189) wrote, "a world in which most of the members of his own sex will be his enemies, in which his major equipment for success must be a capacity for violence, for seeing and avenging insult. . . ." This hostile temperament was shared by men and women; the Mundugumor have "no theory that women differ temperamentally from men. They are believed to be just as violent, just as aggressive, just as jealous. They simply are not quite as strong physically, although a woman can put up a very good fight and a husband who wishes to beat his wife takes care to arm himself with a crocodile jaw and to be sure that she is not armed" (Mead 1963:210).

Turning to the Tchambuli, Mead found another society where the principal themes of temperament and gender were differently defined:

> As the Arapesh made growing food and children the greatest adventure of their lives, and the Mundugumor found greatest satisfaction in fighting and competitive acquisition of women, the Tchambuli may be said to live principally for art. Every man is an artist and most men are skilled not in some one art alone, but in many: in dancing, carving, plaiting, painting and so on. Each man is chiefly concerned with his role upon the stage of his society with the elaboration of his costume, the beauty of the masks that he owns, the skill of his own flute-playing, the finish and elan of his ceremonies, and upon other people's recognition and valuation of his performance. [1963:245]

And while Tchambuli men were preoccupied with art, women had the real power, controlling fishing and the most important manufactures, looking on their menfolk with "kindly tolerance and appreciation" (Mead 1963:255).

Sex and Temperament in Three Primitive Societies was important because at that time in the United States sex roles were viewed—by men and women—as inevitable, natural characteristics of gender differences; Mead showed that these behavior patterns were actually extremely malleable and reflected *cultural* differences.

Mead and Gregory Bateson also explored the cultural bases of personality in their fieldwork in Bali in 1936 to 1938. Their goal was to "translate aspects of culture never successfully recorded by the scientist, although often caught by the artist, into some form of communication sufficiently clear and sufficiently unequivocal to satisfy the requirements of scientific enquiry" (Bateson and Mead 1942:xi). In the absence of a complex scientific vocabulary designed to express a culture's ethos, Mead had relied on ordinary English words—even though their meanings were specific to a cultural setting completely different from Balinese experience (Bateson and Mead 1942:xi). The way out of this dilemma was to combine traditional ethnography with a photographic record so that the observations could be recorded and communicated.

The result is a fascinating anthropological record. Based on their work in the mountain community of Bajoeng Gede, Mead and Bateson document a way of life which is based on orientation. "Orientation," Mead (1942:11) observes, "in time, space, and status are the essentials of social existence . . . ." Mead (1942:7) writes that "Each man's place in the social scheme of his village is known." The status differences are reflected in space (the superior person should sleep on the eastern or inland side of the interior person), vertical elevation (higher chairs for higher statuses), language (using polished language to speak to someone of a higher caste or status), posture and gesture. In Bajoeng Gede, "space and time and social status form an orderly whole, with little stress or strain" and "within the fixed and complicated sets of regulations, obligations, and privileges, the people are relaxed and dreamy" (Mead 1942:10). "Orientation is felt as a protection rather than a straitjacket and its loss provokes extreme anxiety" (Mead 1942:10).

This cultural knowledge is literally transmitted at birth. Mead writes (1942:13):

> When the Balinese baby is born, the midwife, even at the moment of lifting him in her arms, will put words in his mouth, commenting, "I am just a poor little new-born baby, and I don't know how to talk properly, but I am very grateful to you, honorable people, who have entered this pig sty of a house to see me born." And from that moment, all through babyhood, the child is fitted into a frame of behavior, of imputed speech and imputed thought and complex gesture, far beyond his skill and maturity.

Gradually the child adopts these patterns of speech and behavior, a process that Mead describes in a fine metaphor, as "slip[ping] into speech, as into an old garment, worn before, but fitted on another hand" (Mead 1942:13).

"As with speech, so with posture and gesture," Mead writes, and it is in Bateson's photographs that we see mothers pose their children's hands in prayer, dance teachers extending children's arms to instruct by muscular rote, and a mother teasing her son by holding his younger sibling over his head and thus inverting proper relationships of age, status, and elevation. In all Bateson shot some 22,000 feet of 16mm film and 25,000 still photographs; combined with Mead's intensive ethnographic record, as Nancy McDowell (1980:297) observed, "they found themselves with a body of data, particularly photographic material, that was so detailed, extensive, and innovative that no other body of data existed with which they could compare it." It remains a masterpiece of documentation and analysis.

Conclusion

Balinese Character exemplifies a central theme in Mead's work—the relationship between individual and cultural pattern. It is an approach which became known as "culture and personality," and although it shares concerns with Benedict's approach of cultural patterns, Mead's work exhibits a more explicit use of psychological theory, methods of data collection, and a greater awareness of the dynamic between the individual and cultural ethos.

Culture is not just the individual writ large, Mead argued. The individual is a product of cultural behavior that shapes the person in common but unique manners that then are reinterpreted, and reexpressed, relived as the infant becomes an adult, as the child becomes a parent. This interaction between individual and culture is the dynamic, complex process by which humans learn to be humans, but humans of very distinctive sorts.

Like her colleagues Kroeber, Benedict, and Sapir, Mead attempted to discover what it was that made cultures distinctive but coherent. How is it that human societies can be so incredibly different, not just on the surface but at their very cores, and yet within a particular society there can be such unanimity as to values and practice? For the Victorian evolutionists the answer was easy: societies were so different because they represented stages in the "nearly uniform channels" of human progress. The Boasian critique demolished that easy answer, yet put nothing in its place; the best Boas could suggest was to keep collecting good ethnographic data and some day, perhaps, the laws of human culture would become evident.

But that apparently did not satisfy Boas' students, at least not Kroeber, Sapir, Benedict, and Mead. Each sought a different way to explain the coherency of culture: Kroeber turned to the superorganic, Benedict to the core values of culture, Sapir and Whorf to the conceptual categories embedded in language, and Margaret Mead to the processes of human development: the way an infant is bathed, the shared intimacies of husband and wife, or the small gestures that teach a child its place in the world. ✦

Bibliography

Bateson, Gregory and Margaret Mead
1942 Balinese Character: A Photographic Analysis. New York: New York Academy of Sciences.

Bateson, Mary Catherine
1984 With a Daughter's Eye: A Memoir of Margaret Mead and Gregory Bateson. New York: William Morrow and Co.

Freeman, Derek
1983 Margaret Mead and Samoa: The Making and Unmasking of an Anthropological Myth. Cambridge, MA: Harvard University Press.

Gordan, Joan,ed.
1976 Margaret Mead: The Complete Bibliography 1925–1975. The Hague: Mouton.

Holmes, Lowell
1987 Quest for the REAL Samoa: The Mead/Freeman Controversy and Beyond. South Hadley, MA: Bergin and Garvey.

Howard, Jane
1984 Margaret Mead: A Life. New York: Fawcett Columbine.

Leacock, Eleanor Burke
1993 The Problem of Youth in Contemporary Samoa. In From Labrador to Samoa: The Theory and Practice of Eleanor Burke Leacock. C. Sutton, ed. Pp. 115–130. Arlington, VA: Association for Feminist Anthropology/ American Anthropological Association.

Lipset, David
1980 Gregory Bateson: The Legacy of a Scientist. Englewood Cliffs, NJ: Prentice-Hall.

McDowell, Nancy
1980 The Oceanic Ethnography of Margaret Mead. American Anthropologist 82:278–303.

Mead, Margaret
1928 Coming of Age in Samoa: A Psychological Study of Primitive Youth for Western Civilization. New York: William Morrow and Co.
1963 Sex and Temperament in Three Primitive Societies. New York: William Morrow and Co.
1972 Blackberry Winter: My Earlier Years. New York: William Morrow And Co.

Thomas, David H.
1980 Margaret Mead as a Museum Anthropologist. American Anthropologist 82:354–361.

Part Three

The Nature of Society

Beginning in 1920, a fundamental division occurred between American and British anthropology. In the United States, anthropology focused on culture as a set of ideas; in the United Kingdom, it focused on society as the consequence of action. For the American cultural anthropologists, explanation involved showing the relationship between values and cultural behavior. For the British social anthropologists, explanation required analyzing the different segments of society and the institutions which articulate them.

Ironically, British social anthropology has its origins in France. The emphasis on the segmentation and articulation of society was directly derived from Durkheim's discussions of mechanical and organic solidarity, and it was explicitly introduced into British anthropology by Radcliffe-Brown. The foundational trope is a recurrent metaphor in Western thought: the organic analogy which holds that society is like an organism. Just as living things have specific organs that perform certain tasks yet are articulated by nervous, circulatory, and respiratory systems, human societies have distinct subdivisions with different functions that are varyingly tied together through economic, political, and religious institutions. Therefore, explanation of a particular social pattern involves a description of the structure and analysis of its function. Explication of a general social pattern requires demonstrating the cross-cultural utility of its function. Thus, in 1899 Marcel Mauss and Henri Hubert wrote "Essay on the Nature and Function of Magic," marking an approach to social analysis that had no counterpart in America.

American cultural anthropology and British social anthropology developed along different trajectories. First, the nature of an explanation differed dramatically. For Boas an explanation was a historical account, for his students an expression of shared mental constructs. For those operating in the Durkheimian tradition, an explanation was based on laws, statements of regularity about phenomena. This appeal to law-like generalities was explicitly denied by Kroeber (1952:79), who would write, "the findings of history can never be substantiated like proofs of natural science." And yet this is exactly what Malinowski and Radcliffe-Brown proposed.

They argued that functionalist explanations were scientific explanations and the word "science" figures prominently in their writings. The nexus of utility differed: for Malinowski, culture functioned to meet the cumulative social needs that originate in individual biological needs; for Radcliffe-Brown, culture functioned to maintain and reproduce society. But in either case, the cross-cultural occurrence of a specific cultural form resulted from its recurrent utility. The cross-cultural existence of sympathetic magic or Iroquois kinship systems or coil-made pottery was not the product of universal evolution or historical contexts or shared values. These cultural practices reoccur because they meet the same functions in different societies, and their reoccurrence can be characterized with the law-like statements of science.

In addition to differing modes of explanation, British and American anthropology diverged in subject matter. British social anthropology produced an ethnography of societies, analyzing their institutions and operations. The individual social actor was characterized by role and status and shown to act within predetermined sets of behavior. In toto, social forms operated to reinforce each other, insuring the resolution of disruptive conflict and the perpetuation of social structure—in short, the continued functioning of society.

In contrast, American anthropology's emphasis on culture as values led to a greater interest in individuals, and particularly how cultural practices served to shape individual character. There was a tangent point with psychology, and between 1910 and 1950, particularly with Freudian psychology. This created a stream in American anthropology, culture and personality, that had no developed counterpart in Great Britain.

By the 1930s, American cultural anthropology and British social anthropology were on separate tracks, so distinct that anthropologists had difficulty communicating across the theoretical divide. As often occurs, the theoretical debates enmeshed with personal conflicts, making the chance of understanding even more remote. The divide was partly bridged when Radcliffe-Brown and Malinowski began to lecture and teach in the United States, and a group of American functionalists grew in influence. Nevertheless, two distinct trends in anthropology persisted—one ideational, the other behavioral—and never really disappeared. ✦

Chapter 9

Marcel Mauss

Elemental Categories, Total Facts

"I cannot divorce myself from the work of a school," Marcel Mauss (1872–1950) wrote, musing that the common thread of his 50 years of research into the nature of human society was "the conviction that collaborating with others is a drive against isolation and the pretentious search for originality" (Mauss 1983:139). Throughout his academic life, Mauss was tied to the sociological legacy of Durkheim, first as disciple and then as heir. An original member of the group of scholars who surrounded Durkheim and the *Année sociologique*, Mauss spent much of his career working with other scholars or editing the posthumous works of Durkheim, Henri Hubert, and Robert Hertz. "I have perhaps worked too much in collaboration with others," Mauss wrote. Indeed, it is difficult to disentangle Mauss' work or find its distinctive strand.

Marcel Mauss, however, is a pivotal figure in 20th-century anthropology. As a teacher Mauss influenced an enormous number of students, including Maurice Leenhardt, Marcel Griaule, and most explicitly, Claude Lévi-Strauss (1987; see also Clifford 1982). In the United States Mauss' work is unevenly known, largely due to the barrier of language (Nandan 1977:xiv). Mauss was a prolific author, writing over 350 reviews and scores of articles on diverse topics, such as the origin of Australian magic, the notion of the Self, Vedic literature, and Bolshevism (Besnard 1983; Leacock 1954:59; Nandan 1977:270–283). Before his works were collected in a three-volume set (Mauss 1969), his writings were "disseminated in a notoriously fragmented form" (Baker 1987:viii). Only a dozen of Mauss' writings have been translated into English, and his principal works have been available in

English only since the 1960s (Durkheim and Mauss 1963; Hubert and Mauss 1964; Mauss 1967, 1979; Mauss and Beuchat 1979).

Mauss' work touches numerous fields, including economic anthropology, cultural ecology, the history of religion, and the fundamentals of social organization. Though trained as a philosopher, Mauss emphasized the empirical basis for understanding the nature of humanity. "I have never lost sight," Mauss (1983:151) wrote,

> of the only goal of the discipline to which I have dedicated myself: to show and specify the role played by social life in human life through the most precise and direct contact with facts.

Background

Marcel Mauss was born in 1872 into an orthodox Jewish family in Lorraine. Emile Durkheim (Chapter 4) was Mauss' uncle and exerted a tremendous intellectual influence on the young student. Mauss went to the University of Bordeaux to study with Durkheim, who took enormous interest in his nephew's education; for example, he designed a course on the origins of religion simply to fit Mauss' intellectual goals.

Mauss was the first of the group of young scholars that crystallized around Durkheim and established French sociology (Nandan 1977; Besnard 1983). Mauss (1983:140) described himself as a "recruiting agent" for Durkheim, bringing together students in such diverse fields as geography, law, philosophy, linguistics, and criminology to contribute their specialized knowledge to Durkheim's "science of society." In 1898, the first volume of *Année sociologique* was published and it was "the symbol and organ of the Durkheimian School" (Nandan 1977:xxviii). Volume I contained Durkheim' s article on the origins of incest, an article by Georg Simmel on the maintenance of social forms, and over 130 short notes and book reviews, a quarter of them written by Mauss. Mauss was instrumental in creating the dynamic group of bright scholars who surrounded Durkheim not as "a school of blind disciples" but as a coterie of students attracted to Durkheim's science of society (Mauss 1983:140).

But World War I sliced through the young men of the Années and marked even the survivors with tragedy. Robert Hertz, Durkheim's son Andre, and many others were killed on the battlefield, decimating the Années group and perhaps leading to Emile Durkheim's early death in 1917. The Durkheimian mantle fell to Mauss.

After World War I, Mauss edited two volumes of *Année sociologique* (1925–1927). It then failed for financial reasons, but was reborn as the *Annales Sociologiques* and was published from 1934 to 1942 until world war again suspended normal life.

Mauss' erudition is legendary, and his broad learning began at Bordeaux. Mauss wrote that his undergraduate studies "vacillated" between the study of law, the sociology of religions, and a series of studies in collaboration with Durkheim on the history of towns, human spatial organization, and suicide (Mauss 1983:140,144). But Mauss' principal focus was the study of religious phenomena, a field which forced him to combine extended studies in history and languages. Mauss' broad education included a command of English, German, Russian, Greek, Latin, Sanskrit, Celtic, and ancient Hebrew. He was willing to tackle ambitious research projects; thus he chose for one of his two thesis subjects "prayer in all its aspects," a subject he thought would require "a short period of philological studies" but instead led him on a five-year exploration of Vedic Sanskrit, the ancient Hebrew Talmud, and the Christian liturgy, among other topics (Mauss 1983:145). This polymathic learning characterizes Mauss' career. For example, the footnotes to *The Gift* contain mini-essays on the evolution of money, ancient Sanskrit commercial vocabularies, nuances of Germanic law, and forms of Kwakiutl wealth. Active in politics and a committed socialist, Mauss was revered by his students, not only for his learning, but also because he was an affable, informal man (Clifford 1982:154). Mauss' students claimed, "Mauss knows all" (Lévi-Strauss 1945:527).

Mauss spent his adult life in academic institutions. In 1895 he placed third in the national *agrégation* with a degree in philosophy and in 1900 joined the faculty of the Ecole Practique des Hautes Études at the University of Paris. In 1901 Mauss was appointed to the chair in the "History of the Religion of Noncivilized Peoples," a position he held until 1939 when the Nazi occupation of France forced Mauss to retire. In 1925 Mauss, Paul Rivet, and Lucien Lévy-Bruhl established the Institut d'Ethnologie at the University of Paris which became the training ground for an entire generation of French anthropologists. Mauss was renowned as a teacher, and his course summaries indicate the stunning breadth and enormous detail which Mauss brought to his lectures on topics as diverse as "North American Kinship and Religion" (1905), "Primitive Forms of Religious Language" (1913), and "Australian Dramatic Poetry" (1924). James Clifford (1988:123) has written,

> From the perspective of today's intellectual regime, where publication
> is at a premium and where any idea of value tends to be guarded for

the next article or monograph, it is astonishing, indeed moving, to note the tremendous energies that Mauss poured into his teaching at Hautes Études.

Although Mauss never engaged in ethnographic fieldwork, he emphasized the importance of intensive participant observation as the basis for anthropological knowledge. His instructions for making ethnographic observations, such as his *Manuel d'ethnographie* (1947) or his brief instruction on the study of "Body Techniques" (1979), indicate an anthropologist concerned with concrete ethnographic details.

Mauss' greatest contribution to anthropology, however, was his exploration of the fundamental categories of cultural behavior. Mauss wrote that he had contributed to "a social history of the categories of the human mind" (Mauss 1979a:59).

A Social History of Categories

Mauss' social history of cultural categories utilized a methodology employed by Durkheim—the search for elementary forms (see pp. 61–63). Ethnographic comparison could identify essential and primordial elements of human culture through the study of primitive cultures. This search for underlying structure is a recurrent theme in Mauss' research.

For example, in 1899 Mauss coauthored a study of sacrifice with Henri Hubert (Hubert and Mauss 1964:7) described as an attempt "to disentangle the simple and elementary forms of an institution" by comparing Hindu, Old Testament, Greek, and Latin sacrificial rites. Hubert and Mauss identified a schema of sacrificial rites involving separation, consecration, sacrifice, and "exit" or reintegration (a model which anticipates Arnold van Gennep's [1960] insights into rites of passage, see p. 229). Arguing that such diverse rites were not derived from a single form of primitive ritual, Hubert and Mauss found the unity of sacrifice in two principles: that all sacrificial rituals establish "a means of communication between the sacred and profane worlds" via the agent of the victim, but by the same token those two realms are kept distinct because the victim—first consecrated, then killed—is of neither realm; the sacrifice of a victim separates the two realms "while uniting them" (Hubert and Mauss 1964: 97, 100). In the closing pages of their essay, Hubert and Mauss discuss the social origin and function of sacrifice, first contending that it consists of social facts rather than individual confusions about cause and effect (an extension of Durkheim's response to Tylor and Müller's theories of the origins of religion, see pp. 61–63), then outlining the role of sacrifice in maintaining social norms, and finally concluding with a brief synopsis of nonreligious beliefs and practices organized around the sacrifice ritual. Sacrifice, in their analysis, is a primordial social category.

Hubert and Mauss' essay employs the central methods followed by Durkheim and his students: the use of comparative data, the search for elemental categories, and the assumption that primitive societies preserved fundamental social patterns lost in industrialized societies. As discussed in Chapter 4, this rationale led Durkheim to analyze religious beliefs among the Australian aborigines since their beliefs—in Durkheim's view—were most "elementary." Durkheim and Mauss believed that this strategy was superior to philosophical musings about the origins of social concepts since it was based on ethnographic "facts."

Apparently, it never occurred to either Durkheim or Mauss that traditional, less technologically developed societies like the Australian aborigines were other than semifossilized remnants of some prehistoric human condition. In *The Gift*, for example, Mauss describes the Trobrianders and other cases studied as "good representatives of the great neolithic stage of civilization" (1967:69). Such assumptions are not unique to Mauss or Durkheim; they are found in the writings of numerous anthropologists of different theoretical stripes. Mauss never justified his assumption, except to presume that cultural patterns changed from simple to complex and to assume that traditional societies were less complex than modern industrialized ones.

Overlooking this flaw, Mauss—solely and in collaboration with Durkheim and others—pursued bold lines of investigation. For example, in *Primitive Classification* Durkheim and Mauss explored the relationship between social systems and cosmological categories "to investigate the most rudimentary classifications made by mankind, in order to see with what elements they have been constructed" (1963:9). Arguing that systems of classification—categories of space, time, color, organisms, etc.—are too complex for spontaneous invention through individual observation and inference, Durkheim and Mauss conclude that all systems of classification are learned (1963:7–8). But, what was the source or model of original, primitive classifications? Durkheim and Mauss contend that classifications are modeled on the categories of social life, a crucial point which reemerges in Mary Douglas' work (see pp. 251–253).

Turning first to the Australian aborigines, Durkheim and Mauss summarized social organization as based on moieties, dual social classifications which categorize clans into two equal units; all individuals of the tribe are members of a clan which, in turn, is subsumed by one moiety or the other. *"Now the classification of things reproduces this classification of men"* Durkheim and Mauss write (1963:11, original emphasis), and they develop this argument with additional data from Australia, North America (Zuni, Sioux), and classical China. Durkheim and Mauss show that the spatial arrangement of clans within a Zuni pueblo parallels the spatial division of the world, and they analyze the complexities of Chinese cosmologies as shadowy reflections of ancient clan totems. Durkheim and Mauss conclude that different aspects of classification systems point to their *social origins*: the description of relatedness in kinship metaphors ("humans are members of the Family Hominidae"); the hierarchical nature of categories mirroring the nested social units of sub-clan, clan and moiety; and the spatial orderings of people and things. Primitive classifications are not based on the individual, Durkheim and Mauss (1963:87) write, but "society." They continue, "It is this that is objectified, not man."

In an introductory essay to his translation of *Primitive Classification*, Rodney Needham (1963) provides a detailed critique of the logic, method, and evidence employed by Durkheim and Mauss, exposing crippling faults in their essay. Yet, Needham (1963:xxxiv) concludes that the essay's

> great merit, and one which outweighs all its faults, is that it draws attention, for the first time in sociological enquiry, to a topic of fundamental importance in understanding human thought and social life.

With his polymathic brio, Mauss consistently raised key issues for the first time. His combination of insight and erudition characterizes his best-known work, *The Gift*.

The Gift, Total Prestations and Total Phenomena

Mauss' *Essai sur le Don*, as Evans-Pritchard (1967:ix) noted, is essential for understanding Mauss' significance as a scholar. *The Gift* is a cross-cultural assay of an institution which Mauss calls "total prestations": exchanges which may appear to be voluntary but in fact are obligatory and reinforced by recognized sanctions. Mauss (1967:3) situates *The Gift* within a larger study of contracts—economic and social—a theme which runs through French social theory to the Enlightenment and beyond. Mauss contributes to this debate by grounding it in ethnographic detail.

Mauss contends that the "natural economy"—in which individuals compete in a free and open market with exchange value set solely by supply and demand—simply does not exist in traditional societies. Rather, Mauss argued, exchanges in "archaic" societies occurred between groups or representatives of groups (chiefs, clan leaders, groom's family to bride's family, etc.), not between socially isolated individuals.

Further, the exchanges were not only of goods and services, but also of "courtesies, entertainments, ritual, military assistance, women, children, dances, and feasts"; the exchange of wealth was only "one part of a wide and enduring contract" (Mauss 1967:3). Such exchanges, far from being voluntary, "take it or leave it" negotiations between individuals, were surrounded by socially recognized and sanctioned obligations. Although described in the voluntary language implied by the word "gift," such total prestations are defined by a triad of obligations: the obligation to give, the obligation to receive, and the obligation to repay (Mauss 1967:37–41). While not all exchanges take this form, total prestations are recurrent social phenomena.

In an exercise of extraordinary scholarship, Mauss documents total prestations in Oceania, Melanesia, the Northwest Coast, ancient Rome, Classic Hindu law, and tribal Germany. For example, Mauss discusses the potlatch of the Northwest Coast, an economic institution in which vast amounts of wealth are accumulated and given away or even destroyed in elaborate ceremonial displays (see Drucker 1966; Piddocke 1967; Schneider 1974). Mauss analyzes the potlatch as a form of antagonistic prestation in which "consumption and destruction are virtually unlimited." The potlatch is "a war of wealth" (Mauss 1967:35).

To a Western economist, such destructive redistribution of wealth is senseless. Mauss argues that such exchanges are comprehensible only within a certain cultural context. But more importantly, Mauss shows that exchanges like the potlatch or the kula ring are not solely economic transactions: they are *total phenomena*.

The potlatch is certainly an economic institution, but it is also a religious institution since the chief participants are viewed as incarnations of spirits and ancestors. The potlatch is also a social phenomena as different clans, families, and social groups come together, social ties are reestablished, and points of conflict reemerge. The potlatch provides the setting for movement up the social ladder for gift givers and their families. It is thus a pivotal institution in Northwest Coast society, bridging different elements of economic, social, religious, and legal life (Mauss 1967:31–37). Mauss' exploration of total prestations became a key text in the substantivist versus formalist debate in economic anthropology; it showed how the economy was "an embedded process" (Polanyi 1957), undivorceable from other realms of society.

Many American anthropologists approach *The Gift* as a contribution to economic anthropology (e.g., Schneider 1974), but Lévi-Strauss (1987) emphasized Mauss' discussion of total social phenomena. Put another way: American anthropologists consider the work to be a study on economy of which gift exchange is one form; Lévi-Strauss approached the work as a model analysis of total social phenomena using gift exchange as an example (see pp. 220–221).

For Lévi-Strauss, *Essai sur le Don* is Mauss' masterwork, not because it introduced any new facts per se, but because in that work

> for the first time in the history of ethnological thinking . . . an effort was made to transcend empirical observations and to reach deeper realities. For the first time, the social ceases to belong to the domain of pure quality—anecdote, curiosity, material for moralising description or for scholarly comparison—and becomes a system, among whose parts, connections, equivalencies and interdependent aspects can be discovered. [Lévi-Strauss 1987:38]

Mauss was aware of the importance of his concept, writing that nothing "is more urgent or promising than research into 'total' social phenomena" (1966:78). Mauss' concept was to link the individual and social, specific and general, structure and process.

> We are dealing then with something more than a set of themes, more than institutional elements, more than institutions, more even than systems of institutions divisible into legal, economic, religious and other parts. We are concerned with "wholes," with systems in their entirety. . . . It is only by considering them as wholes that we have been able to see their essence, their operation and their living aspect, and to catch the fleeting moment when the society and its members take emotional stock of themselves and their situation as regards others. [Mauss 1966:77–78]

Lévi-Strauss (1988:39–45) argues that Mauss stood on the verge of structuralism (see pp. 219–223), a contestable claim (Clifford 1988:128; Panoff 1970). Seth Leacock offered a more cautious assessment, arguing that Mauss' emphasis on the integration of social phenomena runs throughout his work (Leacock 1954:67). Yet the concept of "total social facts" remains elusive; it is not clear whether all ethnographic facts are potentially total or if some facts are total and others are not. As James Clifford (1988:63–65) has pointed out, it is an ambiguous concept, indistinguishably validating different approaches to ethnographic research. The concept "offers no guidance as to which code, key, or luminuous example is to be preferred," Clifford writes (1988:64). "Social reality and the moral world are viewed as constructed in many possible ways, none of which may be privileged."

Perhaps, Mauss seems most modern at this point; his concerns are echoed in Clifford Geertz's discussion of "thick description" (see pp. 241–243), his emphasis on dynamic social phenomena anticipates Victor Turner's concept of social drama (see pp. 230–232), and Mauss' explorations of multiple alternatives suggest a post-modernism of the early-20th century (pp. 261–263). But any such resonances remained undeveloped and were essentially unintentional. Mauss was primarily concerned with the analysis of diverse, but concrete social phenomena.

Conclusion

A number of objections may be raised to Mauss' work. First, for all his scholarship, Mauss usually cited ethnographic data to support his ideas, not to test them. Mauss rarely accepted contradictory evidence as indicating an incorrect hypothesis; such inconvenient facts could frequently be explained, at least to Mauss' satisfaction.

Second, there is a maddening ambiguity and lack of development in Mauss' work. For example, it is unclear precisely what he meant by "social morphology," and his essay on *Body Techniques* (1979:119) contains a section titled "Techniques of the Care of the Abnormal," which in total reads, "Massages, etc. But let us move on."

Third, Mauss' assumption that non-Western societies expressed archaic survivals of ancient social patterns was never closely scrutinized, an important oversight given the anti-evolutionary critiques of Boas (see pp. 48–50) and other Anglo-American anthropologists of whom Mauss was aware. And finally, one can only wonder how such a creative thinker would have been transformed by an extended period of fieldwork in a living society remote from the École Practique des Hautes Études.

Nevertheless, Mauss made enormous contributions to French sociology and ethnology as a teacher, editor, and scholar. His wide-ranging scholarship and engaging mind continue to provoke, and his work remains an essential starting point for inquiry into the fundamentals of social life. ✦

Bibliography

Baker, Felicity
1987 Translator's Note. *In* An Introduction to the Work of Marcel Mauss, Felicity Baker, tran. Pp. viii–ix. London: Routledge & Kegan Paul.

Besnard, Philippe
1983 The 'Année Sociologique' Team. *In* The Sociological Domain: The Durkheimian School and the Founding of French Sociology. Philippe Besnard, ed. Pp. 11–39. Cambridge: Cambridge University Press.

Besnard, Philippe, ed.
1983 The Sociological Domain: The Durkheimian School and the Founding of French Sociology. Cambridge: Cambridge University Press.

Clifford, James
1982 Person and Myth: Maurice Leenhardt in the Melanesian World. Berkeley: University of California Press.
1988 The Predicament of Culture: Twentieth-Century Ethnography, Literature, and Art. Cambridge, MA: Harvard University Press.

Derrida, Jacques
1992 Given Time: I. Counterfeit Money. P. Kamuf, tran. Chicago: University of Chicago Press.

Durkheim, Emile and Marcel Mauss
1963 Primitive Classification. R. Needham, tran. Chicago: University of Chicago Press. [Originally published as *"De quelques formes primitives de classification: contribution l'étude des représentations collectives."* Année Sociologique vol. 6: pp. 1–72, 1903.]

Hubert, Henri and Marcel Mauss
1964 Sacrifice: Its Nature and Function. W. Halls, tran. Chicago: University of Chicago Press. [Originally published as *"Essai Sur La Nature et La Fonction du Sacrifice."* Année Sociologique 2: 29–138, 1899.]

Leacock, Seth
1954 The Ethnological Theory of Marcel Mauss. American Anthropologist 56:58–73.

Lévi-Strauss, Claude
1987 An Introduction to the Work of Marcel Mauss. Felicity Baker, tran. London: Routledge & Kegan Paul. [Originally published 1950.]

Lukes, Steven
1968 Marcel Mauss. International Encyclopedia of the Social Sciences 10:78–82. New York: MacMillan Co. & Free Press.

Mauss, Marcel
1967 The Gift: Forms and Functions of Exchange in Archaic Societies. I. Cunnison, tran. New York: W. W. Norton & Company. [Originally published as *Essai sur le don, forme archaïque de l'échange,* 1925.]
1979a A Category of the Human Mind: The Notion of Person, the Notion of 'Self'. *In* Sociology and Psychology: Essays. Ben Brewster, tran. Pp. 59–94. London: Routledge & Kegan Paul. [Originally published as *Une catégoire de*

l'espirit humain: la notion de personne, celle de 'moi,' un plan de travail. Journal of the Royal Anthropological Institute 68:263-281, 1938.]
1979b Body Techniques. *In* Sociology and Psychology: Essays. Ben Brewster, tran. Pp. 95–123. London: Routledge & Kegan Paul. [Originally published in Journal de Psychologie Normale et Pathogique, 35ᵉ année, 1935:271–293,1935.]
1979c Seasonal Variations of the Eskimo: A Study in Social Morphology. In Collaboration with Henri Beuchat. James Fox, tran. London: Routledge & Kegan Paul. [Originally published as *"Essai sur les variations saisonnières des sociétés Eskimos: étude de morphologie sociale"* in Sociologie et anthropologie Pt. 7, 1950.]
1983 An Intellectual Self-Portrait. *In* The Sociological Domain: the Durkheimian School and the Founding of French Sociology. Philippe Besnard, ed. Pp. 139–151. Cambridge: Cambridge University Press. [Originally published 1930.]

Nandan, Yash
1977 The Durkheimian School: A Systematic and Comprehensive Bibliography. Westport, Connecticut: Greenwood Press.

Panoff, Michel
1970 Marcel Mauss's The Gift Revisited. Man 5:60–70.

Schnieder, Harold
1974 Economic Man: The Anthropology of Economics. New York: The Free Press.

van Gennep, Arnold
1960 The Rites of Passage. Chicago: University of Chicago Press. [Originally published 1909.]

Chapter 10

Bronislaw Malinowski

The Functions of Culture

Bronislaw Malinowski inspired strong reactions from people, and it is clear he wanted it that way. There are no tepid accounts of Malinowski; they are either hot or cold. Anthropologists tend to evaluate Malinowski on three grounds—as a fieldworker, as a theoretician, or as a personality. As a fieldworker there is near unanimity: Malinowski set new standards for ethnographic research, influencing an entire generation of anthropologists. As a theoretician, opinions of Malinowski diverge. On one hand, the British social anthropologist Audrey I. Richards wrote, "Malinowski's concept of culture, as he first developed it, was one of his most stimulating contributions to the anthropological thought of his day," concluding that this contribution has been "considerably undervalued" (Richards 1957:15). At the other extreme, Edmund Leach contrasted Malinowski's valuable fieldwork with his theoretical contribution:

> [B]esides altering the whole mode and purpose of ethnographic inquiry Malinowski made numerous theoretical pronouncements of a general, abstract, sociological kind, which were supposed to be valid for all cultural situations, regardless of time or space. Here, I consider, he was a failure. For me, Malinowski talking about the Trobrianders is a stimulating genius; but Malinowski discoursing on Culture in general is often a platitudinous bore. [1957:119]

Remarkably, such different opinions appear in the same collection of symposium papers edited by one of Malinowski's first and most loyal former students, Raymond Firth. Writing ten years after his death, the contributors' different assessments of Malinowski's theoretical contributions to anthropology are broadly representative. But if response to his theories was mixed, Malinowski the man was either loved or hated. One supporter said, "He had a really creative mind, an international outlook and the approach and the imagination of an artist" (Karberry cited in Firth 1988:37). In contrast, the anthropologist Clyde Kluckhohn called him "a pretentious Messiah of the credulous"—and this in an obituary in the *Journal of American Folklore* (1943:208). Who was this man who inspired such different reactions?

Background

His life began in Cracow, but it blossomed in the South Seas. Born in 1884, the son of a distinguished professor of Slavic languages, Malinowski was descended from the aristocracy and raised among the intellectuals of Poland (Kubica 1988:88–89; Thorton and Skalník 1993). His 1908 doctorate was in physics and mathematics; his thesis, titled "On the Principle of Economy of Thought," received the highest honor in the Austrian Empire and his Ph.D. was awarded in an elaborate ceremony with a flourish of trumpets (Flis 1988). But sickness and circumstances diverted him from a career in the physical sciences to the study of sociology and anthropology.

In 1910 Malinowski began postgraduate studies at the London School of Economics where he studied with C.G. Seligman. Seligman had been a member of the 1898–1899 Cambridge University expedition to the Torres Straits region, the island-dotted channel between northern Australia and New Guinea. As Kuper describes (1983:5–6), this was a period in which British anthropologists avidly sought to collect empirical data—similar to the "salvage ethnography" of Boas and Kroeber (see pp. 65–67); the Torres Straits expedition introduced systematic field research methods to British anthropology. The ethnographic data on Australia from the Torres expedition and the earlier work on central Australian tribes by Spencer and Gillen (1899) became the fuel for various sociological writers such as Durkheim and Freud. Similarly, Malinowski's first book, *The Family Among the Australian Aborigines*, was based on previously collected ethnographic data, as was his doctorate (awarded in 1913). Nearly 30, Bronislaw Malinowski had yet to do any fieldwork.

But by a fluke, an opportunity occurred: Malinowski was hired as secretary to the anthropologist R.G. Marett who, in his capacity as an officer of the British Association, was traveling to Australia. World War

I broke out while they were there and Malinowski, as an Austrian subject, was classified as an enemy alien. Marett and others intervened
with the Australian authorities, and Malinowski was released and allowed
to remain in Australian territories, including New Guinea, and carry out
fieldwork. It was an opportunity that transformed his career.

Malinowski made three field trips to New Guinea: an initial six-
month visit (September 1914 to March 1915) with the Mailu of Toulon
Island, and two visits with the Trobriand Islanders, first from June
1915 to May 1916 and then from October 1917 to October 1918 (Karberry 1957:77). It was a period of emotional despondency, sexual frus-
tration, hard work, and intellectual excitement, partly recorded in
Malinowski's diaries published 25 years after his death (Malinowski
1967); the diaries and personal letters (Wayne 1995) show a complex,
flawed, but brilliant man.

Malinowski's writings also show an ethnographer very interested
in the systematic collection of ethnographic data, a subject he discusses in the opening pages of his classic study of the Trobriand Islanders, *Argonauts of the Western Pacific*. Malinowski (1922:11) believed that
the ethnographer had to consider:

> the full extent of the phenomena in each aspect of tribal culture stud-
> ied, making no difference between what is commonplace, or drab, or
> ordinary, and what strikes him as astonishing and out-of-the-way. At
> the same time, the whole area of tribal culture *in all its aspects* has to
> be gone over in research. The consistency, the law and order which
> obtain within each aspect make also for joining them into one coher-
> ent whole.

To achieve this, Malinowski advocated a three-part system. First, he
took the idea of the kinship chart in which complex relations are
shown schematically and devised "synoptic charts" to illustrate relationships in other dimensions of culture: economic transactions,
exchanges, legal practices, magical ceremonies, rights to farming lands
and fishing areas, and so on. Synoptic charts expressed relationships
between ethnographic data, and supplemented with genealogies,
maps, plans and diagrams, they served to outline the framework of cultural actions.

But this only covered the bare bones of cultural existence; Malinowski, if nothing else, was always interested in the pulsing complexity of social life. These nuances of behavior and action Malinowski
called the *imponderabilia of actual life*. With that phrase, Malinowski
wanted ethnographers to record the subjective dynamics of daily life as
experienced by another group of human beings, not just the abstract

structure of a primordial society. Arguing that the ethnographer should record the particular actors and spectators in a specific ceremony, Malinowski suggested that he should forget that he understands the stated purpose and structure of the ceremony and

> try to find himself only in the midst of an assembly of human beings, who behave seriously or jocularly, with earnest concentration or with bored frivolity, who are either in the same mood as he finds them every day, or else are screwed up to a high pitch of excitement, and so on and so on. [1922:21]

Although he realized that not every ethnographer could join into native life with equal ease—joking that "perhaps the Slavonic nature is more plastic and more naturally savage than that of Western Europeans"—Malinowski argued that the attempt was an important counterbalance to ethnographic abstractions about society, and to remind the ethnographer that his subjects are living humans and not museum specimens. Even a sharp critic like Adam Kuper (1983:35) acknowledges, ". . . Malinowski's greatness lay in his ability to penetrate the web of theories to the real man, boasting, hypocritical, earthy, reasonable. . . ."

Malinowski knew that not every motive could be reduced to synoptic charts or observed behaviors; one had to reconstruct the subjective mental states of another culture. This information could be derived from a body of "ethnographic statements, characteristic narratives, typical utterances, items of folk-lore and magical formulae . . . as documents of native mentality" (Malinowski 1922:24).

In this manner, Malinowski collected a body of data on the Trobriand Islanders which had deep effects on anthropology. His data on the social dimensions of long-distance exchange in the kula ring influenced Marcel Mauss's *The Gift* (pp. 122–125) and was a key text in the development of the formalist vs. substantive debate in economic anthropology. Malinowski's insights about the nature of magic and science led to greater interest in cognitive anthropology and also figured in the approaches of ecological anthropology that emerged in the 1960s and 1970s (e.g., Rappaport 1967). The Trobriand Islanders became one of the classic ethnographic case studies, and on the strength of that case study Malinowski returned to England to become a major figure in social anthropology.

Kuper (1983:10) contends that Malinowski turned his life story into a "messianic self-image" that served as a "mythical charter" for the new field of social anthropology: a brilliant Polish student,

diverted into anthropology, and imprisoned in the wilderness of Melanesia through a fluke, then returns to civilization to throw out the
ignorant establishment, a battle waged with the assistance of his disciples (for more on Malinowski's self-myth see Firth 1988:31–32). But
this caricature aside, Malinowski began publishing substantive ethnographic articles even before returning to England, and *Argonauts of the
Western Pacific* was published in 1922. He began teaching at the University of London in the early 1920s and by 1927 held the chair in
Social Anthropology, which allowed him to attract numerous students
and increasing international recognition. By the 1930s Malinowski lectured widely in Europe and North America, and the outbreak of World
War II found him in the United States where he remained until his
death in 1942. He was 58 years old.

Malinowski's works remain ethnographic classics, but his contribution to anthropological theory was debated during his lifetime and is
still controversial. His ethnographic concerns were with how culture
met the needs of the individual, and they conflicted with another
viewpoint outlined by A. R. Radcliffe-Brown that emphasized how culture met the needs of society. The two men were labeled "functionalists," a term emphasizing their perspectives on how culture "functioned"
to meet specific needs. From the early-1920s until the late-1930s, Radcliffe-Brown and Malinowski saw themselves as brothers in arms, advo-
cating a new approach to cultures that emphasized them as functionally
integrated wholes (Firth 1988:16–17). Yet each saw a different source of
such needs—Malinowski emphasizing the individual, Radcliffe-Brown
highlighting society—and a growing distance turned into mutual distaste
heightened by a fundamental difference in personalities. But to understand this difference and to evaluate Malinowski's theoretical contribution, one must begin with his theory of needs.

Theory of Needs

Malinowski's theory of needs is central to his functional approach to
culture; it is the theoretical statement linking the individual and society. It is a simple notion: culture exists to meet the basic biological,
psychological, and social needs of the individual. But the theory seems
unduly simplistic if we do not understand Malinowski's notions of
function, the hierarchy of needs, and the role of symbolism, and if we
ignore the intellectual context of Malinowski's thinking.

First, Malinowski (1944:83) viewed function in a physiological sense: "Function, in this simplest and most basic aspect of human behavior, can be defined as the satisfaction of an organic impulse by the appropriate act. Form and function, obviously, are inextricably related to one another." Malinowski developed the physiological analogy further. For example, he argued that if we were to describe *how* a normal lung operates we would be describing the form of the process, but if we attempt to explain *why* the lung is operating in a certain manner then we are concerned with its function. "We could say that the formal approach corresponds to the method of observation and documentation in the statement of a vital sequence," Malinowski (1944:83) wrote, "while function is the restatement of what has happened in terms of scientific principles . . . a full analysis of organic and environmental happenings." This has several implications. First, it means that societies are integrated wholes, requiring an anthropologist to examine the interconnections of different cultural domains. Second, those domains are linked by their complementary functions, and the only anthropological explanations which can be considered to explain those causal links must be functional explanations. Thus any anthropologist unconcerned with the functions of culture is, by definition, not engaged in science.

Malinowski recognized that cultural forms do not have simple or single functions, writing that "no [cultural] institution can be functionally related to one basic need, nor yet as a rule to a simple, cultural need. . . . Culture is not and can not be a replica in terms of specific responses to specific biological needs" (Malinowski 1944:112). Instead, Malinowski wrote that cultural institutions are integrated responses to a variety of needs, and to outline those needs he used a variant of his synoptic charts (Malinowski 1944:91):

Basic Needs	*Cultural Responses*
1. Metabolism	1. Commissariat
2. Reproduction	2. Kinship
3. Bodily Comforts	3. Shelter
4. Safety	4. Protection
5. Movement	5. Activities
6. Growth	6. Training
7. Health	7. Hygiene

Malinowski described each of these needs and cultural responses in detail, but a few examples illustrate his argument. The first human need, *metabolism*, refers to "the processes of food intake, digestion, the collateral secretions, the absorption of nutritive substances, and rejection of waste matter . . . " (Malinowski 1944:91). The cultural response, dubbed *commissariat* (literally a military officer charged with the distribution of food), included 1) how food was grown, prepared, and consumed, 2) where food was consumed and in what social units, 3) the economic and social organization of the distribution of foods (e.g., trade in canned salmon or reciprocal exchange of garden products), 4) the legal and customary rules that ensure the steady operation of food distribution, and 5) the authority that enforces those rules. The basic need, *safety*, simply "refers to the prevention of bodily injuries by mechanical accident, attack from animals or other human beings" (Malinowski 1944:92), but the cultural response, *protection*, may include such different behaviors as placing houses on pilings away from potential tidal waves, the organization of armed responses to aggression, or the magical recruitment of supernatural forces. And *growth*—which in humans is structured by the long dependency of infants—leads to the cultural response of *training* by which humans are taught language, other symbols, and appropriate behaviors for different stages and situations, and are instructed until they are socially and physiologically mature (Malinowski 1944:107).

Obviously Malinowski was not reducing complex cultural systems to simple biological needs: he did not argue that salmon canneries exist in Alaska because humans need to eat. Rather, cultural responses set new conditions—literally new environments—which elicit new cultural responses:

> [I]t is clear that the satisfaction of the organic or basic needs of man and of the races is a minimum set of conditions imposed on each culture. The problems set by man's nutritive, reproductive, and hygienic needs must be solved. They are solved by the construction of a new, secondary, or artificial environment. This environment, *which is neither more nor less than culture itself*, has to be permanently reproduced, maintained, and managed. This creates what might be described in the most general sense of the term as a new standard of living, which depends on the cultural level of the community, on the environment, and on the efficiency of the group. A cultural standard of living, however, means that new needs appear and new imperatives or determinants are imposed on human behavior. [Malinowski 1944:37; emphasis added]

In contrast to the basic needs, these new derived needs or cultural imperatives are "imposed on man by his own tendency to extend his safety and his comforts" (Malinowski 1944:120), but it would be wrong to think of derived needs as somehow dispensable. "Man does not," Malinowski (1944:121) writes, "by biological determinism need to hunt with spears or bow and arrow; use poison darts; nor defend himself by stockades, by shelters, or by armor. But the moment that such devices have become adopted, in order to enhance human adaptability to the environment, they also become necessary conditions for survival." Such items—and the systems of training, raw material exchange, cooperative labor, etc. they require—"are one and all as indispensable under the ultimate sanction of the biological imperative of self-preservation as are any purely physiologically determined elements" (Malinowski 1944:122). New cultural responses to primordial conditions create new situations, literally new environments, to which societies must respond.

Thus culture becomes an enormously complicated behavioral web responding to complex needs that can ultimately—but not always immediately—be traced to the individual. Malinowski (1944:171) summarized his theory of needs with two axioms: first "that every culture must satisfy the biological systems of needs" and second, "that every cultural achievement that implies the use of artifacts and symbolism is an instrumental enhancement of human anatomy, and refers directly or indirectly to the satisfaction of a bodily need." In sum, culture is utilitarian, adaptive, and functionally integrated, and the explanation of culture involves the delineation of function. A classic example of that type of explanation is Malinowski's approach to magic.

The Function of Magic

Magic may seem an improbable case for functional explanation, but it was an integral element in Malinowski's theory because magic was central to Trobriand life. Magic was used to kill enemies and prevent being killed; it was used to ease the birth of a child, to enhance the beauty of dancers, to protect fishermen, or to ensure the harvest. Magic was never mere superstition or empty gesture. Rather, Malinowski argued that

> Magic, as the belief that by spell and rite results can be obtained, . . . always appears in those phases of human action where knowledge fails man. Primitive man cannot manipulate the weather. Experience teaches him that rain and sunshine, wind, heat and cold, cannot be produced by his own hands, however much he might think about or observe such phenomena. He therefore deals with them magically. [Malinowski 1944:198]

Malinowski hypothesized that limited "scientific" knowledge of illness and disease led "primitive" man to conclude that illnesses are caused by sorcery and countered by magic. Malinowski—a man in ill health much of his life—wrote (1944:199):

> The sick man, primitive or civilized, wants to feel that something can be done. He craves for miracles, and the conviction that what has been produced by a malicious sorcerer can be counteracted by a more powerful and friendly witch-doctor, may even assist the organism to resist illness through the belief that something effective is being done. Magic, including sorcery, has thus its practical as well as social characteristics, which allow us to explain its persistence.

Magic persists in societies because it appears to work; it functions. Beyond this apparent utility, Malinowski argued that magic has a profound function in exerting human control over those dimensions that are otherwise outside of our control.

> [Magic] is always strongest there, where vital interests are concerned; where violent passions or emotions are awakened; when mysterious forces are opposed to man's endeavours; and when he has to recognise that there is something which eludes his most careful calculations, his most conscientious preparations and efforts. [Malinowski 1922:395–396]

A classic example is the way that fishing magic is organized: when fishing occurs inside the protected coral reef where "it is possible to make a catch in weather and under conditions in which no other kind of fishing is practicable . . . no magic whatever is practiced in connection with this industry" (1965:17). In contrast, the magic associated with ocean fishing, sailing, and canoes is complex and pervasive, because the dangers and risks are greater.

Similarly, magic surrounding gardening is extensive and considered an indispensable part of cultivation. In terms of economic activity, "agriculture always takes precedence. The districts rich in produce are on the whole politically dominant as well as economically the most wealthy," Malinowski observed (1965:12). "Garden produce is the foundation of wealth throughout the area." Garden magic is public, direct, and extensive; the village garden magician is either the headman, his heir or closest male relative, and therefore he is either the most important or next-most important person in a community. Garden magic and garden work are distinct but inseparable. Malinowski wrote:

> Magic and practical work are, in native ideas, inseparable from each other, though they are not confused. Garden magic and garden work

run in one intertwined series of consecutive effort, form one continuous story, and must be the subject matter of one narrative.

To the natives, magic is as indispensable to the success of gardens as competent and effective husbandry. It is essential to the fertility of the soil: [saying] "The garden magic utters magic by mouth; the magical virtue enters the soil." Magic is to them an almost natural element in the growth of the gardens. I have often been asked: "What is the magic which is done in your country over gardens—is it like ours or is it different?" They did not seem at all to approve of our ways as I described them. . . . [Malinowski 1965:62–63]

We lack the space to describe garden rituals; Malinowski devotes over 150 pages to the horticultural and magical activities associated with gardens and the crop cycle. But the role of magic in cultivation, Malinowski believed, captured its essential function—an attempt to extend control over uncontrollable elements of nature. In this sense, Malinowski's analysis of magic reflects his functional approach to culture.

Conclusion

Malinowski's work has been criticized on numerous grounds. First, there is the valid point that Malinowski extrapolated from the Trobriand case to traditional societies in general. It has been said that Malinowski's thought moved on two levels: the specific case of the Trobrianders, and the abstract, general case of Man and Society—which bore a striking resemblance to the Trobrianders (Nadel 1957). Second, Malinowski's approach has been criticized because it relied on the ability of the anthropologist to perceive some function of a cultural behavior that could rarely be disproved, and because it basically is a crude theory in which all sorts of behaviors are reduced to simplistic notions of utility (Kuper 1983:31). One could ask, "Don't societies do things which are counter-productive for the individual?" or "Aren't there cultural elements which are nonfunctional yet maintained because they are simply customary?" It is not certain that Malinowski developed a useful answer—as opposed to a scathing rebuke—to such questions (e.g., Malinowski 1944:117–119).

Yet Malinowski has been very influential, particularly on lines of anthropological theory emphasizing the adaptive significance of culture. The ecological anthropology of the 1960s and 1970s took Malinowski's basic insights, recast them as hypotheses, and tested them with quantitative data, producing such classics as Roy Rappoport's (1968) study of the role of ritual in regulating subsistence activities. And sociobiology, although its roots are in Darwinian selection and ethology, shares with functionalism the notion that cultural behaviors either impart adaptive advantages, are neutral, or are eliminated.

Of course, not all approaches to culture share in Malinowski's intellectual heritage. But perhaps his most lasting theoretical observation is his most basic one: cultures are not collections of isolated traits, but are interconnected wholes. ✦

Bibliography

Firth, Raymond
1988 Malinowski in the History of Social Anthropology. *In* Malinowski Between Two Worlds: The Polish Roots of an Anthropological Tradition. R. Ellen, E. Gellner, G. Kubica, and J. Mucha, eds. Pp. 12–42. Cambridge: Cambridge University Press.

Flis, Andrzej, ed.
1988 Bronislaw Malinowski's Cracow Doctorate. *In* Malinowski Between Two Worlds: The Polish Roots of an Anthropological Tradition. R. Ellen, E. Gellner, G. Kubica, and J. Mucha, eds. Pp. 195–200. Cambridge: Cambridge University Press.

Kluckhohn, C.
1943 Bronislaw Malinowski 1884–1942. Journal of American Folklore 56:208–219.

Kubica, Grazyna
1988 Malinowski's Years in Poland. *In* Malinowski Between Two Worlds: The Polish Roots of an Anthropological Tradition. R. Ellen, E. Gellner, G. Kubica, and J. Mucha, eds. Pp. 88–104. Cambridge: Cambridge University Press.

Kuper, Adam
1988 Anthropology and Anthropologists: The Modern British School. London: Routledge & Kegan Paul.

Leach, Edmund
1957 The Epistemological Background to Malinowski's Empiricism. *In* Man and Culture: An Evaluation of the Work of Bronislaw Malinowski. R. Firth, ed. Pp. 119–138. New York: Humanities Press.

Malinowski, Bronislaw
1922 Argonauts of the Western Pacific. London: George Routledge & Sons.
1944 A Scientific Theory of Culture and Other Essays. Chapel Hill: University of North Carolina Press.
1965 Coral Gardens and Their Magic: (Volume 1) Soil-Tilling and Agricultural Rites in the Trobriand Islands. Bloomington: Indiana University Press.
1967 A Diary in the Strict Sense of the Term. New York: Harcourt, Brace & World.

Nadel, S. F.
1957 Malinowski on Magic and Religion. *In* Man and Culture: An Evaluation of the Work of Bronislaw Malinowski. R. Firth, ed. Pp. 189–208. New York: Humanities Press.

Piddington, Ralph
1957 Malinowski's Theory of Needs. *In* Man and Culture: An Evaluation of the Work of Bronislaw Malinowski. R. Firth, ed. Pp. 33–51. New York: Humanities Press.

Rappaport, Roy
1968 Pigs for the Ancestors: Ritual in the Ecology of a New Guinea People. New Haven: Yale University Press.

Richards, Audrey
1957 The Concept of Culture in Malinowski's Work. *In* Man and Culture: An Evaluation of the Work of Bronislaw Malinowski. R. Firth, ed. Pp. 15–32. New York: Humanities Press.

Thorton, Robert and Peter Skalník, eds.
1993 The Early Writings of Bronislaw Malinowski. Cambridge: Cambridge University Press.

Wayne, Helena, ed.
1995 The Story of a Marriage: The Letters of Bronislaw Malinowski and Elsie Masson, Volume 1: 1916–20. London: Routledge.

Chapter II

A. R. Radcliffe-Brown

The Structures of Society

A. R. Radcliffe-Brown, Adam Kuper (1977:1) has noted, "has come to stand for a phase of British social anthropology which is currently out of fashion." Kuper suggests that such judgments are only partly deserved and rest on caricatures of Radcliffe-Brown's positions. One such misjudgment yokes Malinowski and Radcliffe-Brown with the theoretical bond of functionalism, and thus, for example, Bohannan and Glazer (1988:294) note "Seen from today's vantage, it is a little difficult to appreciate what the two were arguing about professionally." Yet when a 1948 article (Gregg and Williams 1948) placed Malinowski and Radcliffe-Brown in the same theoretical camp, Radcliffe-Brown responded with strident outrage:

> The authors arbitrarily apply the label functionalist to certain writers on anthropology and sociology . . . they build up an imaginary picture of something they call functionalism which they then present as a body of views held by all the persons they decided to call functionalists. All the canons of scholarly integrity are ignored.

> Malinowski has explained that he is the inventor of functionalism, to which he gave its name. His definition of it is clear; it is the theory or doctrine that every feature of culture of any people past or present is to be explained by reference to seven biological needs of individual human beings. . . . I reject it entirely, regarding it as useless and worse. As a consistent opponent of Malinowski's functionalism, I may be called an anti–functionalist. [Radcliffe-Brown 1949]

In the face of such strident opposition, it seems irresponsible to treat the theories of Malinowski and Radcliffe-Brown as minor variants on the functionalist theme.

Another criticism holds that Radcliffe-Brown conceived of social anthropology as an ahistorical inquiry resulting in a static view of societies unconcerned with diachronic change (e.g., White 1966). There is merit and confusion in such claims. On one hand, Radcliffe-Brown distanced himself from those anthropologists who, "thinking of their study as a kind of historical study, fall back on conjecture and imagination, and invent 'pseudo–historical' or 'pseudo–causal' explanations" (1977a:13). Radcliffe-Brown leaves these anthropologists unnamed, but Tylor's discussion of animism would fit this description (see p. 61). Radcliffe-Brown's distinction between historical and scientific explanations was extended by his American students, including Robert Redfield (1962 [1937]:xi) who wrote that:

> Radcliffe-Brown's signal contribution is . . . derived . . . from his emphasis on a strictly nonhistorical, sharply scientific method in anthropology. The objective of social anthropology is the formulation of general propositions as to society. The social anthropologist deals with classes of social phenomena; early [sic] he names the class with which he deals—sanctions, totemism, Omaha type of kinship system, or whatever; the particular society or institution with which he deals is then of significance only as it represents or modifies the class, type or declared general proposition. History, on the other hand has a logical nature essentially different; its nature [citing Kroeber] ". . . an endeavor at descriptive integration."

This is an extraordinary statement for its time (1937), a clear contrast to the historical particularism of Boas, Kroeber, and others who considered explanation as primarily a historical reconstruction of specific cultural complexes. The notion that one could extract a concept—such as the Omaha type of kinship system—from its specific social context and make that abstraction the object of inquiry did not sit well with Boas or his students. Radcliffe-Brown observed (1952:50), "My objection to conjectural history is not that it is historical but that it is conjectural." Elsewhere, Radcliffe-Brown (1977a:13) condemns conjectural history as "worse than useless," but adds, "this does not in any way imply the rejection of historical explanation but quite the contrary." Radcliffe-Brown's concern was to create a social anthropology which was generalizing and thus a science.

Kuper notes that Radcliffe-Brown has receded from the anthropological spotlight in Great Britain and the United States, although his influence on different anthropologists is evident, e.g., Evans–Pritchard, (Chapter 12), Lévi–Strauss (Chapter 17), and Victor Turner (Chapter 18), among others. The repercussions of Radcliffe-Brown's approach are expressed by those who emulated him and those who vehemently disavow his work. Paradoxically, as Kuper (1977:1) notes, Radcliffe-Brown "remains influential, but, increasingly, indirectly."

Background

Born in 1881, Radcliffe-Brown was educated at Trinity College, Cambridge. The biographical sketches published after his death (Eggan and Warner 1956; Fortes 1956) contain scant information on Radcliffe-Brown's early years or personal life, possibly reflecting a "streak of aloofness" and somewhat reserved nature (Fortes 1956:153). Remembered as warm and gentle by his friends and students, he was considered condescending and pompous by others, particularly by Boas' students. This was complicated by Radcliffe-Brown's tendency to cite the work of his students and ignore the work of others—which effectively slighted all research conducted in America prior to his arrival at the University of Chicago in 1931. It is amazing how unpopular he was with American anthropologists. Mead called him insufferable, sulky, and rude. Benedict wrote, "He seemed to me impenetrably wrapped in his own conceit." Even recent commentators Bohannan and Glazer (1988:295) discuss how Radcliffe-Brown changed his name from "Brown" to the "double–barreled Radcliffe-Brown" with the implicit suggestion of pomposity. Leslie White describes "two traits of Radcliffe-Brown—the tendency to assume originality for himself, and to ignore or depreciate the work of others . . . " (White 1966:32). These personal reactions may have limited Radcliffe-Brown's influence on some, but his contribution to the development of anthropology remains.

Under Haddon's direction, Radcliffe-Brown conducted fieldwork from 1906 to 1908 on the Andaman Islands, a chain of islands off the southern coast of Myanmar (Burma). Radcliffe-Brown finished his thesis in 1909, which was a descriptive account of traditional culture influenced by the work of Haddon and Rivers. In the year after completing his thesis, Radcliffe-Brown became aware of the work of Durkheim and Mauss and began rewriting his thesis to explore this newly–found theoretical position. Although *The Andaman Islanders* was not published until 1922, it became the vehicle through which French comparative sociology shaped the course of British social anthropology.

Radcliffe-Brown conducted ethnographic research among the Kariera and other aboriginal groups in western Australia from 1910 to 1912. He then returned to England and became an overseas education officer during World War I. After the war, Radcliffe-Brown occupied a number of academic positions, frequently establishing new anthropology departments: University of Cape Town (1921–1926), University of Sydney (1926–1931), and the University of Chicago (1931–1937). Next he returned to Oxford where he remained until his retirement in 1946, after which he taught in Cairo and South Africa. Radcliffe-Brown died in England in 1955.

Radcliffe-Brown's impact is evident in the writings of his students. When he left the University of Chicago, his students presented Radcliffe-Brown with a volume titled *Social Anthropology of North American Tribes* (Eggan 1962). That group—including Fred Eggan, Morris Opler, and Sol Tax—all became important figures in American anthropology. Robert Redfield (1962 [1937]:ix) wrote in the introduction:

> Professor Radcliffe-Brown brought to this country a method for the study of society, well–defined and different enough from what prevailed here to require American anthropologists to reconsider the whole matter of method, to scrutinize their objectives, and to attend to new problems and new ways of looking at problems.

Radcliffe-Brown called that approach "social anthropology."

Social Anthropology: Defining A Field

Radcliffe-Brown distinguished "social anthropology" from ethnology. In a 1951 lecture, Radcliffe-Brown pointed out that Boas had set two research objectives: 1) the reconstruction of the cultural history of a particular people or region, and 2) the "investigation of the laws governing social life." Noting that Boas had referred synonymously to the field of inquiry as "ethnology" or "anthropology," Radcliffe-Brown proposed that the terms should mark different lines of inquiry, suggesting that anthropologists:

> . . . refer to those investigations that are concerned with the reconstruction of history as belonging to ethnology and to keep the term social anthropology for the study of discoverable regularities in the development of human society in so far as these can be illustrated or demonstrated by the study of primitive peoples. [1977b:54]

The observation of regularities and search for general laws characterizes Radcliffe-Brown's social anthropology. Although Boas recognized the potential existence of laws of human behavior, in fact most
of Boas' efforts went to the explication of particular cultural developments. Radcliffe-Brown's 1951 lecture was a response, 55 years after
the fact, to Boas' (1896) *The Limitations of the Comparative Method of
Anthropology* in which Boas attacked the Victorian evolutionists (see
pp. 48–50). Boas had argued that focused, intensive fieldwork was
essential, not loose comparisons based on uneven published sources.
Radcliffe-Brown responded that comparative studies were also necessary and that library research was useful when it supplemented ethnographic fieldwork. Radcliffe-Brown (1977b:54) complained that the
modern anthropology graduate student setting out for fieldwork, "is
told that he must consider any feature of social life in its context, in its
relation to the other features of the particular social system in which it is
found. But he is often not taught to look at it in the wider context of
human societies in general." This is what Radcliffe-Brown proposed to do.

Social anthropology was grounded in the comparative method; its
goal was the elucidation of lawlike generalizations about human society. Radcliffe-Brown considered social anthropology to be a subdisci-
pline of comparative sociology—a discipline which he traced to the
French social theorists such as Montesquieu and Comte, but most
directly to Durkheim. Social anthropology differed from comparative
sociology in scope but not in intent. Radcliffe-Brown wrote:

> Comparative sociology, of which social anthropology is a branch, is
> here conceived as a theoretical or nomothetic study of which the aim
> is to provide acceptable generalisations. The theoretical under-
> standing of a particular institution is its interpretation in the light of
> such generalisations. [1977a:13]

"Nomothetic"—from the Greek *nomos* for law—refers to the structure of scientific explanation. Scientific laws—like the Law of Gravity
or the Second Law of Thermodynamics—are generalizing propositions
about the relationship between two or more factors. They are not
idiographic explanations of a particular occurrence, but are broadly
relevant to all cases which express that relationship. Thus, Newton's
Law of Gravity was not an explanation of why a particular apple fell
out of a particular tree one day (to use the apocryphal example), but a
statement about all bodies of matter which have mass and distance.

Radcliffe-Brown envisioned an anthropology that could discover scientific laws about human society, cross–cultural regularities between "structure" and "function."

Structure and Function

Radcliffe-Brown's notion of social structure made his comparative approach possible; they were his unit of comparison. Social structures, Radcliffe-Brown argued, are the relations of association between individuals, and they exist independently of the individual members who might occupy those positions, much in the way that "hero," "heroine," and "villain" define a set of relationships in a melodrama regardless of the actors who play those roles. Social structures are not abstractions; unlike "culture," they exist and may be directly observed:

> We do not observe a "culture", since that word denotes, not any concrete reality, but an abstraction, and as it is commonly used a vague abstraction. But direct observation does reveal to us that . . . human beings are connected by a complex network of social relations. I use the term "social structure" to denote this network of actually existing relations. [Radcliffe-Brown 1952b:190]

Social structure includes all interpersonal relations, the differentiation of individuals and groups by their social roles, and the relationships between a particular group of humans and a larger network of connections.

Although Radcliffe-Brown contends that social structures are concrete realities, they are not what an individual fieldworker observes in a specific society, which Radcliffe-Brown describes as "social forms."

This is confusing and an example is in order. If I am conducting a study of cooperative work groups in a peasant community, over the course of my field work I will observe (hopefully) a number of cases of different groups of people getting together at various times to work in different people's fields. I will take notes on the participants, their efforts, and the interpersonal dynamics of the group. At that point, in Radcliffe-Brown's terminology, I would be describing *social forms*. But if I recorded "as precisely as possible the *general* or *normal* form of this relationship, abstracted from the variations of particular instances, though taking account of those variations" (Radcliffe-Brown 1952b:192, emphasis added) then I would be describing the *social structure* of corvee labor. We will sidestep the issue about whether, thus defined, social structure is a result of observation or an inferred creation;

obviously, Radcliffe-Brown considered social structures to be empiri-
cally knowable and concrete.

This notion of structure, as Adam Kuper (1977:5) observes, "is perhaps the main contemporary stumbling–block to an understanding of
what Radcliffe-Brown was saying." Part of the confusion stems from
alternate uses of the word "structure," most notably in Claude Lévi-
Strauss' structural anthropology (see Chapter 17). For Lévi-Strauss
(1968:279) "The term 'social structure' has nothing to do with empirical reality but with models which are built up after it." Radcliffe-Brown
wrote to Lévi-Strauss:

> As you have recognized, I use the term "social structure" in a way so
> different from yours as to make discussion so difficult as to be
> unlikely to be profitable. While for you social structure has nothing to
> do with reality but in models which are built up, I regard the social
> structure as a reality. When I pick up a particular sea shell on the
> beach, I recognize it as having a particular structure. I may find other
> shells of the same species which have a similar structure so that I can
> say there is a form of structure characteristic of the species. [1977c:42]

Thus we can identify certain social structures—exogamous moieties, joking relationships, corvee labor, cross-cousin marriage, and on
and on—compare those structures as manifested in different societies,
and then attempt to understand the underlying principles that account
for these different social structures. Almost inevitably, Radcliffe-Brown's
explanation of social structures leads to a consideration of function.

For Radcliffe-Brown, the function of cultural institutions was the
role they played in maintaining society, *not* the satisfaction of individuals' needs as Malowinski argued. Like many theories of human society,
the notion is based on the organic analogy, referring to activities meeting
the needs of the structure. Extrapolated to the social realm,

> the continuity of structure is maintained by the process of social life,
> which consists of the activities and interactions of the individual
> human beings and of the organized groups into which they are
> united. The social life of the community is here defined as the *func-
> tioning* of the social structure. The *function* of a crime, or a funeral
> ceremony, is the part it plays in the social life as a whole and there-
> fore the contribution it makes to the maintenance of structural conti-
> nuity. [Radcliffe-Brown 1952c:180; original emphasis]

And

> Such a view implies that a social system . . . has a certain kind of
> unity, which we may speak of as a functional unity. We may define it

as a condition in which all parts of the system work together with a sufficient degree of harmony or internal consistency, i.e., without producing persistent conflicts which can neither be resolved nor regulated. [Radcliffe-Brown 1952c:181]

Such passages have led to the reasonable criticism of Radcliffe-Brown's view as overly static and synchronic. In a footnote to the above quotation, Radcliffe-Brown rather offhandedly comments, "Opposition, i.e., organised and regulated antagonism, is, of course, an essential feature of every social system," a scant recognition of social conflict. Radcliffe-Brown acknowledges the changes traditional societies underwent due to the imposition of European colonialism, but he did not actually analyze such postcolonial changes. Rather, Radcliffe-Brown laments the scarcity of unaltered traditional societies and the absence of precontact historical data and retreats into another attack on pseudohistory (Radcliffe-Brown 1952c:183–184). Clearly diachronic study was not Radcliffe-Brown's preferred mode of inquiry; his contribution was in the analysis of social structures.

Eaglehawk, Crow, and the Cult of the Ancestors

Radcliffe-Brown observed that "The only really satisfactory way of explaining a method is by means of illustration," and two examples make that clear—his analyses of exogamous moieties and of Andaman Islanders' ritual. Exogamous moieties are kin systems in which a population is divided into two social divisions and a man of one moiety must marry a woman of another moiety. Radcliffe-Brown began his analysis with the case of aboriginal groups in the interior of New South Wales in which moieties were matrilineal, exogamous, and the two divisions were named after their respective totems, the Eaglehawk (Kilpara) and the Crow (Makwara). How to explain this? Radcliffe-Brown argues that neither conjectural history nor diffusion provide satisfying explanation and turns to a comparison of social structures. Radcliffe-Brown examines other cases from Australia and finds many cases of exogamous moieties—some patrilineal, others matrilineal—named after birds. Further, other forms of dual organization (such as a system of alternating generational divisions in which you, your grandparents, and your grandchildren are members of a social group different from your parents', children's, and great-grandchildren's) are also named by pairs of birds. A search for more cases finds examples of moieties named by other pairs of animals (two species of kangaroos, for example).

Radcliffe-Brown pursues a series of progressively broader questions, from "Why Eaglehawk vs. Crow?" to "Why all these birds?" to:

> What is the principle by which such pairs as eaglehawk and crow, eagle and raven, coyote and wild cat are chosen as representing the moieties of a dual division? The reason for asking this question is not idle curiousity. We may, it can be held, suppose that an understanding of the principle in question will give us an important insight into the way in which the natives themselves think about the dual division as part of their social structure. [Radcliffe-Brown 1977b:57]

Radcliffe-Brown analyzes stories about Eaglehawk and Crow and other moiety referents to gain insights into native thinking. It is a search for systems of classification similar to those discussed by Durkheim and Mauss (see Chapters 4 and 9). The common element in all these tales may be distilled into a single theme: "The resemblances and differences of animal species are translated into terms of friendship and conflict, solidarity and opposition. In other words the world of animal life is represented in terms of social relations similar to those of human society" (Radcliffe-Brown 1977b:59). Eaglehawk and Crow are both meat eaters but Eaglehawk hunts and Crow steals. Other examples of oppositions between related entities are black cockatoo vs. white cockatoo, coyote vs. wildcat (in California), upstream vs. downstream, and so on. They are all associated with exogamous moieties, leading Radcliffe-Brown (1977b:61) to conclude that "wherever, in Australia, Melanesia or America, there exists a social structure of exogamous moieties, the moieties are thought of as being in a relation of what is here called 'opposition.'"

Radcliffe-Brown presented his analysis of exogamous moieties as an example of the comparative approach and the conceptual utility of social structure. Moving from the specific case to increasing levels of generalization, Radcliffe-Brown posed a series of interesting questions, not just about the societies of New South Wales, but about human societies in general.

Radcliffe-Brown's concern with society in general is clear from a 1945 lecture on "Religion and Society" in which he contrasted totemism and ancestor worship (1977d). He narrowly defines ancestor worship as the worship of a deceased ancestor or ancestors by an associated descent group such as a lineage or clan. Offerings of food and drink are made to the ancestors, which are usually conceived of as sharing a meal with the ancestors (Radcliffe-Brown 1977d:113–114). The rites of ancestor worship also reflect a sense of dependency between the worshiper and the ancestors—ancestors will give him children and well–being, provide blessings if propitiated, send illness and disaster if ignored (Radcliffe-Brown 1977d:125). Not surprisingly, ancestor worship is most developed among societies where unilineal descent is most important:

> In such a society what gives stability to the social structure is the solidarity and continuity of the lineage, and of the wider group (the clan) composed of related lineages. For the individual, his primary duties are those of lineage. These include duties to the members now living, but also to those who have died and to those who are not yet born. In the carrying out of these duties he is controlled and inspired by the complex systems of sentiments of which we may say . . . are centered [on] the lineage itself, past, present and future. It is primarily this system of sentiments that is expressed in the rites of the cult of the ancestors. The social function of the rites is obvious: by giving solemn and collective expression to them the rites reaffirm, renew and strengthen those sentiments on which the social solidarity depends. [Radcliffe-Brown 1977d:114]

Note that Radcliffe-Brown has done more than engage in idle speculation; he has proposed testable hypotheses: "Does ancestor worship only occur in lineage-based societies? Are the sentiments expressed always those of dependency? Does ancestor worship diminish when traditional social forms weaken?" He also produced a broader theoretical statement about "the social function of religions, i.e. the contribution they make to the formation and maintenance of a social order" (Radcliffe-Brown 1977d:104).

Conclusion

Radcliffe-Brown's analysis of social structure and function redirected anthropological inquiry to the institutions of human life and to the role such institutions play in the maintenance and reproduction of society. Today these concerns are not as central as they were between 1930 and 1960 when British social anthropology was at its peak, and consequently Radcliffe-Brown's stature has declined (again, see Kuper 1977). An examination of the two principal social anthropology journals in the United Kingdom and the United States, *Journal of the Royal Anthropological Institute* (formerly *Man*) and *American Ethnologist*, respectively, shows that Radcliffe-Brown was cited only four times in articles published in 1995, usually just to be criticized (Dean 1995; Gupta 1995; Harrison 1995; Keen 1995). Over the last decade, Radcliffe-Brown tends to be cited either when a specific social dimension is discussed—like descent theory (Shapiro 1988) or brother–sister relationship (Joseph 1994)—or in matters relating to Australian kinship systems, e.g. Cowlishaw's (1987: 229–230) brief critical assessment of Radcliffe-Brown's contribution to studies of Australian aborigines.

Adam Kuper (1977:2) writes of Radcliffe-Brown, "the profound yet second–hand nature of his influence on modern anthropology may constitute a real difficulty for the contemporary reader." This suggests that the ideas of Radcliffe-Brown deserve open–minded rereading. ✦

Bibliography

Cowlishaw, Gillian
1987 Colour, Culture and the Aboriginalists. Man 22(2):221–237.

Dean, Bartholomew
1995 Forbidden Fruit: Infidelity, Affinity, and Brideservice among the Urarina of Peruvian Amazonia. Journal of the Royal Anthropological Institute 1:87–110.

Gregg, D. and E. Williams
1948 The Dismal Science of Functionalism. American Anthropologist 50:594–611.

Gupta, Akil
1995 Blurred Boundaries: The Discourse of Corruption, the Culture of Politics and the Imagined State. American Ethnologist 22:335–402.

Harrison, Simon
1995 Four Types of Symbolic Conflict. Journal of the Royal Anthropological Institute 1:255–272.

Joseph, Suad
1994 Brother/Sister Relationships: Connectivity, Cousins and Power in the Reproduction of Patriarchy in Lebanon. American Ethnologist 21:50–73.

Keen, Ian
1995 Metaphor and Metalanguage: "Groups" in Northeast Arnhemland. American Ethnologist 22:502–527.

Kuper, Adam
1977 Preface. In The Social Anthropology of Radcliffe-Brown. A. Kuper, ed. Pp. 1–7. London: Routledge & Kegan Paul.

Redfield, Robert
1962 Introduction. In Social Anthropology of North American Tribes. F. Eggan, ed. Pp. ix–xiv. Chicago: University of Chicago Press. [Originally published 1937.]

Radcliffe-Brown, A. R.
1922 The Andaman Islanders. Cambridge: Cambridge University Press.
1949 Functionalism: A Protest. American Anthropologist 51:320–322.

1952a The Study of Kinship Systems. *In* Structure and Function in Primitive Society. E. Evans–Pritchard and F. Eggan, eds. Pp. 49–89. London: Cohen and West Ltd.

1952b On Social Structure. *In* Structure and Function in Primitive Society. E. Evans–Pritchard and F. Eggan, eds. Pp. 188–204. London: Cohen and West Ltd.

1952c On the Concept of Function in Social Science. *In* Structure and Function in Primitive Society. E. Evans-Pritchard and F. Eggan, eds. Pp. 178–187. London: Cohen and West Ltd.

1977a Introduction. *In* The Social Anthropology of Radcliffe-Brown. A. Kuper, ed. Pp. 11–24. London: Routledge & Kegan Paul.

1977b The Comparative Method in Social Anthropology. *In* The Social Anthropology of Radcliffe-Brown. A. Kuper, ed. Pp. 53–69. London: Routledge & Kegan Paul.

1977c Letter to Lévi-Strauss. *In* The Social Anthropology of Radcliffe-Brown. A. Kuper, ed. P. 42. London: Routledge & Kegan Paul.

1977d Religion and society. *In* The Social Anthropology of Radcliffe-Brown. A. Kuper, ed. Pp. 103–128. London: Routledge & Kegan Paul.

Shapiro Warren
1988 Ritual Kinship, Ritual Incorporation and the Denial of Death. Man 23:275–297.

White, Leslie
1966 The Social Organization of Ethnological Theory. Rice University Studies 52(4). Houston: Rice University.

Chapter 12

Edward Evans-Pritchard
Social Anthropology, Social History

Edward E. Evans-Pritchard (1902–1973) was the errant son of British social anthropology; he first followed its tenets, then later attacked them. During the 1940s, Evans-Pritchard's theoretical outlook changed from a perspective essentially shaped by Radcliffe-Brown to an anthropological vision more attentive to social history and human agency. His early work included classic ethnographies like *Witchcraft, Oracles and Magic Among the Azande* (1937), *The Nuer* (1940), *Kinship and Marriage Among the Nuer* (1951), and edited (with Meyer Fortes) and contributed to *African Political Systems* (1940), a "state-of-the-art" collection, all within the British social anthropology school of thought. Like Radcliffe-Brown, Evans-Pritchard's earlier works emphasize structure and function in social relationships. The articles in *African Political Systems* also tend to be synchronic and isolating, separating 20th-century African societies from their historical past and colonial present. In reference to *African Political Systems*, Marvin Harris (1968:536) points out that 350 years of the slave trade followed by a century of direct European control created enormous cultural change: "Advancing before this scourge [of slavers] were shock waves of wars, migrations, political upheavals, and vast demographic changes. In such a context, restriction to an ethnographic present of the 1930s, in the name of empiricism, has little to commend it."

British social anthropology has fallen out of favor because of this ahistorical perspective, its emphasis on social stasis, and a tendency to reify society and to diminish the role of the individual. Evans-Pritchard's works prior to the 1950s are vulnerable to this criticism. For example, in *The Nuer* (1940) he documented the age-grade system of

the Nuer in which every four years a new group of teenage boys underwent an initiation rite; this cohort formed an age-set and as these
males grew older different behaviors would be expected of them.
Evans-Pritchard called this progression "structural time," calendrical
intervals marked by predictable changes in status.

> Seasonal and lunar changes repeat themselves year after year, so that
> a Nuer standing at any point of time has conceptual knowledge of
> what lies before him and can predict and organize his life accord-
> ingly. A man's structural future is likewise already fixed and ordered
> into different periods, so that the total changes in status a boy will
> undergo in his ordained passage through the social system, if he lives
> long enough, can be foreseen. [Evans-Pritchard 1940:94–95]

In this passage Evans-Pritchard makes even a person's lifecycle
static, reducing the individual to a staircase of status changes. This
analysis is particularly intriguing given that it occurs in the best
known work of an anthropologist who would later become famous for
his emphasis on history and the importance of the individual.

Ten years after the publication of *The Nuer* Evans-Pritchard argued
a very different line distinctly at odds with the British social anthropology tradition: that social anthropology should be recast into social history (Evans-Pritchard 1950). The anthropologist Mary Douglas
(1980:2–3) wrote about his later ideas about the relationship between
individual and society:

> He would not subscribe to mechanistic social theories and resisted sci-
> entific fashions in anthropology. His own rugged individualism for-
> bade him to ignore human agency, and he found uncongenial any
> theorizing that reduced the mind to a mere arena in which social fac-
> tors contend.

So what happened between 1940 and 1950? Why did Evans-
Pritchard's ideas change? What core elements of his thought have
been retained by contemporary anthropology?

Background

Evans-Pritchard's life and work were shaped by the British Empire.
Born in 1902, Evans-Pritchard studied history at Oxford, receiving his
M.A. in Modern History in 1924. He began his anthropological studies
at the London School of Economics where he studied under C. G.
Seligman, one of the members of the Torres Straits expedition directed

by Haddon. According to Beidelman (1974:1), "He left Oxford for London partly for a change of environment but mainly because he wanted to do field research and no one in Oxford had done that." He arrived at the London School of Economics the same term that Malinowski arrived to teach; in fact, Evans-Pritchard and Raymond Firth were Malinowski's first students. Evans-Pritchard was closer to Seligman, however, and apparently kept his distance from Malinowski.

In 1926 Seligman was contracted to provide an ethnographic survey of the indigenous groups of the Anglo-Egyptian Sudan. When Seligman became ill he arranged for Evans-Pritchard to carry on the fieldwork. Nearly 50 years later Evans-Pritchard recalled his professors' advice before his first fieldwork experience:

> I first sought advice from Westermarck. All I got from him was "don't converse with an informant for more than twenty minutes because if you aren't bored by that time he will be." Very good advice, even if somewhat inadequate. I sought instruction from Haddon, a man foremost in field-research. He told me that it was really all quite simple; one should always behave as a gentleman. Also very good advice. My teacher, Seligman, told me to take ten grains of quinine every day and to keep off women. The famous Egyptologist, Sir Flinders Petrie, just told me not to bother about drinking dirty water as one soon became immune to it. Finally, I asked Malinowski and was told not to be a bloody fool. [Evans-Pritchard 1976:240]

There is an amateurish dash about all this, replete with "stiff upper lipisms," but the Anglo-Egyptian government was paying for this ethnographic survey (and most of Evans-Pritchard's subsequent research) because the government had a serious objective.

The goal was empire. The British government wanted to assert imperial control over African peoples like the Azande and Nuer living in the watershed between the Nile and the Congo rivers. Initially British control was via indirect rule in which local political authorities were maintained but depended on colonial administrators, but in the early 1920s imperial authority was more directly applied. The traditional scattered Azande homesteads were forcibly resettled along new Government roads. The expressed intent was to control sleeping sickness; the obvious consequence was to control the Azande (Gillies 1976:viii). In 1930 Evans-Pritchard began his work among the Nuer right after the British military had bloodily suppressed Nuer revolts (Evans-Pritchard 1940:11). He agreed to conduct the study with great hesitation, because, according to Douglas (1980:40), he felt responsible as an anthropologist to serve as a mediator between the Nuer and the government: "The Nuer would fight until they were destroyed." Evans-Pritchard (1940:11) recalled, "When I entered a [Nuer] cattle camp it was not only as a stranger but as an enemy, and they seldom tried to conceal their disgust at my presence, refusing to answer my greetings and even turning away when I addressed them."

Much of Evans-Pritchard's work was conducted under government auspices and was frequently written to inform British administrators (e.g., Evans-Pritchard 1937:3–4). Some of his investigations would raise ethical issues today which he and his contemporaries ignored. But Evans-Pritchard did not engage in espionage; he always made his intentions known to the people he studied and lived with and respected them.

Evans-Pritchard received his Ph.D. in 1927 by writing up the results of his first three months of fieldwork among the Azande for his thesis. Over the next three years he spent 20 months among the Azande. Between field trips he was Lecturer in Social Anthropology at the London School of Economics and in 1932 he became Professor of Sociology at Fuad I University in Cairo. He resigned that post to become a research lecturer in African Sociology at Oxford, a position he held until the outbreak of World War II.

During the war, Evans-Pritchard led a guerrilla force along the Sudanese/Ethiopian border against the Italians, earning this headline in a London newspaper: "OXFORD DON GUERRILLA: LED ABYSSINIAN TRIBESMEN." He also served as an intelligence officer and political officer in Ethiopia, Sudan, Syria, and Libya. Referring to Evans-Pritchard's life, a colleague recalled (Lienhardt 1974:300), "Parts of his own life . . . had a fictional quality."

He returned to England in 1945 and after a year at Cambridge, became professor of social anthropology at Oxford, succeeding Radcliffe-Brown. He remained at Oxford until he retired in 1970. After retirement, he remained very active, however. His bibliography lists 21 publications for 1970 alone, and although many are relatively brief reviews, prefaces, and notes, they range over topics like the sociology of Comte, witchcraft in Tudor and Stuart England, and nine different pieces about the Zande (Evans-Pritchard 1974a). He produced "one of the largest published ethnographic collections in social anthropology" (Lienhardt 1974:304).

But where are Evans-Pritchard's theories of human behavior in all of this ethnographic research? They are present but intentionally hidden. Douglas (1980:24) writes:

> The relation of his ethnographic researches to contemporary speculations or theory was never spelled out in his big fieldwork monographs.

As a matter of principle, these were written with practically no polemics, no controversies, no disputatious thrashing out of definitions.

Instead, his ethnographic research was a presentation of

a coherent story, omitting nothing, twisting nothing, and adding nothing that could not be justified. The theoretical burden would be found in the internal consistency of a large body of ethnographic analysis, in which other ethnographers would discern theoretical innovations. [Douglas 1980:24]

Evans-Pritchard believed that theories were inferred from local realities and that, therefore, general pronouncements should fade into the background. For example, in an early essay Evans-Pritchard attacked some of the theorists working on magic. Accusing theorists of creating an artificial patchwork of indigenous belief, Evans-Pritchard argued:

The resulting pattern of belief may be a fiction since it may never be actually present in a man's consciousness at any given time and may not even be known to him in its entirety. This fact would have emerged if records of everything a savage does and says throughout a single day were recorded, for then we would be able to compare our own thoughts more adequately with the real thoughts of savages instead of with an abstraction pieced together from persistent enquiries conducted in an atmosphere quite unlike that of the savages' ordinary milieu and in which it is the European who evokes the beliefs by his questions. . . . [cited in Douglas 1980:27]

Evans-Pritchard's goal was to present a body of ethnographic work which was entire, coherent, and an accurate presentation of indigenous belief. Yet running through much of his work is an idea that Douglas calls Evans-Pritchard's "theory of accountability."

A Theory of Accountability

Mary Douglas has written brilliantly about Evans-Pritchard, placing his work within a larger theoretical debate (cf. Gellner 1981:xv–xvi). Douglas writes:

One of the present crises in sociology comes from the criticisms of phenomenologists. Maintaining that social understanding must start from the human experience of consciousness and reflection, they despair of truth in any so-called human science that ignores the distinctively human element. [Douglas 1980:2]

Phenomenologists would dismiss theories proposed by White, Harris, and Radcliffe-Brown, for example, because their respective points of view argue that cultural life is knowable independently of the experience of its participants, holding that what informants think or perceive of reality is not necessarily the starting point for inquiry. Phenomenologists basically give explanatory priority to the informant's subjective view. Douglas continues:

> These critics have undermined confidence in the traditional methods and even in the traditional objectives of sociology. Consequently, many scholars sensitive to the criticism have been tempted to give up striving for objectivity and to shift their own writing into a mystical mode, indulgent to their own subjectivity. Others, who would still like to try for objective comparisons, find little alternative but to work on in the old framework of inquiry, and so tend to shirk these issues. In advance of this critical juncture Evans-Pritchard felt the dilemma keenly. [Douglas 1980:2]

The dilemma is this: Where does culture exist other than in the perceptions, beliefs, and actions of individuals? This is the issue Sapir encountered when he read about the contrary Omaha, Two Crows (see pp. 92–94). How can we state, "The Nuer believe X," when we really need to list the individual opinions of each of a finite list of Nuer, as expressed at a particular time? And if culture only exists with the individual, how can comparisons between individuals—let alone between cultures—be made? And finally, and most problematically, how can an anthropologist's statement about another culture be anything more than her or his individual perception of another individual's expression, a flimsy bridge of communication across a chasm of cultural difference?

As Douglas suggests, one response to the dilemma is to say "the hell with it!" and focus on issues that do not require such epistemological turmoil. Another approach is to retreat into a cocoon of hypersubjectivity in which ethnography and autobiography are not distinguished.

Evans-Pritchard, Douglas suggests, attempted to find a way through the dilemma:

> He taught that the essential point for comparison is that at which people meet misfortune. They may accuse others, they may accept responsibility. They count different kinds of misfortune as needing explanation. As they work their ideas of blame and compensation into their social institutions, they invoke existences and powers that are adapted to each particular accounting system. There are ways of

getting valid evidence on these essential moral purposes as they surface from consciousness into action. [Douglas 1980:3]

For example, how do we deal with misfortune in modern America?
We litigate. If we spill scalding coffee on ourselves, we sue the restau-
rant that heated it. If we slip on ice and break a leg, we sue the store
that should have shoveled the sidewalk. In American society, we
appeal to the legal system to establish responsibility—even over "acci-
dents"—and to assess penalties. An exploration of accountability in
American society would readily identify major themes of a cultural life.

Similarly, Evans-Pritchard followed the threads of accountability in
his classic studies of the Azande. He (1967:11) wrote, "I suppose that
the simplest way of assessing an African people's way of looking at life
is to ask to what they attribute misfortune, and for the Azande the
answer is witchcraft."

Azande Witchcraft: The Allocation of Accountability

"Witchcraft is ubiquitous," Evans-Pritchard (1976:18) wrote,

> I had no difficulty in discovering what the Azande think about witch-
> craft, nor in observing what they do to combat it. These ideas and
> actions are on the surface of their life. . . . *Mangu*, witchcraft, was one
> of the first words I heard in Zandeland, and I heard it uttered day by
> day throughout the months. [Evans-Pritchard 1976:1]

Witchcraft may be the cause for misfortune in any element of Zan-
delife:

> There is no niche or corner of Zande culture into which it does not
> twist itself. If blight seizes the ground-nut crop it is witchcraft; if the
> bush is vainly scoured for game it is witchcraft; if women laboriously
> bale water out of a pool and are rewarded with but a few small fish it
> is witchcraft; if termites do not rise when their swarming is due and
> a cold useless night is spent waiting for their flight it is witchcraft; if a
> wife is sulky and unresponsive to her husband it is witchcraft; if a
> prince is cold and distant with his subject it is witchcraft; if a magi-
> cal rite fails to achieve its purpose it is witchcraft; if, in fact, any fail-
> ure or misfortune falls upon anyone at any time and in relation to
> any of the manifold activities of his life it may be due to witchcraft.
> [Evans-Pritchard 1976:63–64]

This does not mean the Azande are unaware of other forms of causation—for example, incompetence or carelessness, breach of taboo or

failure to observe a moral rule, or what we might call "natural processes"—but witchcraft is an important explanatory link.

Evans-Pritchard's classic example of this is the case of the falling granary. Granaries are heavy structures of wattle and daub raised above ground on wooden posts. Evans-Pritchard writes, "sometimes a granary collapses. There is nothing remarkable in this. Every Zande knows that termites eat the supports in course of time and that even the hardest woods decay. . . . " In the heat of the summer the Azande will sit in the shade of the granary:

> Consequently it may happen that there are people sitting beneath the granary when it collapses and they are injured, for it is a heavy structure. . . . Now why should these particular people have been sitting under this particular granary at the particular moment when it collapsed? That it should collapse is easily intelligible, but why should have it collapsed at the particular moment when these particular people were sitting beneath it? Through years it might have collapsed, so why should it fall just when certain people sought its kindly shelter?
>
> Zande philosophy can supply the missing link. The Zande knows that the supports were undermined by termites and that people were sitting beneath the granary in order to escape the heat and glare of the sun. But he knows besides why these two events occurred at a precisely similar moment in time and space. It was due to the action of witchcraft. [Evans-Pritchard 1976:69–70]

Evans-Pritchard discusses Azande witchcraft in over 500 pages impossible to summarize briefly. The Azande believe that witchcraft is located in an organ by the liver and is passed patrilineally from father to son, but that it is not present in the royal lineage. This genetic theory of witchcraft transmission, Douglas observes, "was adapted so that questions about transmission were directed away from those social relationships where claims could not be collected" (Douglas 1980:55). Such selectivity in the organization of human thinking is one of the key points of Evans-Pritchard's theory of accountability. Douglas writes:

> Evans-Pritchard's implicit conception of human knowledge starts from three principles. First, rational thought is exercised only selectively over the possible field of attention. Second, the principle of selectivity depends on the social demand for accountability. Third, the social patterns of accountability which can be elicited by systematic observation provide a structured anchorage for a particular kind of reality, with its own array of beings invested with appropriate powers. In sum, each human society, insofar as its members expect to

hold each other accountable, has its own locally selected reality anchored to agreement about moral objectives. [Douglas 1980:132]

By focusing on the ways different segments of a society hold each other accountable, the structures linking individuals and institutions can be discerned. The identification of such local structures was one of Evans-Pritchard's goals in discussing social anthropology as a form of social history.

Social Anthropology as Social History

In the Preface to *Witchcraft, Sorcery and Magic among the Azande*, Evans-Pritchard wrote, "If I have paid no attention to Zande history this is not because I consider it unimportant but because I consider it so important that I desire to record it in detail elsewhere." In 1971 he published *The Azande: History and Political Institutions*. It is an incredibly complex description of Azande expansion during the 150 years before colonial subjugation, full of battles, royal intrigues, and struggles of succession. But in addition to the historical detail, Evans-Pritchard outlined why history was important for anthropology:

> Anthropological theory often rests on a basis of studies of primitive societies for which there is little recorded history. In the case of African kingdoms, such as those of the Azande, to leave out the historical dimension is to deprive ourselves of knowledge that is both ascertainable and necessary for an understanding of political organizations which have always, to a greater or lesser extent, been transformed by European rule before anthropologists have commenced their study of them, and which, furthermore, have been shaped by events that took place long before Europeans appeared on the scene. That the Azande had been expanding and . . . conquering and assimilating dozens of foreign peoples, as well as taking part in a long series of dynastic wars among themselves, for at least 150 years before Europeans imposed their administrations is surely a fact which cannot be left out of consideration in a study of their institutions and culture. [Evans-Pritchard 1971:267]

Such common sense struck at the heart of Radcliffe-Brown's form of social anthropology; it also formed the basis of Evans-Pritchard's later research agenda.

Evans-Pritchard contended that social history could serve as a model for social anthropology. He argued (1988 [1950]:418–19) that there are three levels of anthropological inquiry of increasing abstraction, each with direct parallels in historical methods. First, the anthropologist attempts to understand another society and translate it to his own. The only difference between anthropology and history is that the anthropologist's data are produced from direct fieldwork experience while the historian relies upon the written record; this was merely "a technical, not a methodological, difference." Second, the anthropologist and historian attempt to make their subjects "sociologically intelligible." Evans-Pritchard writes:

> But even in a single ethnographic study the anthropologist seeks to do more than understand the thought and values of primitive people and translate them to his own culture. He seeks also to discover the structural order of the society, the patterns which, once established, enable him to see it as a whole, as a set of interrelated abstractions. Then the society is not only culturally intelligible, as it is, at the level of consciousness and action, for one of its members or for the foreigner who has learnt its mores and participates in its life, but also becomes sociologically intelligible. [1988 (1950):417]

And finally, "the anthropologist compares the social structures his analysis has revealed in a wide range of societies" (1950 [1988]:419). Thus, Evans-Pritchard was not engaged in historical particularism, but based his comparison on social structures as documented from a historical perspective with abundant ethnographic detail.

Conclusion

Evans-Pritchard currently enjoys a level of respect that other British social anthropologists—Radcliffe-Brown most obviously—are denied. There are several reasons for this. First, in the later half of his career Evans-Pritchard engaged in a virtual point-by-point refutation of Radcliffe-Brown's structural functionalism (Kuper 1977:129–135). Central to this was Evans-Pritchard's argument that anthropology should be modeled on social history rather than a science, and this call for a "humanistic" anthropology resonates with many anthropologists today. "It has seemed to me," Evans-Pritchard wrote in his last book (1974:9), "that anthropologists (include me if you wish) have, in their writings about African societies, dehumanized the Africans into systems and structures and lost the flesh and blood." Evans-Pritchard's stature derives from his attention to placing ethnographic accounts within their local logics, for example, embedding explanations within the specific cultural rationales of Zande culture. Unlike many scholars who articulated a singular view of human behavior, Evans-Pritchard was engaged in a living debate and did not create an "Evans-Pritchardian position let alone dogma," as the late Ernst Gellner observed. E. E. Evans-Pritchard's relation to the anthropological tradition, Gellner (1981:xv) wrote, was "Not that of a prophet, but rather an intellectually restless, ever-questing, sceptical Hamlet." ✦

Bibliography

Beidelman, T. O.
1974 A Biographical Sketch. *In* A Bibliography of the Writings of E. E. Evans-Pritchard. E. E. Evans-Pritchard and T. Beidelman, eds. Pp. 1–13. London: Tavistock Publications.

Douglas, Mary
1980 Edward Evans-Pritchard. New York: The Viking Press.

Evans-Pritchard, Edward
1937 Witchcraft, Oracles and Magic among the Azande. Oxford: Oxford University Press.
1940 The Nuer: A Description of the Modes of Livelihood and Political Institutions of A Nilotic People. Oxford: Oxford University Press.
1948 The Divine Kingship of the Shilluk of the Nilotic Sudan. Cambridge: Cambridge University Press.
1949 The Sansusi of Cyrenaica. Oxford: Clarendon Press.
1950 Social Anthropology: Past and Present. Man 198:118–124. [Reprinted in Highpoints in Anthropology. P. Bohannon and J. Glazer, eds. Pp. 410–421.]
1951 Kinship and Marriage among the Nuer. Oxford: Oxford University Press.
1965 Theories of Primitive Religion. Oxford: Clarendon Press.
1967 The Zande Trickster. Oxford: Oxford University Press.
1971 The Azande: History and Political Institutions. Oxford: Oxford University Press.
1974a A Bibliography of the Writings of E. E. Evans-Pritchard. Compiled by E. E. Evans-Pritchard, amended and corrected by T. Beidelman. London: Tavistock Publications.
1974b Man and Woman among the Azande. New York: The Free Press.
1976 Witchcraft, Oracles, and Magic among the Azande. Abridged with an introduction by E. Gillies. Oxford: Clarendon Press.

Fortes, Meyer and E. E. Evans-Pritchard, eds.
1940 African Political Systems. Oxford: Oxford University Press.

Gellner, Ernst
1981 Introduction. *In* A History of Anthropological Theory by E. E. Evans-Pritchard. A. Singer, ed. Pp. xiii–xxxvi. New York: Basic Books.

Gillies, E.
1976 Introduction. *In* Witchcraft, Oracles, and Magic among the Azande by E. E. Evans-Pritchard. Abridged with an introduction by E. Gillies. Oxford: Clarendon Press.

Harris, Marvin
1968 Rise of Anthropological Theory: A History of Theories of Culture. New York: Thomas Y. Crowell and Co.

Kuper, Adam
1983 Anthropology and Anthropologists: The Modern British School. London: Routledge & Kegan Paul.

Lienhardt, Geoffrey
1974 Evans-Pritchard: A Personal View. Man (n.s.) 9(2):299–304.

Part Four

Evolutionary, Adaptationist, and Materialist Theories

Evolution reemerges in American anthropology in the 1930s. It is explicitly anti-Boasian, frequently revivalistic, and only implicitly Marxist. In contrast to Boasian historical anthropology, the 20th-century evolutionists—Leslie White, Julian Steward, Marvin Harris, and Eleanor Burke Leacock, among others—proposed a series of explicit, scientific laws linking cultural change to different spheres of material existence. Evolution's proponents revived the works of Morgan and Tylor, considered theoretically irrelevant by many, especially some of the hyperparticularistic followers of Boas. Due to reactionary politics within the United States, these scholars couldn't do more than implicitly address the contributions of Marx until the 1970s. In the 1920s and 1930s, Marxist ideas were commonplace in American universities; by the 1950s their espousal was cause for dismissal as the witch hunts of McCarthyism spread and the Cold War deepened.

As a consequence, American anthropologists disguised their indebtedness to Marx and Engels and emphasized their connection to Tylor and Morgan. This is not surprising given that redbaiting occurred in anthropological journals as well as before the House Un-American Activities Committee. A classic example is Morris Opler's comment about the conceptual "tool kit" proposed by evolutionary anthropologists, that "its main contents seems to be a somewhat shopworn hammer and sickle" (Opler 1961:13). Such innuendo, labeling anthropologists as "communists," did no one's career any good. White resisted numerous efforts to fire him during the McCarthy era, Steward distanced himself from Marxist approaches, and Leacock carefully avoided mentioning Marx and Engels in her doctoral research even though she was a

committed radical and active in politics. By the 1960s the reactionary movement in academia had slightly abated, but an openly Marxist
anthropology would not emerge in the United States until the 1970s.

Evolutionary models became extremely important in America,
much more so than in Great Britain where prehistorian V. Gordon
Childe's evolutionary writings had broad impact in archaeology but
not in social anthropology. In the United States, anthropologists
tended to have a deeper diachronic perspective than advocated by the
synchronic studies of British social anthropology. The idea of looking
for systematic cultural changes through time fit better into American
anthropology because it included archaeology. In spite of its reaction
to anything tainted by Marxism, American anthropology saw a important role for examining general historical processes of change.

The 20th-century evolutionists' signal contribution was a concern
with the causes of change. Their causal explanations are materialist, in
contrast to idealist or historical. Changes in the modes of production,
whether caused by economic reorganizations or fluctuations in the
environment, have consequences in other arenas of culture, and thus
material factors have causal priority. Although claiming antecedents in
Morgan and Tylor, or Marx and Engels, the so-called "neo-evolution-
ists" emphasized the importance of providing causal explanations
rather than historical reconstructions.

For Leslie White, culture was humanity's means of adapting to the
physical and social environments. Like any other organism, humans
must capture energy in order to survive and reproduce and those societies which capture more energy or use it most efficiently are at a competitive advantage over societies who do not. White contended that
the history of human cultural evolution is essentially characterized by
changes in quantity of energy and the efficiency of its use.

This adaptationist element is also found in the work of Steward
and Harris, although it takes different forms. For Steward, cultures
evolved as adaptations to the environment; similar cultural patterns
reflect parallel adaptations to analogous environmental situations,
not—as Morgan and Tylor argued—that all cultures have passed
through similar evolutionary stages. Thus Steward argues for a multi-
lineal rather than a unilineal form of evolution.

Harris' concept, which he called cultural materialism, explains cultural patterns in terms of three sets of human life—infrastructure, structure, and superstructure—the most important being infrastructure.
"Infrastructure" relates to the social control of production and
reproduction, encompassing such aspects as technology, demography,

subsistence, and environment—it's the cultural interface between humans and nature. Cultural materialism can serve to explain specific cultural practices and broad evolutionary trends, providing explanations rooted in material factors rather than ideological constructs.

Eleanor Burke Leacock's contributions are the most explicitly Marxist. For Leacock, changes in the mode of production (whatever their specific nature) are ultimately the source of social evolution. In that, Leacock directly follows Morgan, Engels, and Marx. Leacock's particular emphasis was to examine how changes in production relations caused by the expansion of capitalism affected traditional, egalitarian band societies, giving particular attention to the subjugation of women. Leacock's writings emulate those of Engels, both as a historical model and as a social critique.

These materialist explanations, which were linked at their roots, branched off in many directions. From 1960 to 1980 these ideas were central in American anthropology. Since the mid-1970s, materialist and idealist approaches have vied for popularity, a conflict within American anthropology which continues. ✦

Chapter 13

Leslie White

Evolution Emergent

In a variety of ways, Franz Boas cast a very large shadow over the development of American anthropology, but his influence threw theories of cultural evolution into pitch darkness. Boas' position—that cultural patterns were best explained by specific historical references rather than general cultural laws—had two effects. First, it erased most references to stages of cultural evolution or to lawlike generalizations from American anthropology, consigning to irrelevancy the 19th-century social evolutionists like Morgan, Tylor, and Karl Marx. Second, it refocused anthropological inquiry onto particular cultures—specific societies that exhibited a set of cultural behaviors at a certain place and time. The Boasian perspective prohibited—or at least inhibited—general theories about "culture." The anti-evolutionary and nongeneralizing influences of historical particularism were widespread in American anthropology from the early 1900s well into the 1950s. Berthold Laufer's glowing 1918 review of Robert Lowie's anti-evolutionary *Culture and Ethnology* characterized that perspective: "The theory of cultural evolution [is] to my mind the most inane, sterile, and pernicious theory ever conceived in the history of science" (cited in White 1959a:vii).

Leslie White's work ran headlong into this position on both scores. First, White advocated a theory of cultural evolution which, as he put it, "does not differ one whit in principle from that expressed in Tylor's *Anthropology* in 1881, although of course the development, expression and demonstration of the theory may—and does—differ at some points" (1959a:ix). Second, White advocated a general science of *culture*—not of *cultures,* but of Culture—which he called "Culturology" (1949a).

White's theory of cultural evolution and his science of culture were not separate endeavors, but two prongs of the same general attack against historical particularism (cf. Service 1976:613). White, writing of himself in the third person, explained:

> The author absorbed the anti-evolutionist doctrines of the Boas school as a graduate student. But as he began to teach, he found, first, that he could not defend this point of view, and later that he could no longer hold it. . . . He has attacked the position of the anti-evolutionists in a number of articles. [White 1959a:ix]

It did not make him a popular man.

Background

Leslie White was born in 1900. He studied psychology at Columbia (B.A. 1923, M.A. 1924) and anthropology and sociology at the New School for Social Research under Alexander Goldenweiser, Thorstein Veblen, and John B. Watson. White began graduate work in anthropology at the University of Chicago, where he studied under Sapir and Fay Cooper-Cole. His 1927 Ph.D. was a study of medicine societies among the Southwest Indians. That same year White began teaching sociology and anthropology at the University of Rochester and the Buffalo Museum of Science. Fieldwork at the nearby Seneca reservations led to an interest in Morgan's work on the Iroquois (see Chapter 2) and ultimately to White's reassessment of the Boasian critique (1937, 1942a, 1944, 1951, 1957, 1959b). In addition, every summer White conducted research in the American Southwest in the Native American communities of Acoma (1932a), the Pueblo of San Felipe (1932b), the Pueblo of Santo Domingo (1934), and the Pueblo of Santa Ana (1942b). Each of these studies were major ethnographies, establishing White as an authority on the Southwest.

In 1930 White moved to the University of Michigan where, over the next 40 years, he was instrumental in developing one of the best anthropology departments in the United States. Michigan produced a number of anthropologists who shared White's evolutionary interests, although White hired faculty who didn't necessarily share his views.

White's evolutionary theories were so at odds with most anthropological thinking that they probably hampered his career. Anthropologist Elman Service (1976) suggests that White did not receive professional honors until late in life because he was unpopular with some anthropologists. But if his ideas offended some scholars, they whipped certain elements of the public into a froth. His Michigan lectures emphasized cultural determinism—as opposed to free will or deism—leading to attacks from irate parents. The Catholic Church lobbied state legislators against White and called for his dismissal from the University of Michigan (Service 1976; Beardsley 1976). Yet White's lectures were well attended, his articles were extensively reprinted, he was interviewed on radio shows, and in a variety of ways his ideas were widely disseminated. After retiring from Michigan in 1970, he moved to the University of California, Santa Barbara where he was visiting professor emeritus until his death in 1975.

What were White's provocative ideas about the evolution and science of culture? In order to understand them, we first need to recognize the functionalist core of White's approach to culture.

Evolution and The Functional Core

White's personal odyssey from historical particularism to cultural evolution is discussed below, but it is important to mention the similarities between White's theory of culture and Malinowski's functionalism (see pp. 132–135). Central to White's evolutionary theory is a functionalist conception of culture.

There are important differences between the two positions. Malinowski ultimately saw culture as functioning to meet individual needs, whereas White posited that culture met the needs of the species. This difference is not insignificant: Malinowski was interested in accounting for specific cultural patterns—usually exhibited by the Trobriand Islanders—while White was concerned with broader cultural developments exhibited by humanity, as White himself explained:

> Man is unique: he is the only living species that has a culture. By culture we mean an extrasomatic, temporal continuum of things and events dependent upon symboling. [1959a:3]

By extrasomatic—from the Greek *soma* for body, therefore, literally, "external to the body"—White stipulated that culture had a "suprabiological character":

> . . . although culture is produced and perpetuated only by the human species, and therefore has its origins and basis in the biological make-up of man . . . after it has come into existence and become established as a tradition, culture exists and behaves and is related to man as if it were *nonbiological in character*. [White 1959a:12; original emphasis]

Culture exists separately from the individuals who are born and die in a society. A baby learns culture from other individuals; culture is not genetically transmitted. But this is not to suggest that culture has no biological functions; in fact, White writes, "The purpose and function of culture are to make life secure and enduring for the human species." In contrast to other, cultureless organisms:

> . . . man employs the extrasomatic tradition that we call culture in order to sustain and perpetuate his existence and give it full expression.
>
> Specifically, the functions of culture are to relate man to his environment—his terrestrial habitat and the circumambient cosmos—on the one hand, and to relate man to man, on the other. [White 1959a:8]

This functional notion is a key element in White's theory of evolution. It is a utilitarian notion that Elman Service has traced back to the 19th-century evolutionist Herbert Spencer. According to Service, (1976:614) White, by his own admission, borrowed this utilitarian notion "more or less unwittingly." Regardless of White's intent, the consequences of his emphasis on the functions of culture are diverse and profound in American anthropology. This is particularly true for American archaeology, which fully embraced that position from the mid-1960s until very recently.

This functionalist interpretation of culture was central to White's theory of evolution because it implied that the most important dimensions of culture were those that imparted adaptive, biological advantages. It logically followed that the most important cultural realm is the one which transforms energy and makes it available for human use—technology. And, by extension, the evolution of cultures could be measured by their relative capacities to obtain and divert energy. Those two concepts underlie White's theory of evolution.

Theory of Cultural Evolution

The first element in White's theory of cultural evolution is a division of culture into three subsystems: technological, sociological, and ideological.

> The technological system is composed of the material, mechanical, physical and chemical instruments, together with the techniques of their use, by of which man, as an animal species, is articulated with his natural habitat. . . . The sociological system is made up of interpersonal relations expressed in patterns of behavior, collective as well as

individual. The ideological system is composed of ideas, beliefs, knowledge, expressed in articulate speech or other symbolic form. [1949:362–363]

In a latter work, White (1959a:6–7) suggested four categories of culture: technological, sociological, ideological, and "sentimental or attitudinal." The attitudinal category attempts to capture "the feelings or attitudes that constitute the subjective aspect." White did not really develop this category, it is almost an afterthought. He briefly refers to the culturally transmitted feelings about things—"loathing of milk, attitudes toward chastity, snakes, bats, death, etc."—a motley assortment of sentiments that reinforce the haphazard impression of this element of White's theory.

This reflects the firm priority that White gave to the technological realm of culture. White viewed the technological, sociological, and ideological systems as a three-part hierarchy of causation, with technology the foundation on which social and ideological systems are raised. White wrote:

> The technological system is basic and primary. Social systems are functions of technologies; and philosophies express technological forces and reflect social systems. The technological factor is therefore *the* determinant of a cultural system as a whole. . . . This is not to say, of course, that social systems do not condition the operation of technologies, or that social and technological systems are not affected by technologies. They do and are. But to condition is one thing; to determine, quite another. [1949:366]

Why does technology—broadly defined—have a determinant role? Why does White posit that technology is the basis of cultural evolution? First, there is the obvious fact that all organisms must meet basic energy requirements, be protected from the elements, and defend themselves from enemies. These life-sustaining, life-perpetuating processes, White writes (1959a:19), "are technological in a broad, but valid, sense, i.e., they are carried on by material, mechanical, biophysical, and biochemical means." By meeting these fundamental requisites of life, the technological dimensions allow other elements of culture to occur. "The technological system is therefore both primary and basic in importance: all human life and culture rest and depend upon it" (White 1949:365).

But more than technological potential, technology itself *determines* the nature of social and ideological systems:

> [T]he social organization of a people is not only dependent upon their technology but is determined to a great extent, if not wholly, by it

both in form and content. . . . The activities of hunting, fishing, gathering, farming, tending herds and flocks, mining, and all the processes by means of which raw materials are transformed and made ready for human consumption are not merely technological processes; they are social processes as well. [White 1959a:19–20]

And thus—to cite some of White's examples—a railroad workers' union is based on the technological fact of having a railroad and the social institutions formed by the existence of the railroad (1959a:21). Technology determines concepts of female beauty (White 1959a:21):

In cultures where technological control over food supply is slight and food is frequently scarce as a consequence, a fat woman is often regarded as beautiful. In cultures where food is abundant and women work little, obesity is likely to be regarded as unsightly [!].

We will object to the accuracy of such claims below, but for the moment it is more important to understand the logic behind White's theory: technology determines other aspects of culture. Thus White—echoing Malinowski's statements about the relationship between magic and science—suggests that as technological control increases, belief in the supernatural diminishes, stating for example, that "where the ceramic art is well developed, a minimum of magic is employed" (White 1959a:23). Again, this may not be accurate, but the argument is clear.

By arguing that technological dimensions were primary factors, that technology was the bedrock of cultural development, White set the stage for his theory of cultural evolution. If technology was an attempt to solve the problems of survival and if this ultimately meant capturing enough energy and diverting it to human needs, then those societies that captured more energy and used it most efficiently were at an adaptive advantage; they were, in an evolutionary sense, more advanced. Note here that by energy White is thinking like a physicist, considering energy in all of its states: as human effort, as fossil fuel, as kilocalories stored in corn or other domesticated foods, as falling water, as explosives, and on and on. From White's perspective,

Culture thus confronts us as an elaborate thermodynamic, mechanical system. . . . The functioning of culture as a whole therefore rests upon and is determined by the amount of energy harnessed and by the way it is put to work. [White 1949:367–368]

This implied that the differences between cultures could be measured, not by some rough qualitative scale or "ethnical periods," but precisely in terms of horsepower or kilocalories or another unit of measure.

> . . . the degree of cultural development, measured in terms of amount of human need-serving goods and services produced per capita, is determined by the amount of energy harnessed per capita and by the efficiency of the technological means with which it is put to work. We express this concisely and succinctly with the following formula: $E \times T \rightarrow C$, in which C represents the degree of cultural development, E the amount of energy harnessed per capita per year, and T the quality of efficiency of the tools employed in the expenditure of energy. We can now formulate the basic law of cultural evolution: Other factors remaining constant, *culture evolves as the amount of energy harnessed per capita per year is increased, or as the efficiency of the instrumental means of putting the energy to work is increased.* Both factors may increase simultaneously of course. [1949:368–369]

With this elegant argument, White made thermodynamics into the bridging argument of cultural evolution, transforming intuitive classification of different societies into a series of propositions which were logical, testable, and lawlike. If, as Marvin Harris (1968:636) argues, White's law of evolution "is neither a law nor a definition but rather a statement of research strategy," it is worthwhile noting that previous evolutionary approaches lacked this predictive quality, instead being ex post facto classifications. White's statement was lawlike in a scientific sense, not a legal one: it stated a relationship between a set of observable phenomena which could be proven incorrect or falsified. This property of refutability sets scientific statements apart from other kinds of statements, and it suggests White's intentions when he outlined a science of culture.

The Science of Culture

Elman Service (1976:613) suggested that White's theories about the evolution of culture and the science of culture were two separate, completely independent bodies of theory: *"Culturology,* the science of culture as he presented it, is not the same thing as, nor does it even imply a connection to, his ideas about the *evolution of culture."* This may be slightly overstated, because White's notions of the evolution of culture certainly exemplify what he thought a science of culture should contain: 1) it should be science, 2) it should be about culture, not cultures, and 3) it should be deterministic, i.e., denying appeals to Free Will, the Individual, or to any cause other than Culture.

For White, humans had two ways of dealing with experience—science and art. "The purpose of science and art is one: to render experience intelligible," White wrote, but these two ways of knowing approached experience from different directions. "Art deals with universals in terms of particulars. . . ." In contrast, science was not merely a collection of facts and formulae, but a way of knowing by dealing with particulars from universals. "Art and science thus grasp a common experience, or reality, by opposite but inseparable poles," White concludes.

Therefore, if we are interested in a science of culture, our task is to discover and delineate the universal principles that explain particular phenomena. Note that these phenomena exist independently of the subjective viewer; White approvingly cites Einstein's statement, "The belief in an external world independent of the perceiving subject is the basis of all natural science." Such phenomena—existing in space, time, and having particular formal properties—can be viewed from different frames of reference. Thus a raindrop may be viewed as one event in the evolution of the cosmos, as a mass changing its spatial relationship with other masses like the earth and clouds, or as a mass which changes form through time (White 1949:13). Although we define the different frames of reference, the reality exists separate from the viewer. Whereas some changes in form are repetitive and reversible—water may become ice and then melt again—the temporal order of events is not: "only in *Through the Looking Glass* do Queens scream before they prick their fingers, or Alices pass the cake before they cut it. The evolutionary process, *being temporal as well as formal*, is likewise irreversible" (White 1949:13, emphasis added).

This developmental argument sets the stage for White's deterministic approach to cultural evolution. New cultural forms develop out of preceding cultural forms, regardless of the role of individuals. The theory of natural selection was *discovered* by Darwin and Alfred Russel Wallace; it was not created from thin air by either man, but was a crystallization of previously existing, culturally expressed knowledge. Calculus was "invented" by both Leibnitz and Newton, but calculus would have been developed even if both men had died as infants. "The development of mathematics, like the development of technology or medicine, is an evolutionary process: new forms grow out of preceding forms" (White 1949:14). We may not be able to predict the name of an inventor or when another innovation will occur, but the fact that such an innovation will occur is predictable because of the inevitability of cultural evolution. White lavished great care on his article "Ikhnaton: the Great Man vs. the Culture Process," which considered the case of the pharaoh Ikhnaton who introduced monotheism to replace the multitude of gods in ancient Egypt in the 14th century B.C. Ikhnaton has been variously lauded as a seer or damned as a heretic, but universally characterized as a "Great Man," a singular individual who brought about a truly original innovation. Not so, White argued: all the elements which made the acceptance of monotheism possible existed independently of Ikhnaton:

> In the process of cultural development, a Great Man is but the neural medium through which an important synthesis of culture takes place. Darwin, Newton, Beethoven, and Edison were men of this type. They were the neurological loci of important cultural events. To be sure, they were superior organisms. But had they been reared as swineherders, Greatness would not have found them. [1949:280]

A science of culture, White argued, is concerned with the general principles that define and predict relationships in cultural phenomena. It is not interested in defining specific cultural traits, but instead in understanding general cultural patterns. "Particular cultures vary among themselves in specific form and content, but all are alike in general respects; i.e., all have tools, language, customs, beliefs, music, etc. And every cultural system functions as a means of relating man to the earth and cosmos, and as a means of relating man to man. *The science of culture will therefore concern itself with the structure and function of cultural systems*" (White 1959a:29, emphasis added).

Not only is such a science uninterested in particular cultures except as examples of universals, but it could consider culture as a realm of phenomena, "as if it had an existence of its own, independently of the human species" (White 1959a:16). Considered this way, a science of culture is one which posits generalizations about culture that are verifiable through the study of culture.

Conclusion

White's unsparingly deterministic view of human development led to criticisms of his work by church and state and by anthropologists as well. First, there is the notion that culture somehow exists independently of specific societies and thus is a phenomenon separate from its particular expressions. One may immediately ask "Is this true, or are White's lawlike statements about Culture actually generaliza tions about *some* cultures to which *other* cultures are exceptions?" For example, White's contention that "In cultures where food is abundant and women work little, obesity is likely to be regarded as unsightly" (White 1959a:21)—presumably a reference to 20th-century America and Europe—is only remotely valid if you classify "women's work" as not really work. It is also a very simplistic explanation of why anorexia and other eating disorders affect so many people—women *and* men—in Europe, Japan, and the United States (all ethnic groups).

Second, White's three categories of culture—technological, sociological, and ideological—are not equivalent; technology has priority because, according to White's definition, it involves the capture and transformation of energy which is essential for life in all organisms; all other dimensions of culture are therefore based on technology. But, humans do not rely on instinctual means to obtain energy directly from the environment. For example, breast feeding involves learned behavior on the part of both infant and mother. The infant is born with a rooting reflex, but it may take several days before she or he learns how to nurse; the new mother learns about feeding from her relatives, her doctor, pages of advice, and the cries of her infant which she learns to distinguish between hunger, wetness, and tiredness. All of that is learned social and symbolic behavior. If breast feeding—one of the most elementary energy transfers in human society—is learned behavior based on symbols, why isn't it that systems of meaning, rather than technology, constitute the fundamental cultural realm? White anticipated this point (1950:19), but simply denied it out of hand.

A final point concerns the definition of cultural development. The critique turns on the concept of tautology, a fallacious restatement about cause and effect. For example, "I am taller than other people because most people are shorter than I am" is a tautology. White's version of this tautology is to state:

> 1) Like all systems comprised of matter, culture is a "thermodynamic system" that requires the constant acquisition and transformation of energy (White 1959a:38).

> 2) Since it is fundamental that humans as organisms must capture and use energy, "it follows that this must be the basic function of culture also" (White 1959a:39). The basic purpose of cultural systems is to obtain and utilize energy.

3) Cultural systems vary in their effectiveness in harnessing and using energy; this effectiveness can be measured in terms of per capita horsepower, kilocalories or some other measure of energy. And therefore:

4) *"Culture advances as the amount of energy harnessed per capita per year increases, or as the efficiency or economy of the means of controlling energy is increased, or both"* (1959a:56, original emphasis).

Consider what happens to the logic if we substitute other desiderata for that of energy capture and efficiency. How would we evaluate cultures if energy *conservation* were the goal or to meet basic human needs with the minimum of effort or to have the maximum number of socially well-adjusted offspring? Couldn't we substitute any or all of these alternate goals for White's thermodynamic one? If we did the entire logic of the argument would be reshaped.

White's theories of cultural evolution and culturology were extremely influential, and they form part of the backdrop to a current debate in American anthropology. White's adaptationist and utilitarian views of culture influenced a large school of American anthropology, particularly during the 1960s and 1970s when many of White's ideas about the energetics of cultural systems, the role of energy and structure in the organization of the state, and the notion that understanding past societies should be based on interpreting material remains as remnants of environmental, social, and ideological behaviors (Binford 1964) were pursued in fields such as ecological anthropology, comparative ethnology, and the New Archaeology. The last twenty years of debates in anthropology are partially a reaction to the theoretical positions inspired by White and others.

But perhaps White's most significant accomplishment was a more general one: the reintroduction of anthropological theories as legitimate topics of discussion. As Richard Beardsley concludes in his obituary of White:

Even the many contemporary anthropologists to whom these subjects [about cultural evolution] are not matters of central concern share at least an indirect heritage from Leslie A. White. Their interests and ideas are possible in part because he fought successfully to restore to respectability a concern for grand theory. [Beardsley 1976:619–620]

And thus White's contribution to anthropology was not only to propose a particular theory of culture, but to reintroduce theory building as a creative anthropological enterprise. ✦

Bibliography

Beardsley, Richard
1976 An Appraisal of Leslie A. White's Scholarly Influence. American Anthropologist 78:617–620.

Service, Elman
1976 Leslie Alvin White, 1900–1975. American Anthropologist 78:612–617.

White, Leslie
1932a The Acoma Indians. Bureau of American Ethnology, 47th Annual Report. Pp. 1–192. Washington, D.C.: Smithsonian Institution. [Reprinted 1973. Glorieta, N.M.: The Rio Grande Press.]
1932b The Pueblo of San Felipe. American Anthropological Association, Memoir No. 38. [Reprinted 1964. New York: Krauss Reprint Company.]
1934 The Pueblo of Santo Domingo. American Anthropological Association, Memoir No. 43. [Reprinted 1964. New York: Krauss Reprint Company.]
1937 Extracts from the European Travel Journal of Lewis H. Morgan. Rochester Historical Society Publications XVI:221–390.
1942a Lewis H. Morgan's Journal of a Trip to Southwestern Colorado and New Mexico, 1878. American Antiquity 8:1–26.
1942b The Pueblo of Santa Ana, New Mexico. American Anthropologist 44(4), Part 2. American Anthropological Association, Memoir 60. [Reprinted 1969. New York: Krauss Reprint Company.]
1944 Morgan's Attitude Toward Religion and Science. American Anthropologist 46:218–230.
1949 The Science of Culture: A Study of Man and Civilization. New York: Grove Press.
1951 Lewis H. Morgan's Western Field Trips. American Anthropologist 53:11–18.
1957 How Morgan Came to Write Systems of Consanguinity and Affinity. Papers of the Michigan Academy of Science, Arts, and Letters XLII.
1959a The Evolution of Culture: the Development of Civilization to the Fall of Rome. New York: McGraw-Hill.
1959b Lewis Henry Morgan: His Life and Researches. In The Indian Journals, 1859–1862. L. White, ed. Pp. 3–12. Ann Arbor: The University of Michigan Press.

Chapter 14

Julian Steward

Cultural Ecology and Multilinear Evolution

The materialist approaches of Julian Steward have been extremely influential in American anthropology, particularly in the 1950s and 1960s. His ideas were a bridge between the historical particularism of Boas and Kroeber and the cultural evolution of Leslie White. On the one hand, Steward criticized the particularist approaches as nonexplanatory, arguing that clear similarities between different cultures could be explained as parallel adaptations to structurally similar natural environments. On the other hand, he contended that not all societies passed through similar stages of cultural development and that unilineal models of evolution were, therefore, too sweeping to be interesting.

Steward's ideas had a crucial impact on American archaeology, shifting archaeological focus from cultural history to cultural evolution. During the 1960s and 1970s, the changing conception of archaeology—dubbed the New Archaeology—relied heavily on his ideas. Steward's work was relevant to archaeology because it considered the relationship been human society and environment, and because it focused on social changes through time. Both were issues archaeologists could address with their data.

Steward's contributions to anthropology were diverse. He was a major figure in the development of area studies programs, in turning anthropological inquiry to problems of culture change and Third World development, and in leading large research projects with teams of investigators. He also made a major contribution to anthropological theory with two significant concepts: cultural ecology and multilinear evolution.

Background

Born in Washington, D.C. in 1902, Julian Haynes Steward's most important formative years were spent in the American West. At the age of sixteen Steward went to a preparatory school in Owens Valley, California on the western margin of the Great Basin, a region to which he would return for his first sustained anthropological fieldwork as a graduate student. After spending his freshman year at U.C. Berkeley where he was exposed to the teachings of Alfred Kroeber and Robert Lowie, Steward transferred east to Cornell University to complete his B.A. in 1925. He returned to Berkeley for graduate training. Under Kroeber and Lowie, Berkeley graduate students primarily studied North American Indian groups, and Steward was no exception. His 1929 dissertation, "The Ceremonial Buffoon of the American Indian," was based on library research, which was a common practice at the time; ethnographic fieldwork was presented in descriptive monographs and comparative studies in dissertations were based on published materials (Murphy 1975:4). A study of role reversal and cross-cultural patterns of social humor and ritual clowning, Steward's dissertation exhibits no obvious connection to his subsequent research (for a synopsis, see Steward 1977a).

Steward became a professional anthropologist as the Great Depression began. In 1928 he was one of the first anthropology instructors at the University of Michigan; in 1930 he moved to the University of Utah where he established a program of research and instruction, conducting archaeological excavations at Pueblo sites (Manners 1973:889; Murphy 1977:4–5). But Steward's research was not sharply focused until he resumed his ethnographic investigations in the Great Basin. He returned to Berkeley as a lecturer for the 1933–34 academic year and then began a two-year research project focusing on Shoshone and Northern Paiute communities in eastern California, Nevada, Utah and Idaho.

The Shoshone and Northern Paiute were to Julian Steward what the Trobriand Islanders were to Bronislaw Malinowski (see pp. 130–133): a pivotal ethnographic case which exemplified broad cultural patterns. For Steward, the fundamental pattern of Shoshonean society was derived from the fact that "Pursuits concerned with the problems of daily existence dominated their activities to an extraordinary degree and limited and conditioned their [social] institutions" (Steward 1938:1–2). As Steward documented the limited natural resources, simple technology, and seasonal movements of Great Basin food collectors from arid basins to alpine piñon groves, a general model of hunting and gathering societies emerged. This model emphasized the egalitarianism and social fluidity of bands (Steward 1938:258–260; 1977b). Anthropologist Robert Murphy writes:

> Living in a forbidding country of high desert and harsh landscape, the single dominant fact of their lives was the necessity to eke out subsistence through the seasons of the year. Given the simple technology at their disposal, the environment offered few alternatives to the ways in which they lived, and their very patterns of social life had to be understood as an adjustment to bleak physical reality. Steward grasped and developed this essential truth of Shoshoni [sic] society and made it into a general theory. [1977:6]

Steward's early researches on band society outlined parallels between such scattered societies as the Shoshone, Australian Aborigines, the San and other so-called "Bushmen" groups of southern Africa, and the Semang of Malaysia. He argued that they exhibited similar adaptations shaped by low population density, reliance on foot transportation, and hunting of scattered and nonmigratory game (Steward 1936). Today Steward's ideas are accepted as basic anthropological insights, so it is somewhat surprising to realize his early article on the topic was rejected by American anthropological journals as too speculative (Manners 1973:890).

The cool response to Steward's early work stems from three innovations that ran counter to American anthropology in the 1930s. First, he conducted ethnographic fieldwork that focused on a specific problem rather than attempted to "complete" a description of another culture. Just as descriptive ethnography and comparative ethnology were separated when Julian Steward was a graduate student, many anthropologists viewed problem-oriented fieldwork as somehow preconceived and biased. Second, Steward was not interested in cultural traits, styles, or norms—common concerns of American anthropologists—but instead in the adaptive relationships between humans and their environments. And finally, he proposed that regular patterns existed in human adaptations, between groups like the Australian aborigines and the Great Basin Shoshone who had never been in contact. Steward emphasized cultural parallels due to adaptation rather than historical diffusion or migration. This made his work suspect to many American anthropologists but also produced, in Marvin Harris' phrase, "the first coherent statement of how the interaction between culture and environment could be studied in causal terms" (Harris 1968:666). That search for causal relationships would occupy the balance of Steward's career.

In 1935 Steward joined the Bureau of American Ethnology of the Smithsonian Institution where he remained until 1946. The most successful of a number of large research projects he headed at the Smithsonian was a program of library and field research on the native peoples of South America. The multivolume *Handbook of South American Indians* employed almost every ethnographer and archaeologist who had worked in South America: Alfred Kroeber, Robert Lowie, Alfred Metraux, Claude Lévi-Strauss, Gordon Willey, John Rowe, Paul Kirchoff, John Murra, Luis Valcarcel, Wendell Bennett, and W.D. Strong, among many others. Fifty years after its publication, the *Handbook of South American Indians* remains a major resource for anthropologists (Steward [ed.] 1946–50). Its organization and emphasis on the cultural developments of native South American societies reflect the research interests of Julian Steward.

In 1946 Steward left the Smithsonian and joined the Department of Anthropology at Columbia University where the graduate program had swelled as postwar students entered school on the GI Bill; Steward chaired 35 doctoral dissertations in the six years he was at Columbia, a staggering quantity of work. His students included Stanley Diamond, Eric Wolf, Robert Murphy, and Sidney Mintz, among others. Steward also initiated a large research program in Puerto Rico (Steward et al. 1956) coordinating the investigations of five graduate students and establishing one of the first area studies of a complex society and its historical context.

In 1952 Steward accepted a research professorship at the University of Illinois where he remained until his retirement in 1968. Freed of all teaching responsibilities—except for seminars he chose to offer— Steward initiated yet another large research project, focusing on social and economic changes in 20th-century traditional societies. Eleven fieldworkers investigated traditional societies and documented patterns of culture change in Third World countries on four continents (Steward [ed.] 1967). Steward also published prolifically during his time at Illinois: he wrote *Theory of Culture Change: The Method of Multilinear Evolution* (1955); a biographical sketch of Alfred Kroeber (1973); a major synthesis entitled *Native Peoples of South America* (Steward and Faron 1959); and a stream of articles and reviews on cultural evolution, irrigation agriculture, and native societies in the Great Basin. Until the end of his life, Julian Steward maintained an active interest in diverse areas of research, but these were bound together by two central, unifying concepts: cultural ecology and multilinear evolution.

Cultural Ecology

"Cultural ecology," Steward (1968:337) wrote, "is the study of the processes by which a society adapts to its environment. Its principal problem is to determine whether these adaptations initiate internal social transformations of evolutionary change." Like biological ecology, which analyzes adaptation to the complex interconnections that make up an environment, cultural ecology is a view of "man in the web of life" (Steward 1973a:31). That web consisted of both natural and cultural realities:

> Cultural ecology is broadly similar to biological ecology in its method of examining the interactions of all social and natural phenomena within an area, but it does not equate social features with biological species or assume that competition is the major process. It distinguishes different kinds of sociocultural systems and institutions, it recognizes both cooperation and competition as processes of interaction, and it postulates that environmental adaptations depend on the technology, needs and structure of the society and on the nature of the environment. It includes analysis of adaptation to the social environment. . . . [Steward 1968:337]

The web of life of a human group "may extend far beyond the immediate physical environment and biotic assemblage. In states, nations, and empires, the nature of the local group may be determined by these larger institutions no less than by its local adaptation" (Steward 1973a:32). Steward argued that the links between environment and culture were particularly clear in societies like the Shoshone where the margins of survival were slim. In contrast, in societies that "have adequately solved subsistence problems, the effect of ecology becomes more difficult to ascertain. In complex societies certain components of the social superstructure rather than ecology seem increasingly to be determinants of further developments. With greater cultural complexity analysis becomes increasingly difficult" (Steward 1938:262).

Steward viewed cultural ecology as a research agenda rather than a religious dogma; other processes of cultural change—for example, diffusion or innovation—were not precluded by the culture ecological approach. And cultural ecology provided a key advantage: cross-cultural parallels in social patterns could be explained as adaptations to similar environments. That interest in causes distinguished cultural ecology from the historical particularism of Boas and his students. Relying on mechanisms of diffusion, innovation, and migration, cultural-historical "explanations," Steward argued (1973a:35), were not really explanations since they relied on the inexplicable tendency "of societies to develop in unlike ways." The explanations of historical particularism were actually reconstructed accounts of the "divergences in culture history," with the cause of diversity remaining mysterious.

Further, Steward wrote (1973a:35), in cultural-historical explanations the environment was relegated to a secondary role in explaining cultural differences. Ironically, cultural-historical explanations relied on the "culture area" concept, a scheme used by Clark Wissler and Alfred Kroeber to subdivide culture patterns—such as the American Southwest or the Great Plains—based on shared cultural traits exhibited in similar environments. If, Steward asked, there were such clear patterns between environment and culture, how could environment be ignored?

Steward (1973a:40–42) outlined three basic steps for a cultural-ecological investigation. "First, the interrelationship of exploitative or productive technology and environment must be analyzed," i.e., the relationship between material culture and natural resources. "Second, the behavior patterns involved in the exploitation of a particular area by means of a particular technology must be analyzed." For example, certain game is best stalked by individual hunters while other game can be captured in communal hunts; different social behaviors are involved in the exploitation of different resources. The third step in the analysis is to determine how "behavior patterns entailed in exploiting the environment affect other aspects of culture" (Steward 1973a:41). This three-step empirical analysis identifies the cultural core, "the constellation of features which are most closely related to subsistence activities and economic arrangements" (Steward 1973a:37).

Cultural ecology was not a form of unilineal evolution, but an attempt "to explain the origin of particular cultural features and patterns which characterize different areas rather than to derive general principles applicable to any cultural-environmental area" (Steward 1973a:36). Although it differed from the 19th-century unilineal evolutionary theories of Tylor (Chapter 1), Morgan (Chapter 2), or Marx and Engels, and lacked the broad, generalizing character of the 20th-century theories of Leslie White (Chapter 13) and Marvin Harris (Chapter 15), cultural ecology was, nevertheless, a clear materialist strategy. Marvin Harris writes:

> The essence of cultural materialism is that it directs attention to the interaction between behavior and environment as mediated by the human organism and its cultural apparatus. It does so as an order of priority with the prediction that group structure and ideology are

responsive to these classes of material conditions. Turning to Steward's statement of the research strategy of cultural ecology [as summarized above], we find all of these attributes of cultural materialism clearly delineated. [Harris 1968:659]

By emphasizing human adaptation and the varying relationships between human societies and natural resources, cultural ecology provided both the analytical focus and the empirical bases for Steward's theory of culture change—multilinear evolution.

Multilinear Evolution

Steward's concept of cultural evolution rested on two key concepts: "First, it postulates that genuine parallels of form and function develop in historically independent sequences or cultural traditions. Second, it explains these parallels by the independent operation of identical causality in each case" (Steward 1973a:14). Thus, understanding cultural evolution involved discovering "parallels and similarities which recur cross-culturally" and proposing "lawlike" statements about the causes of such parallels. Steward's approach was to find and explain similarities between societies without assuming that all societies passed through identical stages of development. Multilinear evolution, he (1973a:19) wrote, "deals only with those limited parallels of form, function, and sequence which have empirical validity. What is lost in universality will be gained in concreteness and specificity."

For example, Steward compared the prehistoric patterns of developments in five independent centers of ancient civilization—Mesopotamia, Egypt, China, Mesoamerica, and the Andes. These centers shared "parallels of form, function, and sequence" based on having developed in arid and semi-arid environments in which the economic basis was irrigation and flood-water agriculture. Agriculture created food surpluses which allowed for nonsubsistence activities and population growth. When population growth reached the limits of agricultural productivity, competition over natural resources intensified, warfare ensued, and political leadership shifted from temple priest to warrior king. As some communities prospered and others suffered, empires were forged that instituted strong political controls over vast regions (Steward 1973a:206–208).

Steward traced the evolutionary similarities in the five ancient civilizations. Although the chronology of events differed, Steward argued that there were striking parallels in the pattern of cultural evolution, not because there were universal stages of cultural development or due to the diffusion of civilization between regions, but because these five cultural traditions emerged in similar arid and semi-arid environments where agriculture had been able to flourish. This development of agrarian civilizations in arid and semi-arid environments was one "line" of the multilinear evolution which Steward proposed. Thus, Steward's multilinear evolution intentionally avoided sweeping statements about culture in general, applying more limited models to specific sets of cultures.

Conclusion

Julian Steward's theory of multilinear evolution has fallen out of favor among many anthropologists, but some of his insights are the anthropological equivalent of gospel. Steward's basic insights about the organization of band societies, the importance of cultural ecology, and the search for cross-cultural similarities are all firmly embedded in anthropological thought and practice. Steward's form of materialism emphasized, 1) the central relationship between environment and culture and its implications for other aspects of social life, 2) the search for patterned regularities and similarities between societies, and 3) the importance of causal explanations of parallel developments over historical reconstructions. These central tenets of Steward's thought are recurrent themes in a body of work that was written over 30 years and originated in the arid landscape of the American West. ✦

Bibliography

Harris, Marvin
1968 The Rise of Anthropological Theory: A History of Theories of Culture. New York: Thomas Crowell Company.

Leone, Mark, ed.
1972 Contemporary Archaeology: A Guide to Theory and Contributions. Carbondale, IL: Southern Illinois University Press.

Manners, Robert
1973 Julian Haynes Steward, 1902–1972. American Anthropologist 75:886–903.

Murphy, Robert
1977 The Anthropological Theories of Julian Steward. In Evolution and Ecology: Essays on Social Transformation. J. Steward and R. Murphy, eds. Pp. 1–39. Urbana: University of Illinois Press.

Steward, Julian
1938 Basin-Plateau Aboriginal Sociopolitical Groups. Bureau of American Ethnology, Bulletin 120. Washington, DC: Smithsonian Institution.
1968 Cultural Ecology. *In* International Encyclopedia of the Social Sciences, Vol. 4. D. Sills, ed. Pp. 337–344. New York: Macmillan Company.
1973a Theory of Culture Change: The Methodology of Multilinear Evolution. Urbana: University of Illinois Press.
1973b Alfred Kroeber. New York: Columbia University Press.
1977a The Ceremonial Buffoon of the American Indian. *In* Evolution and Ecology: Essays on Social Transformation. J. Steward and R. Murphy, eds. Pp. 347–365. Urbana: University of Illinois Press.
1977b The Foundations of Basin-Plateau Society. *In* Evolution and Ecology: Essays on Social Transformation. J. Steward and R. Murphy, eds. Pp. 366–406. Urbana: University of Illinois Press.

Steward, Julian, ed.
1946–50 Handbook of the South American Indians. Bureau of American Ethnology, Bulletin 143, Vols. 1–6. Washington, DC: Smithsonian Institution.

Steward, Julian and Louis Faron
1959 Native Peoples of South America. New York: Columbia University Press.

Chapter 15

Marvin Harris
Cultural Materialism

The work of Marvin Harris is solidly identified with the notion of cultural materialism, which, as he put it, "is based on the simple premise that human social life is a response to the practical problems of earthly existence" (1979:ix). It is a point of view thoroughly associated with Harris; as he says, "Although I did not invent 'cultural materialism,' I am responsible for giving it its name" (1979:x). Though intellectually indebted to Marx and Engels, Harris has outlined a distinctive materialist approach to culture. In his numerous provocative and often provoking writings, Harris has developed a coherent body of anthropological theory.

Background

Harris received his Ph.D. in 1953 from Columbia University, where he taught until 1981, at which time he moved to the University of Florida. Harris' ethnographic research and theoretical concerns are clearly connected. His research has focused on Latin America, primarily Brazil, which led him to look at Angola and Mozambique, former African colonies of Portugal. His first book, *Town and Country in Brazil* (1956), was based on fieldwork in Minas Velhas—literally "Old Mines" in Portuguese—located in the state of Bahia, Brazil. A straightforward ethnography, *Town and Country in Brazil* describes the growth of an isolated gold rush settlement which quickly became a regional center, but then faded in glory as the mines were worked out. Surrounding regions with more secure economies grew in importance, and Minas

Velhas settled into a genteel oblivion distant from national life. Harris questioned classifying Brazil as a "rural" developing nation because "many of its rural areas cannot be understood at all except in relation to hundreds of deeply entrenched urban nuclei" like Minas Velhas spawned by the odd economics of mining.

Town and Country in Brazil is an early introduction to Harris' research agenda and his emphasis on *infrastructure*, which he later defines as the ". . . technological, economic, demographic, and environmental activities and conditions directly related to sustaining health and well-being through the social control of production and reproduction" (Harris 1992:297). In his first book Harris documented economic pursuits, the public economy, and class and race, but the distinctive factors in Minas Velhas were its establishment as a mining community and the importance of an urban ethos (1956:279–280), a "complex of interconnected values" emphasizing the "preference for living in a town rather than in the country." It might seem that Harris had lapsed into idealism, but he quickly observed that there are "dynamic, functional factors which account for the persistence of these traits" and that once societies reach "the stage of technology and social organization in which a large number of people can be freed from food-producing activities and occupational specialization becomes feasible on a large scale, there is little likelihood of reverting to more homogeneous arrangements" (Harris 1956:283). The urban ethos of Minas Velhas reproduces and reinforces a social arrangement initially defined by infrastructure.

Harris' work in Brazil led to issues of race, as discussed in *Minorities in the New World* (1958), which he co-authored with Charles Wagley, and his later book, *Patterns of Race in the Americas* (1964). *Patterns of Race in the Americas* is a brief (99 pages), densely packed discussion of the roots of racism in the Americas, and it was published during the Civil Rights Movement—the march on Selma, the Freedom Riders, and the awe-inspiring oratory of Dr. Martin Luther King, Jr. Harris contributed a powerful analysis of the economic origins of racism, constantly comparing the history of racism in Latin America and the United States. He traces the varying contours of unequal race relations between American Indians, Africans, and Europeans in the Americas to the differing impositions of economic systems of plantations, haciendas, or small farm holdings. It is interesting that in the 1960s, at a time in the United States when racism was considered a matter of unequal rights, Harris argued that it had an economic basis—an analysis that is extremely current.

But again, Harris gives explanatory priority to infrastructure, and that emphasis is fundamental in his 1968 magnum opus, *The Rise of Anthropological Theory*. If *Patterns of Race in the Americas* is a marvel of compression, *The Rise of Anthropological Theory* is a sprawling critique of Western thinking about the nature of culture and its evolution. Harris assesses the contributions of thinkers—from Plato to Montesquieu to Hegel—and anthropological schools—from culture and personality to structuralism to cultural evolution. In the process, he expresses an opinion—frequently negative—on almost every social thinker since the Enlightenment. Although Harris apologizes in advance for his severe attacks on anthropologists past and present, he feels justified because "at this particular moment in the development of anthropological theory . . . critical judgments deserve priority over polite ones" (Harris 1968:7). Harris attacks the "dubious factual foundation on which [Ruth] Benedict reared her psychologistic portraits" (1968:404), accuses Alfred Kroeber of making statements about changes in style and artistic achievement based on "the effete standards of salon gossip" (Harris 1968:331), and suggests that Claude Lévi-Strauss—far from plumbing the hidden structures of another culture—"may not even understand what's going on in his own head" (1968:511).

But why is Marvin Harris so mad? Harris' agenda has two tasks. First, he is attacking the atheoretical legacy of Boas, arguing that historical particularism, far from being a neutral presentation of "just the facts," was a theoretical position characterized by a misinterpretation of 19th-century evolutionary social theorists and a murky view of science. Harris argues for the importance of anthropological theory in general, and against a current of American anthropology in which hypothesis was used as a synonym for "guess" and "theory" for vague supposition.

Second, Harris advances his own theoretical point of view, distinguishing it from other theories and claiming its greater logical utility. He dubbed that theory "cultural materialism."

Cultural Materialism

In the introduction of *The Rise of Anthropological Theory*, Harris describes cultural materialism as the sociocultural analog of Darwinian selection and immediately identifies it as nonidealist and evolutionary. There will be no appeal to human nature, to the utter uniqueness of different cultures, or to such intangibles as core values, deep structures, or superorganic configurations. Instead, Harris will develop

> . . . the principle of techno-environmental and techno-economic determinism. This principle holds that similar technologies applied to similar environments tend to produce similar arrangements of labor in production and distribution, and that these in turn call forth similar kinds of social groupings, which justify and co-ordinate their activities by means of similar systems of values and beliefs. Translated into a research strategy, the principle of techno-environmental, techno-economic determinism assigns priority to the study of the material conditions of sociocultural life, much as the principle of natural selection assigns priority to the study of differential reproductive success. [1968:4]

Harris distinguished his position, "cultural materialism," from philosophical materialism—e.g., questions of the priority of matter or mind—and from dialectical materialism, the body of concepts formulated by Marx and Engels. He considered philosophical materialism irrelevant to considerations of sociocultural phenomena and subsumed dialectical materialism as a subset of cultural materialism. In the opening pages of *The Rise of Anthropological Theory* Harris (1968:5) states, "I shall demonstrate that the failure to apply the cultural-materialist strategy resulted not from any reasonable program of oriented research, but from the covert pressures of the sociocultural milieu in which anthropology has achieved its disciplinary identity." With that, the challenge has been made.

Harris' most concise and also complete presentation of his theory is *Cultural Materialism: The Struggle for a Science of Culture,* (Harris 1979). It begins by outlining the epistemological basis for cultural materialism considering

> how scientific knowledge . . . can be acquired. Alone among the things and organisms studied by science, the human "object" is also a subject; the "objects" have well-developed thoughts about their own and other people's thoughts and behaviors.
>
> . . . No aspect of a research strategy more decisively characterizes it than the way in which it treats the relationship between what people say and think as subjects and what they say and think and do as objects of scientific inquiry. [Harris 1979:29]

Harris insists (1979:31–32) that the relevant question is not "the reality" of the actions versus the ideas of people, or of sociocultural phenomena as observed versus sociocultural phenomena as experienced. Instead, we must make two sets of distinctions: "first, the distinction between mental and behavioral events, and second, between emic and etic events." Behavioral events are simply "all the body motions and environmental effects produced by such motions, large and small, of all the human beings who ever lived." Mental events, on the other hand, "are all the thoughts and feelings that we humans experience within our minds." The second set of distinctions is between *emic* and *etic*. Emic perspectives convey a participant's point of view; etic perspectives are from an observer's point of view. These two ways of knowing imply different research approaches and agendas:

> Emic operations have as their hallmark the elevation of the native informant to the status of ultimate judge of the adequacy of the observer's descriptions and analyses. The test of the adequacy of emic analyses is their ability to generate statements the native accepts as real, meaningful, or appropriate.

> Etic operations have as their hallmark the elevation of observers to the status of ultimate judges of the categories and concepts used in descriptions and analyses. The test of the adequacy of etic accounts is simply their ability to generate scientifically productive theories about the causes of sociocultural differences and similarities. Rather than employ concepts that are necessarily real, meaningful, and appropriate from the native point of view, the observer is free to use alien categories and rules derived from the data language of science. Frequently, etic operations involve the measurement and juxtaposition of activities and events that native informants may find inappropriate or meaningless. [Harris 1979:32]

These distinctions lead to specific categories of human actions and thoughts. First, are those relating to the needs of meeting subsistence requirements, the *etic behavioral mode of production*. Second, are the actions taken to insure the existence of the population, the *etic behavioral mode of reproduction*. Third, are actions taken by each society to maintain "secure and orderly behavioral relationships among its constituent groups and with other societies" and because this is a principal area of discord an associated set of behaviors are "the economic processes which allocate labor and the material products of labor to individuals and groups" (Harris 1979:51). Therefore, we are concerned with the *etic behavioral domestic economies* and *etic behavioral political economies*. A final etic category, *behavioral superstructure*, consists of acts related to the importance of symbolic processes for the human psyche—from art to advertising, ritual to sport. Harris then lumps—for no clear reason—modes of production and reproduction under the rubric "infrastructure," and domestic and political economies under the name "structure." When "behavioral superstructure" is added to these two categories, *voilà*—a tripartite scheme of etic behavior emerges: *infrastructure, structure*, and *superstructure*. Although Harris briefly sketches a parallel tripartite scheme for mental and emic components, he is uninterested in the effort and collapses the framework as soon as it is constructed, leaving us with infrastructure, structure, and superstructure (all etic categories) and the fourth catch-all, *mental and emic superstructure* (Harris 1979:54).

This is a circuitous route to arrive at a foregone destination, the principle of infrastructural determinism. "Infrastructure," Harris writes (1979:57),

> . . . is the principal interface between culture and nature, the boundary across which the ecological, chemical, and physical restraints to which human action is subject interact with the principal sociocultural practices aimed at overcoming or modifying those restraints.

Harris argues that studies focused on infrastructure have a "strategic priority" for anthropological research (and funding), justifying this claim on two points. First, if the goal of science is to create an ordered body of knowledge based on lawlike generalizations, then one should begin with those sociocultural arenas "under the greatest direct restraints from the givens of nature" (Harris 1979:57). Second, innovations in infrastructure tend to produce greater systemic changes since their reverberations are felt in the other arenas of structure, superstructure and mental/emic superstructure (Harris 1979:71–73). This does not mean that structure and superstructure "are insignificant, epiphenomenal reflexes of infrastructural forces." Rather, such dimensions often serve as regulating mechanisms that may counteract changes or enhance and amplify them. Innovations, Harris (1979:73) writes,

> . . . are unlikely to be propagated and amplified if they are functionally incompatible with the existing modes of production and reproduction—more unlikely than in the reverse. . . . This is what cultural materialists mean when they say that in the long run and in the largest number of cases, etic behavioral infrastructure determines the nature of structure and superstructure.

In short, understanding cultural patterns first requires explaining phenomena in terms of infrastructure—the culture/nature interface, as expressed by such dimensions as subsistence, settlement, population, demography, and so on—and then understanding how such changes reshape structure and superstructure. Harris employs this strategy in an evolutionary sketch of world history (Harris 1979:79–113), but also uses it to explain specific, contemporary social phenomena (Harris 1974, 1977, 1985) like the sacred cows of India and the collapse of the Soviet Empire.

Sacred Cows and the End of Empire

Harris' cultural materialist approach is exemplified in analyses which explain perplexing social patterns by examining the nature of infrastructure. Two examples are, "Why are there so many sacred cows in India?" and "Why did the Soviet Union collapse?"

To someone from the meat-eating West, the notion of cows wandering freely in India while people starve is a paradoxical waste of protein (Harris 1985). The Hindu ban on the slaughter of cattle and the consumption of beef would seem nonadaptive, a case where cultural rules run roughshod over common sense and, by extension, an illustration that mental superstructure, and not infrastructure, is causally prior.

The religious, symbolic, and political regulations associated with sacred cattle in India are well-known. There are laws regulating the slaughter of cows in India's constitution, all but two states' laws forbid the slaughter of India's native hump-backed zebu cow, and a complete ban on cow slaughter is a common flash point of political agitation. In Hindu sacred literature the god Krishna is described as a cowherd and protector of cows; and milk, butter, curds, urine and dung are blended into a sacred nectar used to anoint religious statues and worshippers. Cows are decorated with flowers, placed in animal shelters when they are old and sick, in short, venerated and worshipped. The worship of cows is associated with the adoration of human motherhood. It is a major theme in political life; a constant friction between Muslims and Hindus is that Muslims eat beef. Similarly, British beef-eating was a rallying cause during India's independence movement, and one source of Mohandas Gandhi's political support was his ardent belief in the sacredness of the cow.

Consequently, India has more cows than any other nation in the world—an estimated 180 million plus 50 million water buffalo—a seeming waste created by illogical religious belief. Not surprisingly, Harris disagrees:

> Both politics and religion obviously play a role in reinforcing and perpetuating the beef and slaughter taboos, but neither politics nor religion explains why cattle slaughter and beef eating have achieved

symbolic prominence. Why the cow and not the pig, horse, or camel? I do not doubt the symbolic power of the sacred cow. What I doubt is that the investment of symbolic power in one particular kind of animal and one particular kind of meat results from an arbitrary and capricious mental choice rather than from a definite set of practical constraints. Religion has affected India's foodways, but India's foodways have affected India's religion even more. [Harris 1985:51]

How has infrastructure produced the sacred cow? Harris' detailed answer can be distilled to a simple point—the need for oxen. Harris cites Vedic texts describing a beef-eating past (before 600 B.C.) when cattle were slaughtered for communal, carnivorous feasts. But as the human population increased and grazing lands were converted to farmlands, beef became too expensive and eventually was limited only to privileged castes. Beginning in the 5th century B.C., religions developed which banned killing—Buddhism and Jainism—and during subsequent centuries milk, not meat, became the ritual food and cow worship became part of Hinduism.

But the need for oxen as plow animals meant that cows were always necessary. Draft animals are needed on small farms. Today tractors are only more efficient on larger farms, and they break down and are expensive to repair. The poorest of India's farmers are the real owners of the supposedly stray animals wandering in the landscape; with no pasturage the cows scavenge food from roadside vegetation, food stands, and garbage heaps. Producing little milk and only an occasional ox, the cow is nonetheless cost-efficient—sufficient reason for protection from slaughter:

> [N]ot only did she give milk but she was the mother of the cheapest and most efficient traction animal for India's soils and climate. In return for Hindu safeguards against the reemergence of energetically costly and socially divisive beef-eating foodways, she made it possible for the land to teem with human life. [Harris 1985:66]

This is the interface between nature and culture: infrastructure pure and simple.

A second case is Harris' (1992) analysis of the demise of the Soviet Union. The deterioration of Soviet state communism was not, as some contend, due to the triumph of capitalism, the unforeseen consequences of perestroika, or the political foresight of American foreign policy. Instead, Harris argues that the Soviet Union collapsed because of infrastructural devolution.

On the eve of perestroika, per capita economic growth in the Soviet Union was at zero or less, grain production was unchanged over the previous decade in spite of heavy investments, and between 1970 and 1987 output per unit of input declined at the rate of one percent per year. Factories, agricultural equipment, generation plants, and transmission systems were worn and antiquated. The diffusion of technological innovations took three times longer in the Soviet economy than it did in the Western economies. Inadequate distribution systems meant that 20 percent to 50 percent of the wheat, potato, sugar beet and fruit harvests were lost between farm and store. A broad range of pollution—from the radiation of Chernobyl to the poisoning of the Baltic, Black, and Caspian Seas—was a further index of decline, as was the decrease in life expectancy for Soviet males (Harris 1992:298).

Such problems at the level of infrastructure were compounded by impediments at the structural level of the Soviet command economy. State-owned factories' budgets were allocated based on the number of employees rather than on the efficiency of production, creating payrolls of unneeded workers. Production quotas were stated in terms of output without quality control. "This meant that the penalties for inefficient and irrational management, such as excessive inventory, overemployment, and excess investment, were minimal and did not lead to the extinction of the enterprise" (Harris 1992:299). The command economy unevenly distributed the trickle of resulting production. Thus the interminable queues and unpredictable shortages that people endured in Moscow were paralleled by inequities between the republics. Russia gained more from the other republics than it redistributed. Harris (1992:300) points out that in the 1970s–1980s infant mortality increased in Kazakhstan by 14 percent, Turkmenia by 22 percent and in Uzbekistan by 48 percent. The perception that Russia was benefiting at the expense of the other republics intensified nationalistic movements. "[T]he collapse of state communism and the Soviet empire," Harris (1992: 300) concluded, was "a case of selection against a political economy that increasingly impeded and degraded the performance of its infrastructure."

Harris' analysis of the Soviet Empire was presented as a distinguished lecture to the American Anthropological Association, and he directed a number of comments to his fellow anthropologists. He notes that

> . . . infrastructural, structural and symbolic-ideational features are equally necessary components of human social life. It is no more possible to imagine a human society without a symbolic-ideational or structural sector than it is possible to imagine one without a mode of production and reproduction. Nonetheless, these sectors do not play a

symmetrical role in influencing the retention or extinction of sociocultural innovations. [Harris 1992:297]

Rather, the realm of infrastructure is determinant. Innovations in the realm of infrastructure will tend to change structural and symbolic-ideational systems, while innovations in structural and symbolic-ideational systems which reduce the efficiency of the infrastructure, as measured "by the efficiency of productive and reproductive processes that sustain [human] health and well-being," will be selected against. And that, Harris argues, is what happened to the Soviet Union.

Conclusion

As noted above, Harris gives causal priority to infrastructure in explanations of sociocultural innovations; he does not suggest that structural or symbolic-ideational realms are irrelevant or unimportant for understanding cultural change. There is a simply greater probability that innovations in infrastructure will cause changes in other realms than there is the reverse: symbolic-ideational innovations will not cause innovations if they are fundamentally incompatible with the infrastructure.

In his address to the American Anthropological Association, Harris (1992:302) pointed out that the causal primacy of infrastructure does not

> . . . diminish our freedom to intervene and direct the selection of alternate futures. For along with the restraints come opportunities— opportunities that can deepen the benefits of social life for all of humankind. Recognition of the primacy of infrastructure does not diminish the importance of conscious human agency. Rather, it merely increases the importance of having robust theories of history that can guide conscious human choice.

But wait—what does this tell us about other dimensions of culture? How do aspects of culture without direct adaptive consequences develop, spread, or get maintained? Let us grant, for the sake of argument, that Harris is correct that the infrastructural domain is likely to be regulated by laws. Why does that make other aspects of culture uninteresting? Harris' argument is this: anthropology is a science, science is based on laws, infrastructure is (most likely) governed by laws, therefore anthropology should focus on infrastructure. But what if anthropology is not a search for lawlike generalizations? What if it is a humanistic discipline, as Evans-Pritchard argued (see pp. 160–161), or one which "is not an experimental science in search of law, but an interpretive one in search of meaning," as Clifford Geertz (see pp. 241–242) stated?

And finally, how can we be so dismissive of the informant's emic viewpoint if culture is rooted in values and meanings held by individuals? Why should we give research priority to etic research focused on infrastructure when as anthropologists we are interested in the rich diversity of human cultures? Doesn't cultural materialism reduce human culture to mere matters of eating and breeding?

These are some of the issues which emerge in the 1970s as American anthropology splits into two major camps: those who argue for an anthropology grounded in the humanities and those—like Marvin Harris—who advocate an anthropology modeled on natural science. ✦

Bibliography

Harris, Marvin
1956 Town and Country in Brazil. New York: Columbia University Press.
1964 Patterns of Race in the Americas. New York: Walker and Company.
1968 The Rise of Anthropological Theory: A History of Theories of Culture. New York: Thomas Y. Crowell Company.
1974 Cows, Pigs, Wars and Witches: The Riddles of Culture. New York: Random House.
1977 Cannibals and Kings: The Origins of Cultures. New York: Random House.
1979 Cultural Materialism: The Struggle for a Science of Culture. New York: Random House.
1985 Good to Eat: Riddles of Food and Culture. New York: Simon and Schuster.
1992 Distinguished Lecture: Anthropology and the Theoretical and Paradigmatic Significance of the Collapse of Soviet and East European Communism. American Anthropologist 94:295–305.

Chapter 16

Eleanor Burke Leacock
Feminism, Marxism, and History

Eleanor Burke Leacock was the leading Marxist feminist in American anthropology, and her contributions to the field were wide and profound. At her death in 1987, her field research had spanned forty years and covered such diverse topics as hunter-gatherer economies of Labrador, child rearing in Europe, educational ethnography in urban America and rural Zambia, the ethnohistory of the North American fur trade, and the problems of urban adolescents in Samoa. Leacock was a radical and leading exponent of Marxist analyses of human society, producing critical essays on Engels' *The Origins of the Family, Private Property, and the State* and on Morgan's *Ancient Society* (Leacock 1963, 1972). A central focus to Leacock's work was her argument that the subordination of women was the consequence of capitalism, not an innate reflection of gender differences. This argument was documented with rich ethnohistoric detail in her earliest writings and remained a central theme throughout her life (Leacock 1954, 1978, 1982a).

Leacock's theoretical contributions were fundamental: she was one of the first American anthropologists to apply an explicitly Marxist approach to understanding ethnographic realities, particularly the historical transformation of women's status (Gailey 1993). She contributed to the postwar reemergence of evolutionary thinking in American anthropology, but advocated a materialist approach markedly different from those of White, Steward, or Harris (Leacock 1958, 1982b). Lauded for her detailed research (Grumet 1993), her dissertation was published as a memoir of the American Anthropological Association (Leacock 1954)—a clear recognition of her scholarly contribution and academic promise.

Yet Eleanor Burke Leacock was excluded from academic anthropology, marginalized by a discipline to which she contributed so much. She obtained her first tenure track position fifteen years after completing her Ph.D. at Columbia. In contrast, her male contemporaries at Columbia—including fellow radicals Elman Service, Morton Fried, and Stanley Diamond—were quickly hired by universities. In the pages of the *International Dictionary of Anthropologists* (Winter 1981), there is not even a brief mention of Eleanor Burke Leacock.

Why did this occur? Simply because, as Stanley Diamond (1993:114) writes, "Being an honest scholar, a radical and a feminist, the going was rough." But the most difficult barrier Eleanor Burke Leacock faced was simply being a woman in American society.

Background

Eleanor Burke was born in 1922 into a family enmeshed in radical and literary politics. Her father was the critic and writer Kenneth Burke, and her mother Lily was trained as a mathematician. In the early 1920s, Kenneth Burke became a full-time freelance critic, and as a biographer notes, "He began to earn enough to live in poverty" (Jay 1988:6). The family lived a mobile lifestyle, spending Easter to Thanksgiving on a rustic farm in northern New Jersey where the family gardened, cut wood, and hauled water and then moving to Greenwich Village each winter (Leacock 1993). It was an unconventional lifestyle, but it led Eleanor Burke to absorb values that "mixed the respect for manual work that characterized the marginal farming community . . . with the high esteem for intellectual integrity and independence that characterized the Bohemian circle of writers and artists in Greenwich Village" (Leacock 1993:5).

Burke began college at Radcliffe where she was exposed to the books of evolutionary archaeologist V. Gordon Childe and to the misogyny of Mayanist Alfred Tozzer, who announced to his class of Radcliffe women "bluntly and unsympathetically, that they should not go into anthropology unless they had independent incomes, because they would never get jobs" (Leacock 1993:7). Burke absorbed anthropology courses, participated in radical student groups, and in 1941 married Richard Leacock, a filmmaker who would work with Robert Flaherty and later direct the film studies program at M.I.T.

Leacock returned to New York to complete her undergraduate education at Barnard and began graduate studies at Columbia, where she was influenced by Gene Weltfish and William Duncan Strong. Welt-fish lectured on the political consequences of anthropological research, a concern Leacock took to heart (Leacock 1993:13–14). Strong's influence was also formative. An archaeologist and ethnologist who worked throughout the Americas (Solecki and Wagley 1963), Strong had conducted ethnographic research in Labrador in 1927–28 (Leacock and Rothschild 1993) and was marginally involved in an anthropological debate over the social and economic organization of the Montagnais-Naskapi of the Labrador peninsula. Unlike many academic squabbles, this debate had content and consequence.

Property, Colonialism, and the Montagnais-Naskapi

In 1915 the anthropologist Frank Speck had documented that the Montagnais-Naskapi bands of Labrador held territory, essentially showing that private property ownership existed among hunters and gatherers and arguing that this was an aboriginal, precontact economic pattern (Speck 1915, 1923; Speck and Eiseley 1939). Speck's evidence for private land ownership countered claims by Morgan, Marx, and Engels that collective—not private—ownership was fundamental to hunting and gathering societies. Speck's study became more than an ethnographic obscurity when it was whipped into a "disproof" of Morgan, Marx, and Engels by anti-evolutionists like Robert Lowie (1920, 1927).

Sparked by Strong's unpublished data from Labrador (Leacock 1993:15; Leacock and Rothschild 1993), Leacock studied the early Jesuit accounts about Labrador at the Biblioteque Nacionale in Paris and examined other historical sources for the 16th to 19th centuries. A basic point emerged from her ethnohistoric research: Montagnais-Naskapi social life had been dramatically restructured due to the fur trade.

In 1950 Leacock went to Labrador to conduct ethnographic research with the Montagnais-Naskapi. By collecting genealogies and mapping hunting territories, she was able to reconstruct the historical transformations of the hunting economy and Montagnais-Naskapi property relations. The combination of ethnohistoric and ethnographic sources deepened Leacock's knowledge of the Montagnais-Naskapi and the historical changes they had experienced. Individual ownership resulted from the changes in property relationships triggered by the fur trade; it was not, as Speck argued, an aboriginal economic institution. In her tightly documented monograph, "The Montagnais 'Hunting Territory'

and the Fur Trade," Leacock (1954) carefully builds the argument.
Speck had argued that the fur trade was relatively recent (since the
1700s) and its impacts too short-lived to create completely new property relations. Leacock shows how indirect trade began in the early
1500s and was of major importance by the early 1600s (Leacock
1954:10–12). Citing historical accounts, Leacock documents 1) that
prior to the 18th century hunting bands were fluid social groups freely
ranging over large territories, 2) that individual ownership emerged in
the 18th century, 3) that even in the 20th century property rules distinguished between hunting for food and trapping for sale, and 4) that
Jesuits, Hudson Bay factors, and government officials had been actively
changing Montagnais-Naskapi social and economic structures for 400
years (Leacock 1954). Leacock (1954:43) concludes:

> It is becoming increasingly evident that Indian tribal life as recorded
> in the nineteenth and even late eighteenth centuries reflected impor-
> tant changes which had already come about as a result of the Indians
> taking an active part in the world-wide growth of trade and com-
> merce. . . . The present study has taken the position that the [Montag-
> nais-Naskapi] are no exception. Their apparent "primitivity" is
> deceptive. In order to reconstruct their aboriginal culture, one cannot
> simply record their recent life and subtract those traits that are of
> obvious European origin. One must work from the understanding
> that fundamental socioeconomic changes have been taking place in
> some parts of their area for over three hundred years, one aspect of
> which is the development of the family hunting territory.

Apart from its substantive merits, Leacock's monograph contained
two important, if tangential, points. First, the historical changes of the
Montagnais-Naskapi showed that traditional, non-Western societies
are not static—they change. This seems like an obvious point today,
but it was not so clear to anthropology prior to 1950 when "primitive"
cultures frequently were characterized as conservative and stable rather
than innovative and dynamic. Thus, Tylor could view non-Western
societies as fossilized representatives of earlier stages of human progress
(see pp. 23–25), Radcliffe-Brown could view social structures as expressions of the stabilizing forces that maintain society (see pp. 145–147),
and Benedict could view the Native American world view as representing stable cultural configurations (see pp. 81–85).

Second, Leacock's emphasis on the transformations caused by the
fur trade highlighted two dimensions of change: changing concepts of
property and gender relations. Although sparked by an interest in primitive communism, Leacock intentionally camouflaged her interests in

Marxism and evolution. Writing her dissertation at the height of the McCarthy era, Leacock buried her theoretical interests in dense ethnographic detail. Years later she wrote that when she discussed the historical transformations of production in Montagnais-Naskapi society, "I cited, not Marx as I should have, but a chance statement of the far-from-Marxist [Melville] Herskovits" (Leacock 1982b:255). In 1954 it was simply too dangerous to admit to an interest in Marxism. Over the next 20 years the situation would change, and Eleanor Leacock emerged as a leading Marxist anthropologist.

Marxism and Feminism

In a personal reflection Leacock (1993) traced her radical roots to her upbringing and political experiences, but her personal outlook found support in the works of Lewis Henry Morgan and Friedrich Engels. Leacock wrote that her appreciation of Morgan "is born out of a perverse reaction to the virtually universal criticism of Morgan encountered in my student days, and reinforced both by my field experience and by the recognition that far more of Morgan's theory is already incorporated into the science of anthropology than is generally conceded" (Leacock 1981:106).

Christine Gailey notes that from the early 1960s Eleanor Leacock "would focus on the transformation of societies through colonially catalyzed class and state formation" giving particular attention to "the imposition or encouragement of capitalist development in the post-colonial period" and to consequent changes in women's authority and autonomy (Gailey 1992:68).

Leacock's central argument stemmed directly from her field experience in Labrador. First, band-organized, gathering-hunting societies tend to be characterized by communal ownership (particularly of land), egalitarian social relations, and nonhierarchical gender relationships (Leacock 1982a). Second, the evolution of class societies and the development of capitalism also produced changes from a) kin-based societies which hold property communally and unify societies as collectivities, into b) social systems which define groups that compete for resources and control of labor—an argument advanced by Morgan (Leacock 1982b:247; see pp. 36–38). In particular, the expansion of capitalist systems and the creation of commodity production and exchange resulted in the restructuring of social control over production and products—a point made by Marx (Leacock 1981a:14).

And finally, the subordination of women is an inevitable outcome of these economic changes. In her Labrador research, Leacock analyzed a very explicit program of economic and social changes implemented by the 17th-century Jesuit Paul le Jeune, who, as superior of the Jesuit mission of Quebec, studied Montagnais culture in order to convert and "civilize" the Indians (Leacock 1980; 1981c). This program involved several steps: the establishment of permanent settlements instead of traditional, mobile camps; the creation of chiefs; the introduction of corporal punishment, particularly of children; and finally the imposition of Catholic family values based on patriarchy, monogamy, female sexual fidelity, and the abolition of divorce.

How could such different cultural values be successfully imposed on the Montagnais? "The answer," Leacock (1980:38) wrote, "is that the Jesuits and their teachings arrived in New France a full century after the economic basis for unquestioned cooperation, reciprocity, and respect for individual autonomy had been undercut by the trading of furs for European goods." With the spread of the fur trade and the expansion of capitalism, women progressively were deprived of control over their labor, although the Montagnais retained a higher degree of respect and autonomy between the sexes than is found in other societies (Leacock 1980:40–41).

Leacock expanded her analysis beyond Labrador. In an extremely influential article, "Women's Status in Egalitarian Society: Implications for Social Evolution," Leacock (1978) showed how anthropologists' assumption that women had inferior status in most traditional societies reflected poor ethnographic research and the extension of biases inherent in the anthropologists' own class societies. Too many anthropologists had dealt with women's roles in other societies "with brief remarks about food preparation and child care" and comments on the sexual division of labor (Leacock 1978). Anthropologists had overlooked the degree of autonomy women in egalitarian societies have over their lives and activities, assuming that separate was unequal. Consequently, anthropologists, extrapolating from their own class-based societies, found women everywhere of lower status and then contended that female inferiority was cross-cultural. Leacock argued that this was false.

Leacock's feminist anthropology, as Rapp argues, insisted "on the importance of locating family forms in evolutionary and historical processes, and on the explicitly political nature of monogamy, patriarchy, private property, and class relations" (Rapp 1993:90). Thus Leacock's theoretical approach directly stems from Morgan, Engels, and Marx, but her ethnographic analyses are so richly documented and tightly argued that they read more like the writings of Franz Boas.

For Eleanor Leacock, feminist anthropology was a principal element of a broader radical critique, one grounded in detailed attention to historical processes. Although colonialism and capitalism had common consequences, the ethnographic situations had to be understood based on specific, well-documented historical cases. Leacock (1978:168) wrote:

> Colonization characteristically brought disruption and devastation to foraging peoples and it is necessary to point this out. However, for ethical and political as well as scientific reasons, it is equally necessary to note and to document the resiliency and creativity with which different peoples moved to survive in, cope with, and take what advantage they could of new situations in which they found themselves. . . . They evolved new cultural forms which, although much changed from aboriginal times, continued to be distinctively theirs.

Conclusion

Eleanor Burke Leacock's work covered many different topics, but they shared a common set of themes. First, Leacock argued that the subordination of women was a product of history, not a universal condition (Sutton and Lee 1993:137). Second, Leacock emphasized the historical transformations caused by the development of class societies and the expansion of Western capitalism, causing anthropologists to be cautious in their assumptions about the "aboriginal" patterns in other societies. Finally, Leacock merged the Boasian tradition of establishing the historical context of cultural patterns with a Marxist tradition of engagement, creating a unique body of scholarship and activism. ✦

Bibliography

Diamond, Stanley
1993 Eleanor Leacock's Political Vision. *In* From Labrador to Samoa: The Theory and Practice of Eleanor Burke Leacock. C. Sutton, ed. Pp. 111–114. Arlington, Virginia: Association for Feminist Anthropology/American Anthropological Association.

Gailey, Christine
1993 Egalitarian and Class Societies: Transitions and Transformations. *In* From Labrador to Samoa: The Theory and Practice of Eleanor Burke Leacock. C.

Sutton, ed. Pp. 67–76. Arlington, Virginia: Association for Feminist Anthropology/American Anthropological Association.

Grumet, Robert
1993 Contributions to Native North American Studies. *In* From Labrador to Samoa: The Theory and Practice of Eleanor Burke Leacock. C. Sutton, ed. Pp. 47–55. Arlington, Virginia: Association for Feminist Anthropology/American Anthropological Association.

Jay, Paul
1988 Introduction: Part One. *In* The Selected Correspondence of Kenneth Burke and Malcolm Cowley, 1915–1981. P. Jay, ed. Pp. 3–7. New York: Viking Press.

Leacock, Eleanor Burke
1954 The Montagnais "Hunting Territory" and the Fur Trade. American Anthropologist Vol. 56, No. 5, Part 2, Memoir 78. Washington, DC: American Anthropological Association.
1955 Matrilocality in a Simple Hunting Economy (Montagnais-Naskapi). Southwestern Journal of Anthropology 11(1):31–47.
1958 Social Stratification and Evolutionary Theory: Introduction to a Symposium. Ethnohistory 5(3):193–199.
1963 Introduction. *In* Ancient Society. Lewis Henry Morgan. New York: World Publishing.
1972 Introduction. *In* The Origin of the Family, Private Property and the State. Friedrich Engels. Pp. 7–67. New York: International Publishers.
1978 Women's Status in Egalitarian Society: Implications for Social Evolution. Current Anthropology 19(2):247–275.
1980 Montagnais Women and the Jesuit Program for Colonization. *In* Women and Colonization: Anthropological Perspectives. M. Etienne and E. Leacock, eds. Pp. 25–42. New York: Praeger Publishers.
1981a Introduction: Engels and the History of Women's Oppression. *In* Myths of Male Dominance. Collected by E. Leacock. Pp. 13–29. New York: Monthly Review Press.
1981b Introduction to Lewis Henry Morgan, Ancient Society, Parts I, II, III, IV. *In* Myths of Male Dominance. Collected by E. Leacock. Pp. 85–132. New York: Monthly Review Press.
1981c Seventeenth-Century Montaganais Social Relations and Values. *In* Handbook of North American Indians, Vol. 6. Subarctic. J. Helm, ed. Pp. 190–195. Washington, DC: Smithsonian Institution.
1982a Relations of Production in Band Society. *In* Politics and History in Band Societies. E. Leacock and R. Lee, eds. Pp. 159–170. Cambridge: Cambridge University Press.
1982b Marxism and Anthropology. *In* The Left Academy: Marxist Scholarship on American Campuses. B. Ollman and E. Vernoff, eds. Pp. 242–276. New York: McGraw-Hill.
1993 On Being an Anthropologist. *In* From Labrador to Samoa: The Theory and Practice of Eleanor Burke Leacock. C. Sutton, ed. Pp. 1–31. Arlington, Virginia: Association for Feminist Anthropology/American Anthropological Association.

Leacock, Eleanor and Nan Rothschild, eds.
1993 William Duncan Strong's Labrador Winter. Washington, D.C.: Smithsonian Institution.

Lowie, Robert
1920 Primitive Society. New York: Boni and Liveright.
1927 The Origin of the State. New York: Harcourt, Brace, and Co.

Rapp, Rayna
1993 Eleanor Leacock's Contributions to the Anthropological Study of Gender. *In* From Labrador to Samoa: The Theory and Practice of Eleanor Burke Leacock. C. Sutton, ed. Pp. 87–94. Arlington, Virginia: Association for Feminist Anthropology/American Anthropological Association.

Solecki, R. and C. Wagley
1963 William Duncan Strong 1899–1962. American Anthropologist 65:1102–1111.

Speck, Frank
1915 The Family Hunting Band as the Basis of Algonkian Social Organization. American Anthropologist 17:289–305.
1923 Mistassini Hunting Territories in the Labrador Peninsula. American Anthropologist 25:452–471.

Speck, Frank and Loren Eiseley
1939 The Significance of the Hunting Territory Systems of the Algonkian in Social Theory. American Anthropologist 41:269–280.

Winter, Christopher, ed.
1981 International Dictionary of Anthropologists. New York: Garland Publishing.

Part Five

Structures, Symbols, and Meanings

Since the 1960s anthropological theory has been characterized by divergence. Unlike previous periods when a few theoretical positions dominated the field, the last decades have been characterized by a multiplicity of unreconcilable theoretical points of view. As anthropologist Sherry Ortner wrote in 1984,

> The field appears to be a thing of shreds and patches, of individuals and small coteries pursuing disjunctive investigations and talking mainly to themselves. We do not even hear stirring arguments any more. Although anthropology was never actually unified in the sense of adopting a single shared paradigm, there was at least a period when there were a few large categories of theoretical affiliation, a set of identifiable camps or schools, and a few simple epithets one could hurl at one's opponents. [Ortner 1984:126–127]

And yet certain themes do seem to run through anthropological theories since the 1960s, and they point to the idealist nature of current explanations. There has been a general movement away from materialist theories, like those discussed in the previous section, which treat culture as humanity's principal means of adaptation to the physical and social environment. In addition, there is an increased emphasis on the way in which individual actions creatively shape culture, and, by extension, a diminished effort to reify culture as somehow separable from the individual, as Kroeber argued (see Chapter 5).

Finally, the symbolic nature of culture has come to dominate definitions of culture, and this has had several consequences. A symbolic approach to culture means that ethnographic studies which emphasize ecological, economic, or other materialist concerns have fallen into disfavor in some anthropological circles.

Perhaps more importantly, a symbolic approach to culture inevitably leads to a concern with meanings: if culture is symbolic, then it follows that it is used to create and convey meanings since that is the purpose of symbols. If meanings are the end products of culture, then understanding culture requires understanding the meanings of its creators and users. And if that is true, then culture is unknowable to the etic observer, since the meanings are only obtainable from the emic insider's point of view.

And this shift has led to a subtle atomization of theoretical models. As theoretical definitions have highlighted culture's symbolic aspects, explanations of cultural patterns have become increasing localized. If, for example, culture is the creation of symbolic meanings and these meanings differ even among the individuals involved in a single cultural exchange (such as a ritual, a conversation, or a coronation), then there can be, to recall Edward Sapir's phrase, "as many cultures as there are individuals in a population." And since symbols contain multiple layers of meaning, explaining cultural behavior becomes an interpretive task in which the anthropologist unravels tangled skeins of significances as seen from the insiders' points of view.

The shifting points of view discernible in the works of Claude Lévi-Strauss, Victor Turner, Clifford Geertz, Mary Douglas, and James Fernandez are a long way from the simple definition of culture used by Edward Tylor.

For Lévi-Strauss, culture involves a variety of communicative exchanges in the domains of kinship, myth, and language. For all their superficial variety, these exchanges follow a relatively small set of basic forms or "deep structures." These structures reflect a universal grammar of culture that is rooted in the subconscious properties of the human mind and exposes the principles by which humans classify. With a legacy in the Durkheimian concern with *representations*, Lévi-Strauss' structuralism views culture as the symbolic expression of the human mind.

The works of Victor Turner equally emphasize the symbolic nature of culture but place its explanation within the dynamics of social life. Symbols are used and meanings are created in public, social exchanges. Symbols have specific properties: they are powerful concentrates of meaning, their meanings are multiple, and the meanings vary for different members of a society. Understanding cultural life requires isolating symbols, identifying their meanings, and showing how symbols resonate within a specific, dynamic cultural context.

Clifford Geertz shares this interest in the symbolic basis of culture. For Geertz, culture involves the acting out of world view, values, and ethos—the particular "core values," to use Benedict's phrase—that give societies their distinctive styles. This process, however, is extremely complex because the use of symbols and the creation of meaning inevitably involves misunderstandings, differences of opinions about meaning, and conflicts between individuals in their use of symbols. Thus, one cannot make global statements about "Culture X believes . . ." which are common in earlier ethnographies. Explication involves situating an event in a particular cultural actor(s)' motives, values, and intentions. In turn, the anthropologist's role is not to explain a cultural event within an overarching, universal framework, but to interpret it within a specific code of meanings.

In her ethnographic works, Mary Douglas explores the social categories of cultural meanings. Extending a line of analysis which clearly originates in the ideas of Durkheim and Mauss, Douglas examines the ways in which cultural statements about symbolic purity and contamination—food taboos, behavioral prohibitions, avoidance rules—are restatements of ideas about society. Douglas analyzes how humans articulate symbolic systems and social institutions to make meaningful and unique assertions about who they are.

The progressive shift to local explication is clear in James Fernandez's writings, and those of other post-modernist anthropologists such as James Clifford (1988; Clifford and Marcus 1986), George E. Marcus (1992; Marcus and Fischer 1986; Marcus and Myers 1995), and Michael M.J. Fischer (Fischer and Abedi 1990), among others. The symbolic nature of culture almost insures that competing understandings should coexist. Rather than reduce such conflicts or classify some proposed meanings as central and others as marginal, post-modernist approaches accept, in fact revel in, the diversity of points of view. Chaos is not the failure to make sense of social phenomena, but inherent in the nature of phenomena. The description of "what is going on" requires locating social life within specific and multiple frames. The current situation, George E. Marcus and Michael M.J. Fischer write,

> . . . is a pregnant moment in which every individual project of ethnographic research and writing is potentially an experiment. Collectively, these are in the process of reconstructing the edifices of anthropological theory from the bottom up, by exploring new ways to fulfill the promises on which modern anthropology was founded: to offer worthwhile and interesting critiques of our own society; to enlighten us about other human possibilities, engendering an awareness

that we are merely one pattern among many; to make accessible the normally unexamined assumptions by which we operate and through which we encounter other cultures. [Marcus and Fischer 1986:ix]

As anthropological theories have shifted there has been increasing attention on the role of the anthropological observer. If culture is the creation of meanings and explanation is their interpretation, then how does the anthropologist influence meaning? How can these different experiences be translated faithfully and how can veracity be measured? Is the anthropologist writing an account of another culture or always and inevitably writing autobiography? How do the genres we use to describe another society shape understanding? If we treat others as subjects described in a scientific format, are we dehumanizing them?

Anthropologists did not really worry about such issues before 1970, or if they did, they kept it to themselves. But the increasing emphasis on the symbolic nature of culture and the interpretive basis of explanation leads almost inevitably to these concerns which dominate current debates in anthropological theory. ✦

Bibliography

Clifford, James
1988 The Predicament of Culture: Twentieth-century Ethnography, Literature, and Art. Cambridge, MA: Harvard University Press.

Clifford, James and George E. Marcus, eds.
1986 Writing Culture: The Poetics and Politics of Ethnography. Berkeley: University of California Press.

Fischer, Michael M.J. and Mehdi Abedi
1990 Debating Muslims: Cultural Dialogues in Postmodernity and Tradition. Madison: University of Wisconsin Press.

Marcus, George E.
1992 Rereading Cultural Anthropology. Durham, N.C.: Duke University Press.

Marcus, George E. and Michael M.J. Fischer
1986 Anthropology as Cultural Critique: An Experimental Moment in the Human Sciences. Chicago: University of Chicago Press.

Ortner, Sherry
1984 Theory in Anthropology Since the Sixties. Comparative Studies in Society and History 26:126–166.

Chapter 17

Claude Lévi-Strauss

Structuralism

The anthropologist Claude Lévi-Strauss (b. 1908) occupies a unique position in the development of anthropological theory and the intellectual life of the 20th century. In anthropology Lévi-Strauss is known as the founder of structuralism, an approach which emerged uniquely in his work. The ideas of Lévi-Strauss seemed fully developed and utterly original at first sight, yet the importance of his anthropological ideas were recognized belatedly in the United States, similar to American anthropologists' treatment of Emile Durkheim. The anthropologist Robert Murphy (1970:165) wrote that *Les structures élémentaires de la parenté* was read "by most French anthropologists, many English anthropologists, and few American anthropologists—a gradient that reflected facility with French rather than doctrinal schisms."

The cultural critic George Steiner (1977:241) wrote that the relevance of Lévi-Strauss' "work on the notion of culture, on our understanding of language and mental process, on our interpretation of history is so direct and novel that an awareness of Lévi-Strauss' thought is part of cultural literacy." And the essayist and novelist Susan Sontag (1966:69–81), describing the modern search for moral place, wrote: "The anthropologist is thus not only the mourner of the cold world of the primitives, but its custodian as well. Lamenting among the shadows, struggling to distinguish the archaic from the pseudoarchaic, he acts out a heroic, diligent, and complex modern pessimism." Claude Lévi-Strauss was, in Sontag's well-known phrase, "The anthropologist as hero."

The ascent of Lévi-Strauss to such pinnacles of esteem has confounded any number of commentators and the heroic anthropologist himself. Lévi-Strauss' popularity was the French intellectual's equivalent of the hula hoop, as Sanche de Gramont (1970:8) observed. Steiner (1977:239) wondered if those who invoked "Lévi-Strauss" and "structuralism," like the words of a magic spell had actually read his works. And Robert Murphy (1970:165) groused that Lévi-Strauss' "vogue has spread throughout the United States . . . making him as unavoidable at cocktail parties as the cheese dip."

Even Lévi-Strauss seems mystified by the intense popularity of structuralism in the 1960s and 1970s. Part of the intensity was created by the verbal jousting between Lévi-Strauss and Sartre, a debate that began in the last chapter of *The Savage Mind* (1966 [1962]) but quickly spilled into the pages of intellectual journals and personified the conflicts between existentialism and structuralism as reigning systems of thought. Lévi-Strauss commented on the fadish popularity of structuralism:

> The educated public in France is bulimic. For a while, it fed on structuralism. People thought it carried a message. That fashion has passed. A fashion lasts for five or ten years. . . . That's how things go in Paris. I have neither nostalgia nor regret. . . . [Lévi-Strauss and Eribon 1991:91–92]

But beyond mere fad, Lévi-Strauss achieved this intense interest among the reading public because of the depth of his insights and the breadth of his prose. Anthropologist Bob Scholte (1970:146) describes him as "a French *savant* par excellence, a man of extraordinary sensitivity and human wisdom, an encompassing mode of considerable erudition and philosophical scope, a deliberate stylist with profound convictions and convincing arguments."

Claude Lévi-Strauss is an institution in French intellectual life. Although he has lived most of his life in Paris, his central experience was to encounter that "single, awe-inspiring presence: the New World" (Lévi-Strauss 1974:80).

Background

Claude Lévi-Strauss was born in 1908. The son of a painter whose fortunes diminished with the waning tastes for the Belle Epoque, Lévi-Strauss was raised in a household which was very rich intellectually but not without "struggles with material difficulties" (Lévi-Strauss and Eribon 1991:5). After graduating from the Sorbonne in 1932 with degrees in philosophy and law, Lévi-Strauss taught at a lycée for the next two years and was active in socialist politics. Tiring of teaching, Lévi-Strauss returned to the university to pursue postgraduate studies in sociology, which was still very much Durkheim's science of society (and incorporated anthropology).

In 1935 he got the chance to join a French educational mission involved in establishing the University of Sao Paulo, Brazil, which only had a few dozen students. Lévi-Strauss developed his interest in anthropology, and at the end of his first academic year began field-work among the Indian tribes of the Mato Grosso in western Brazil. He wrote of his first encounter with a group of Tibagy, a group of encul-turated Native Americans, which had been contacted by the Brazilian Indian Protection service and then thrown back on their own resources:

> So, to my great disappointment, the Tibagy Indians were neither com-pletely "true Indians", nor what was more important, "savages". But, by removing the poetry from my naive vision of what experiences lay ahead, they taught me, as a beginner in anthropology, a lesson in prudence and objectivity. Although I had found them to be less unspoiled than I had hoped, I was to discover that they were more mysterious than their external appearance might lead one to believe. [Lévi-Strauss 1974:154]

In 1936 Lévi-Strauss published his first anthropological article, "Contribution . . . l'étude de l'organisation des Indiens Bororo" in the *Journal de la Société des Américanistes*, and soon his work was known by Americanists like Robert Lowie, Curt Nimuendaju, and Alfred Metraux. Over the next few years Lévi-Strauss made brief trips into the interior of Brazil, but in 1938 he obtained French support for a longer expedi-tion. He traveled to the far northwestern corner of Brazil, along the border with Bolivia, where he carried out research among the Nambi-kwara and Tupi-Kawahib, an experience beautifully described in *Tristes Tropiques*. In the beginning of 1939, however, Lévi-Strauss returned to Europe where he hoped to organize his collections, prepare a thesis, and reenter academic life in France.

World War II made that impossible. After a few months of military service, Lévi-Strauss, along with the rest of the French army except for DeGaulle's Free French, was demobilized by the Vichy government. For a brief period he returned to teaching until the imposition of racial laws ended his job. Though his parents did not practice their Judaism, Lévi-Strauss' maternal grandfather was a rabbi; his Jewish heritage made him an obvious target when the Nazis occupied France in 1940. Fortunately, it was still possible to leave Vichy France, and Lowie and Metraux were able to obtain a position for Lévi-Strauss at the New

School of Social Research in New York. The Rockefeller Foundation was actively involved in rescuing European intellectuals at risk from the Nazis, and New York became a vast expatriate community of artists and scholars.

After a squalid sea voyage in a ship crammed with refugees, Lévi-Strauss arrived in New York. He taught at the New School from 1942 to 1945, interacting with anthropologists at Columbia—Boas, Linton, Benedict, Mead—and others like Kroeber and Lowie who visited New York. This personal exposure to American cultural anthropology with its emphasis on values and ethos influenced Lévi-Strauss and complemented his concerns with classifications and representations derived from Durkheim and Mauss.

During his exile in New York, Lévi-Strauss began work on his first major book, *The Elementary Structures of Kinship* (1969a). At the end of the war Lévi-Strauss was assigned the position of cultural counselor to the French Embassy; his duties kept him in New York and he continued to write. He returned to France in 1947 where he presented *Les structures élémentaires de la parenté* as a doctoral thesis at the Sorbonne, receiving his Doctorat et Lettres in 1948. He served as assistant curator of ethnology at the Musée de l'Homme and was then elected to a chair at the Ecole de Hautes Études, the same position that Marcel Mauss once held.

With the publication of *Les structures élémentaires de la parenté* in 1949, *Tristes Tropiques* in 1955, and *Antropologie structurale* (Vol. 1) in 1958 (Vol. 2 appeared in 1973), Lévi-Strauss became very well known in French letters. His books were widely reviewed in leading intellectual journals, he participated in international organizations, and after two unsuccessful nominations, was made a member of the illustrious College de France in 1959 where he taught until 1982. The pinnacle of French academia, the College consists of fifty elite professors, each elected by fellow faculty, whose responsibilities are to teach one course annually, but each on a new topic (Lévi-Strauss 1987:1–3). Those courses were the testing ground for Lévi-Strauss' ideas on structural anthropology, which appeared in such works such as *The Savage Mind* (1966) and *Totemism* (1963), and his monumental studies of the nature of myth, which resulted in the publication of four volumes in his Mythologiques series: *The Raw and the Cooked* (1969b), *From Honey to Ashes* (1973), *The Origin of Table Manners* (1978), and *The Naked Man* (1981). It represents a prodigious creation and analysis. These are difficult, demanding writings in which logical constructs are devised only to be dismantled by new tacks of analysis. Sanche de Gramont (1970:16) wrote, "His books are possibly the greatest collection of riddles since the Sphinx."

In retirement Lévi-Strauss has continued to work, writing the *View from Afar* (1985), and *The Jealous Potter* (1988), and recently (1995) publishing a collection of photographs from his ethnographic explorations in the Matto Grosso. Lévi-Strauss has written deeply on his personal attraction to anthropology:

> Anthropology affords me intellectual satisfaction: as a form of history, linking up at opposite ends with world history and my own history, it thus reveals the rationale common to both. In proposing the study of mankind, anthropology frees me from doubt, since it examines those differences and changes in mankind which have a meaning for all men, and excludes those peculiar to a single civilization, which dissolve into nothingness under the gaze of an outside observer. Lastly it appeases that restless and destructive appetite [for new knowledge and intellectual challenges] I have already referred to, by ensuring me a virtually inexhaustible supply of material, thanks to the diversity of manners, customs and institutions. It allows me to reconcile my character with my life. [Lévi-Strauss 1974:58–59]

That restless process of reconciliation has led to one of the great intellectual searches of the 20th century: the search for structures of the unconscious that shape the forms of cultural life.

Structural Anthropology

Lévi-Strauss (1963:3) argues that "Social anthropology is devoted especially to the study of institutions considered as systems of representations." Lévi-Strauss uses "representations" as did Durkheim, to refer to beliefs, sentiments, norms, values, attitudes, meanings. Those institutions are cultural expressions that are usually unexamined by their users; in that narrow but fundamental sense anthropology examines the *unconscious* foundations of social life: "anthropology draws its originality from the unconscious nature of collective phenomena" (Lévi-Strauss 1963:18). This search for the underlying structures of social life led Lévi-Strauss to explore three principal areas: systems of classification, kinship theory, and the logic of myth.

Edmund Leach, not usually sympathetic to Lévi-Strauss, provides a handy paraphrase of the basic argument of structuralism:

> The general argument runs something like this: what we know about the external world we apprehend through our senses. The phenomena

which we perceive have the characteristics which we attribute to them because of the way our senses operate and the way the human brain is designed to order and interpret the stimuli which are fed into it. One very important feature of this ordering process is that we cut up the continua of space and time with which we are surrounded into segments so that we are predisposed to think of the environment as consisting of vast numbers of separate things belonging to named classes, and to think of the passage of time as consisting of sequences of separate events. Correspondingly, when, as men, we construct artificial things (artifacts of all kinds), or devise ceremonials, or write histories of the past, we imitate our apprehension of Nature: the products of our Culture are segmented and ordered in the same way as we suppose the products of Nature to be segmented and ordered. [Leach 1970:21]

The segmentation and imposition of form on inherently formless phenomena (like space or time) reflect deeply held structures from the bedrock of humanness.

At this point, the theoretical parallels between linguistics and the study of language, and anthropology and the study of culture, become important. Structuralism is not a mere restatement of the Sapir-Whorf hypothesis; Lévi-Strauss does not argue that language shapes cultural perceptions in that direct manner (1963:73,85). Rather, there are parallels between language and certain aspects of culture such as kinship, exchange, and myths, because they are all forms of communication:

In any society, communication operates on three different levels: communication of women, communication of goods and services, communication of messages. Therefore kinship studies, economics, and linguistics approach the same kinds of problems on different strategic [i.e., methodological] levels and really pertain to the same field. [Lévi-Strauss 1963:296]

The path of analysis had been blazed by the development of structural linguistics, which Lévi-Strauss was introduced to by the linguist and Slavic specialist Roman Jakobson during their shared exile in New York. Lévi-Strauss states, "At the time I was a kind of naive structuralist, a structuralist without knowing it" (Lévi-Strauss and Eribon 1991:41), but learning of the advances in linguistics was "a revelation." According to Lévi-Strauss (1963:33), the revolutionary aspects of these developments were 1) the shift of linguistic focus from conscious behavior to unconscious structure, 2) the new focus on the relations *between* terms rather than *on* terms, 3) the importance of proving the concrete existence of systems of relationships of meaning, and 4) the goal of discovering general laws. Those became Lévi-Strauss' analytical objectives as he turned to examinations of kinship, exchange, art, ritual, and myth—all of which are forms of communication analogous to language (Lévi-Strauss 1963:83–84).

Phonemes are the minimal units of sound which a group of speakers consider distinct; for example, the aspirated /t'/ in "top" and the unaspirated /t/ in "stop" are considered to be the same sound "t" in English but are different sounds in Thai. Lévi-Strauss (1963:34) argues that phonemes and kinship terms are both elements of meaning, although meaningful only in reference to systems which "are built by the mind on the level of unconscious thought." A kinship system, like language, "exists only in human consciousness; it is an arbitrary system of representations" (Lévi-Strauss 1963:50), but representations whose organizations reflect unconscious structures. Consequently, Lévi-Strauss holds that "the unconscious activity of the mind consists in imposing forms upon content, and if these forms are fundamentally the same for all minds—ancient and modern, primitive and civilized (as the study of the symbolic function, expressed in language, so strikingly indicates)—it is necessary and sufficient to grasp the unconscious structure underlying each institution and custom . . ." (Lévi-Strauss 1963:21).

A Structural Approach to Kinship: Analysis of the Avunculate

In *The Elementary Structures of Kinship* Lévi-Strauss provides an encyclopedic summary of kinship systems but focuses on a central theme: kinship systems are about the exchange of women, defining the categories of potential spouses and prohibited mates. "Marriage is thus a dramatic encounter between nature and culture, between alliance and kinship. . . . [M]arriage is an arbitration between two loves, parental and conjugal" (1969b:489). The value of this way of seeing kin relationships is demonstrated by his analysis of the relationship between a young man (Ego) and his Mother's Brother, an institution called the *avunculate*.

The avunculate is a recurrent problem in kinship literature. Kin systems which recognized a special bond between Ego and his maternal uncle—often expressed in a joking relationship—had been interpreted as remnants of matrilineal systems, until it was shown to exist in patrilineal systems as well. Yet the avunculate relationship expresses not only a system of kin terminology, but also a system of attitudes, and Lévi-Strauss (1963:40), following Radcliffe-Brown, argued that the "avunculate covers two antithetical systems of attitudes": one in which the uncle is feared and respected and one in which the relationship is easy and familiar. Further, there is an inverse relationship in the attitudes between Ego and his maternal uncle and Ego and his father; when the relationship between Ego and Mother's Brother is familiar, the relationship between Ego and Father is formal, and vice-versa.

Even more interesting is that these relationships (Ego: Father and Ego: Mother's Brother) are linked to other relationships, namely between Ego's father and mother or husband and wife (Father: Mother) and between brother and sister, in this case Ego's mother and Ego's mother's brother (Mother: Mother's Brother). The relationship between Ego and his maternal uncle fits into a set of relationships in which the relationships between Ego and Father and Ego and Maternal Uncle are inversely correlated and the relationships between Father and Mother (or husband and wife) and Mother and Mother's Brother (or brother and sister) are always inverse. This produces the possible arrangements shown below.

	A	B	C	D
Ego and Father	+	+	–	–
Ego and Mother's Brother	–	–	+	+
Father and Mother	+	–	–	+
Mother and Mother's Brother	–	+	+	–

+ = familiar relationship; – = formal or hostile relationship

The avunculate only makes sense as one relationship within a system, a structure in which there are attitudinal oppositions between generations and between husband and wife and brother/sister, constituting "the most elementary form of kinship that can exist. It is properly speaking, *the unit of kinship*" (Lévi-Strauss 1963:46). It expresses the fundamental relationships of consanguinity, affinity, and descent in a formal, structured manner. That same search for structure led Lévi-Strauss to another domain of cultural phenomena—the study of myth.

Structural Approach to Myth: The Story of Asdiwal

Lévi-Strauss expanded his search for structure by turning to the study of myth, because "The elements of mythical thought . . . lie half-way between precepts and concepts" (Lévi-Strauss 1966:18), relying on both concrete situations and the notions to which they refer. Mythical thought "builds up structured sets, not directly with other structured sets," but by using the odds and ends of experience, building "ideological castles out of the debris of what once was a social discourse" (Lévi-Strauss 1966:21–22). Thus, "The myth is certainly related to given facts, but not as a *representation* of them. The relationship is of a dialectic kind, and the [social] institutions described in the myths can be the very opposite of the real institutions" (Lévi-Strauss 1976:172). It is, therefore, incorrect to see myths as reflections of social reality; rather, they are created transformations of social existence. "The conception of the relation of myth to reality," Lévi-Strauss (1976:173) writes, "no doubt limits the use of the former as a documentary source. But it opens the way for other possibilities; for, in abandoning the search for a constantly accurate picture of ethnographic reality in the myth, we gain, on occasions, a means of unconscious categories."

In the first volume of *Structural Anthropology*, Lévi-Strauss lays out his hypothesis explicitly:

> Mythology has no obvious practical function: unlike the phenomena previously studied, it is not directly linked with a different kind of reality, which is endowed with a higher degree of objectivity than its own and whose injunctions it might therefore transmit to minds that seem perfectly free to indulge their creative spontaneity. And so, if it were possible to prove in this instance too [as in the case with kinship classifications] that the apparent arbitrariness of the mind, its supposedly spontaneous flow of inspiration, and its seemingly uncontrolled inventiveness imply the existence of laws operating at a deeper level, we would inevitably be forced to conclude that when the mind is left to commune with itself and no longer has to come to term with objects, *it is in a sense reduced to imitating itself as an object* . . . [Lévi-Strauss 1969b:10; emphasis added]

If basic unconscious structures were found in myth, then that might reflect the existence of fundamental mental structures that provide the organizing categories of cultural phenomena.

Mythology was the subject of four volumes in his *Mythologiques* (literally "logics of myth") series, *The Raw and the Cooked, From Honey to Ashes, The Origins of Table Manners,* and *The Naked Man.* The series, as Lévi-Strauss points out, progressively expands its geographic focus, beginning with myths from central and eastern Brazil and then expanding to much of South America and moving north to focus on North America. In a parallel manner, the studies treat "progressively more complex problems" considered by different myths (Lévi-Strauss and Eribon 1991:135). Levi-Strauss also addressed the complex problems reflected by myth throughout his writings.

One example is his analysis of the story of Asdiwal, a myth Boas had recorded among the Tsimshian of British Columbia. "The Story of Asdiwal" is Lévi-Strauss's most commonly reprinted analysis of myth, published in the second volume of *Structural Anthropology* (1976) and in several edited collections (Bohannan and Glazer 1988; Dundes 1984; Leach 1968). It is a complex story, and the reader is urged to examine the detailed synopsis which Lévi-Strauss provides in his article. Doing little justice to the myth, it can be summarized in the following schematic form (Levi-Strauss 1976:149–152):

1) During the famine of winter, a mother and daughter, both widowed, leave their respective villages and meet on the banks of the Skeena River where they suffer, finding only a single rotten berry to eat.

2) The women are visited by a mysterious stranger, Hatsenas, the bird of good omen. They begin to find food, Hatsenas sires a son with the younger woman, and the culture hero, Asdiwal, is born.

3) After Hastenas' disappearance and the older woman's death, Asdiwal and his mother head west to the mother's native village. There Asdiwal hunts a white she-bear which leads him up a ladder into the heavens where the she-bear is transformed into the beautiful girl, Evening-Star, who successfully lures Asdiwal to the house of her father, the Sun. Asdiwal and Evening-Star marry, but only after a series of trials does Asdiwal win the Sun's approval.

4) Asdiwal longs to see his mother and to return to earth, which he does with four inexhaustible baskets of food. Asdiwal commits adultery with a woman from his home village, the marriage with Evening-Star ends, and Asdiwal's mother dies. Loose of all social bonds, he sets off downstream.

5) Asdiwal arrives at a downstream village, marries a woman there, then antagonizes his new wife's brothers who break camp taking Asdiwal's wife with them. Asdiwal meets another band, marries a woman from that band, enjoys fortune and then, bragging that he can hunt sea lions better than his newest set of brothers-in-law, is stranded on a reef as a large storm occurs. Fortunately, Hastenas appears and Asdiwal is transformed into a bird that can hover above the waves.

6) Asdiwal falls asleep exhausted when the storm finally ends, but a mouse wakes him and leads him to the subterranean lair of the sea lion that Asdiwal has wounded. Since Asdiwal's arrows are magic and invisible, the sea lions think they are dying from an epidemic and are grateful to Asdiwal when he cures them by extracting the arrows. In repayment, the king of the sea lions helps Asdiwal reach land. There

Asdiwal carves wooden killer whales which come to life and attack the boats of his brothers-in-law, avenging Asdiwal for their treachery.

7) After a long and eventful life, Asdiwal goes on a winter hunting trip when he becomes lost. Asdiwal is transformed into stone where he may be seen on a peak on the Skeena River.

Lévi-Strauss identifies four levels of representations within this myth: geographic, techno-economic, sociological, and cosmological. The myth describes rivers, place names, famines, postmarital residence patterns, and relationships between affinal kin; these descriptions are not distorted reflections of reality; but a multilayered model of structural relationships. Lévi-Strauss (1976:161–165) proposes that there are two aspects in the construction of the myth: the *sequence of events* which form the apparent content of what happened, and the *schemata* of the myth, which represent the different planes of abstraction on which the sequence is organized. On the geographic level, there is the basic opposition between east and west, while on the cosmological level, there are oppositions of the highest heaven and the subterranean world. There are integration schema such as water/land and sea hunting/land hunting which cross geographic and cosmological schema. There are sociological schema, such as the changes in postmarital residence patterns from patrilocal to neolocal to matrilocal, (e.g. Asdiwal's mother and grandmother leave their husbands' villages and establish a new settlement and then in the next generation Asdiwal settles in Evening-Star's village). Structural analysis clarifies the multiple levels of meanings in the story of Asdiwal:

Asdiwal's two journeys—from east to west and from west to east— were correlated with types of residence, matrilocal and patrilocal, respectively. But in fact the Tsimshian have patrilocal residence, and from this we can . . . draw the conclusion that one of the orientations corresponds to the direction implicit in a real-life "reading" of their institutions, the other to the opposite direction. [Lévi-Strauss 1976:173]

Lévi-Strauss views the east-west axis as the structural parallel between imaginary and real, and therefore Imaginary/Real, Matrilocal/Patrilocal, Journey West/Journey East, Sea/Land, and Sea Hunting/Land Hunting form parallel oppositions on the different schematic planes of the story of Asdiwal.

The oppositions do not exist in Tsimshian society, "but rather with its inherent possibilities and its latent potentialities. Such speculations . . . do not seek to depict what is real, but to justify the shortcomings of reality, since the extreme positions are only *imagined* in order to show that they are *untenable"* (Lévi-Strauss 1976:173). Yet, these different considerations all reflect a similar underlying structure, which shapes the substratum of consciousness.

Conclusion

The work of Lévi-Strauss has been criticized intensely on varying levels; a bibliography (Nordquist 1987) lists over one hundred critical writings in English alone. And yet even those who criticize his work acknowledge the impact Lévi-Strauss has had on the way we think about culture and consciousness. Mary Douglas, who has attacked his analysis of the story of Asdiwal, nonetheless considers Lévi-Strauss to be one of three 20th-century thinkers—along with Piaget and Chomsky—who have changed our way of viewing the nature of human thought processes (Douglas 1980:129). The British social anthropologist Edmund Leach (1983:10), with grudging respect, has written that social anthropology

> . . . would not exist in its present form if it had not, in recent years, developed a dialectical relationship with the work of Claude Lévi-Strauss. I know of no British social anthropologist who has ever declared an unqualified enthusiasm for structuralist anthropology of a Lévi-Straussian sort, but likewise there is today no British social anthropologist who has not been deeply influenced by Lévi-Strauss' work. ✦

Bibliography

Douglas, Mary
1980 Edward Evans-Pritchard. New York: Viking Press.

de Gramont, Sanche
1970 There Are No Superior Societies. *In* Claude Levi-Strauss: The Anthropologist as Hero. E. Hayes and T. Hayes, eds. Pp. 3–21. Cambridge, MA: MIT Press.

Leach, Edmund
1970 Lévi-Strauss. London: Fontana/Collins.
1983 Roman Jakobson and Social Anthropology. *In* A Tribute to Roman Jakobson. P. Gray, ed. Pp. 10–16. Berlin: Mouton Publishers.

Lévi-Strauss, Claude
1963 Structural Anthropology, Vol. 1. New York: Basic Books.
1963 Totemism. New York: Basic Books. [Originally published as *Le Totemisme aujourd'hi*, 1962.]
1966 The Savage Mind. Chicago: The University of Chicago Press. [Originally published as *La Pensée sauvage*, 1962.]

1969a The Elementary Structures of Kinship. Boston: Beacon Press.
1969b The Raw and the Cooked. New York: Harper & Row. [Originally published as *Le Cru et le cuit*, 1964.]
1973 From Honey to Ashes. New York: Harpers and Row. [Originally published as *Du Miel aux cendres*, 1967.]
1974 Triste Tropiques. New York: Atheneum.
1977 Structural Anthropology, Vol. 2. New York: Basic Books.
1978 The Origins of Table Manners. New York: Harper and Row. [Originally published as *L'Origine des Manieres de Table*, 1968.]
1981 The Naked Man. New York: Harper and Row. [Originally published as *L'Homme nu*, 1971.]
1985 The View from Afar. New York: Basic Books. [Originally published as *Le Regard eloigne*, 1983.]
1987 Anthropology and Myth, Lectures 1951–1982. Oxford: Basil Blackwell.
1988 The Jealous Potter. Chicago: University of Chicago Press. [Originally published as *La potiere jalouse*, 1985.]
1995 Saudades do Brasil: A Photographic Memoir. Seattle: University of Washington Press.

Lévi-Strauss, Claude and Didier Eribon
1991 Conversations with Lévi-Strauss. Chicago: University of Chicago Press.

Murphy, Robert
1970 Connaissez-vous Lévi-Strauss? *In* Claude Lévi-Strauss: The Anthropologist as Hero, E. Hayes and T. Hayes, eds. Pp. 164–169. Cambridge, MA: MIT Press.

Nordquist, Joan
1987 Claude Lévi-Strauss: A Bibliography. Santa Cruz, CA: Reference and Research Services.

Pace, David
1983 Claude Lévi-Strauss: The Bearer of Ashes, Boston: Routledge & Kegan Paul.

Sontag, Susan
1966 The Anthropologist as Hero. *In* Against Interpretation. Pp. 69–81. New York: Farrar, Straus & Giroux.

Steiner, George
1977 Orpheus with His Myths: Claude Lévi-Strauss. *In* Language and Silence: Essays on Language, Literature and the Inhuman. Pp. 239–250. New York: Atheneum.

Chapter 18

Victor Turner

Symbols, Pilgrims, and Drama

Victor Turner was one of the most creative thinkers in British-American social anthropology. As a developer of new anthropological insights, Turner has few peers. And only rarely have anthropologists achieved the dazzling quality of Turner's writings, which are marked by global knowledge, captivating prose, and stubborn common sense. Take, for example, Turner's explanation of his term *communitas*, which refers to a transitional state experienced during out-of-the-ordinary situations like rites of passage or pilgrimages:

> Communitas is almost always thought of or portrayed by actors as a timeless condition, an eternal now, as "a moment in and out of time," or as a state to which the structural view of time is not applicable. Such is frequently the character of at least parts of the seclusion periods found in many protracted initiation rites. Such is the character, too, I have found, of pilgrimage journeys in several religions. In ritual seclusion, for example, one day replicates another for many weeks. The novices in tribal initiations waken and rest at fixed hours, often at sunrise and sunset, as in the monastic life in Christianity and Buddhism. They receive instruction in tribal lore, or in singing and dancing from the same elders or adepts at the same time. At other set times they may hunt or perform routine tasks under the eyes of the elders. Every day is, in a sense, the same day, writ large or repeated. [1974:238–239]

Turner's work is replete with paragraphs like this one, which illustrates the breadth of his knowledge: he alludes to his ethnographic research on ritual among the Ndembu of Zambia and on pilgrimages in Mexico, and to historical researches into major religions. The basic idea—that one element of communitas is its existence outside of structured time—is, as far as I know, Turner's unique insight. The poetry is evident throughout, but particularly in the last sentence. His common-sense nature is also in evidence: Turner does not become captive of his own metaphors.

It is curious how frequently anthropological theorists have turned to key metaphors to explain their insights (e.g., the organic analogy), and then have treated those metaphors as if they had a social rather than only a heuristic existence. The unexamined metamorphosis from metaphor to scientific law occurs frequently among anthropological theorists, but Victor Turner avoided that pitfall—a remarkable accomplishment considering that Turner's work is full of metaphors, analogies, and striking images. Turner clearly states when he is speaking metaphorically and when he is speaking literally (see, for example, Turner 1974:21–32). For example, when he develops Van Gennep's division of rites of passage into preliminal, liminal, and postliminal states—a metaphor based on *limen*, Latin for "threshold," and applied to stages of separation, transition, and reintegration of social statuses—it is clear Turner is speaking metaphorically. It is equally clear that when Turner writes of rituals as social dramas, he means it quite literally: they are performances; he is not saying "rituals are like performances" (Turner 1985a:180–181). That precision adds enormously to Turner's writing.

Victor Turner's work is dense, complex, and of enormous value. Turner's theoretical contribution has three major nuclei: the nature of symbols, the social process of pilgrimage, and analysis of social performance. It is a body of theory with its origins in British social anthropology, but it is uniquely the creation of Victor Turner.

Background

Born in Glasgow in 1920, Turner studied at the University of London and did graduate work at Manchester University under Max Gluckman. Turner's education was interrupted by World War II in which he served as a conscientious objector digging up unexploded bombs (E. Turner 1985:1). Turner found Mead's *Coming of Age in Samoa* and Radcliffe-Brown's *The Andaman Islanders* in the local library and after reading them said, as his wife recalled, "I'm going to be an anthropologist." Turner married Edith Davis in 1943, and for the next forty years they shared a very creative life of fieldwork, writing, and family, coauthoring

(1978) *Image and Pilgrimage in Christian Culture: Anthropological Perspectives.*

Gluckman arranged a grant for Turner with the Rhodes-Livingstone Institute, and Turner carried out fieldwork from 1950 to 1954 among the Ndembu of northwestern Zambia on the border between Zaire and Angola. A community of some 17,000 people with matrilineal descent and virilocal residence, the Ndembu had a high level of personal mobility, particularly due to marriage, divorce, and remarriage, "each of which normally entails a change of domicile. . . ." Paradoxically, even though "the majority of local groups in Ndembu society are relatively transient and unstable," Turner (1981:10) wrote, "the organizational principles on which they are formed and reformed are enduring." Ndembu social organization was the subject of *Schism and Continuity in an African Society* (Turner 1957), which Gluckman decreed would be the subject of Turner's dissertation. "Until you've mastered that, you're in no position to analyze ritual," Gluckman admonished (E. Turner 1985:4). The topic implied the need to analyze social organization within a functionalist framework, but Turner was disenchanted with a view of society predicated on the organic analogy. Turner recalled that when he began fieldwork, the "normal science of British social anthropology tried to present a unified theory of order and change based on a biological metaphor." In this conception, the nature of change is hidden but present in the social structure, and "The simple, like the grain of mustard seed, *grows* into the complex, through various preordained stages," (Turner 1974:31). Writing about the Ndembu of Zambia, Turner found that

> it was quite useful to think "biologically" about "village life-cycles," and "domestic cycles," the "origin," "growth," and "decay" of villages, families and lineages, but not too helpful to think about change as immanent in the structure of Ndembu society, when there was clearly "a wind of change," economic, political, social, religious, legal, and so on, sweeping the whole of central Africa and originating outside all village societies. [Turner 1974:31-32]

Buffeted by external forces, it was nonsense to think that change was immanent in social structure or that it was cyclical or repetitive.

> With my conviction as to the dynamic nature of social relations I saw movement as much as structure, persistence as much as change, indeed, persistence as a striking aspect of change. I saw people interacting, and, as day succeeded day, the consequence of their interactions. I then began to perceive a form in the process of social time. This form was essentially *dramatic.* [Turner 1974:3]

Edith Turner (1985:5) recalls how Turner and a colleague, both writing their dissertations, went out to commiserate over beers in a pub. Turner was concerned with how to analyze the extended Ndembu conflicts which were serious perturbations in an otherwise smoothly operating social system. The phrase "social drama" came to Turner, and that night he wrote out his paper for Gluckman's seminar. It analyzed conflict surrounding the sorcerer Sandombu:

> With controlled excitement he read the story of Sandombu; and he analyzed its stages—breach, crises, redress, reintegration—the social drama as the window into Ndembu social organization and values. Now you see the living heart. Max sat his hands folded on top of his bowed bald head. When it was over he raised his head, his eyes burning, "You've got it! That's it." [E. Turner 1985:5]

It is ironic, but appropriate, that the story of the conceptual birth of social drama would itself have the elements of breach, crisis, redress, and reintegration. But beyond that, Turner (1974:33) argued "When the interests and attitudes of groups and individuals stood in obvious opposition, social dramas did seem to me to constitute isolable and minutely describable units of social process."

The social drama becomes a potential unit of analysis because it has a beginning, a middle, and an end. Social dramas also possess "a regularly recurring 'processional form' or 'diachronic profile'—in other words, crisis situations tended to have a regular series of phases" (Turner 1985b:74). Drawing on his Ndembu research, Turner plotted how conflict began with a breach of a rule or norm that would rapidly escalate to a division in society to the largest level opposition of social groups involved in the conflict. Some procedures of adjustment or redress would then occur, "ranging from informal arbitration to elaborate rituals, that result either in healing the breach or public recognition of its irremediable character." Not all social processes are dramatic; for example, Turner describes "social enterprises" which are based on cooperative efforts and have different profiles (Turner 1974:34). But social dramas were recurrent units of social life, and although "each society's social drama could be expected to have its own 'style'" (Turner 1985b:74), there were sufficient similarities for comparison without erasing social actors, eliminating temporal depth, or making the organic assumptions of Radcliffe-Brown. "I felt that I had to bring the 'humanistic coefficient' into my model if I was to make sense of human social process," Turner (1974:33) wrote. He clearly did.

Turner's analysis of social dramas led him from the Ndembu (1967, 1969), to a study of Icelandic sagas (1985b), to an analysis of social dramas in the 1810 Mexican Revolution. It eventually led him to theater:

> Theater is one of the many inheritors of that great multifaceted system of preindustrial ritual which embraces ideas and images of cosmos and chaos, interdigitates clowns and their foolery with gods and their solemnity, and uses all the sensory codes to produce symphonies in more than music: the intertwining of dance, body languages of many kinds, song, chant, architectural forms (temples, amphitheaters), incense, burnt offerings, ritualized feastings and drinking, painting, body painting, body marking of many kinds, including circumcision and scarification, the application of lotions and the drinking of potions, the enacting of mythic and heroic plots drawn from oral traditions. [Turner 1985c:295]

It is writing like this—vivid, dense with thought, provocative—that makes Victor Turner such a major figure in anthropological theory. It embodies his emphasis on process—dynamic, communicative, and cultural—an emphasis also represented in his approach to symbols.

Symbols

It is worth recalling that anthropologists of very different theoretical stripes agree that symbols mark the threshold of culture. For example, an arch-materialist like Leslie White writes, "The symbol is the universe of humanity" (1949:22). Yet relatively few anthropologists were concerned with how symbols mean. Sapir (1929), for example, distinguished between primary symbols, which directly mimic an object—the picture of a dog that means "dog"—and secondary symbols, in which "a connection is no longer directly traceable between words, or combinations of words, and what they refer to," as in the sentence, "The red, white, and blue stands for freedom." Turner's contribution—and an example of his sophisticated common sense—was to consider symbols within specific fields of social action. In analyzing Ndembu ritual, Turner wrote:

> I found I could not analyze ritual symbols without studying them in a time series in relation to other "events," for symbols are essentially involved in social processes. I came to see performances of ritual as distinct phases in social processes whereby groups become adjusted to internal changes and adapted to their external environment. From this standpoint the ritual symbol becomes a factor in social action, a

positive force in an activity field. The symbol becomes associated with human interests, purposes, ends, and means, whether these are explicitly formulated or have to be inferred from the observed behavior. The structure and properties of a symbol become those of a dynamic entity, at least within its appropriate context of action. [Turner 1967:20]

Thus, the symbol of the American flag takes on different meanings if it is flapping on a flag post in a school yard, hanging in the back of a Chevrolet van, or draped across the casket of a slain president. The image is the same, but the meanings associated with it are different in kind and intensity.

Turner (1974:55) considers cultural symbols, including ritual symbols, "as originating in and sustaining processes involving temporal changes in social relations, and not as timeless entities. . . ." Symbols have some basic properties in common. They are powerful condensations of meaning: "Many things and actions are represented in a single formation" (Turner 1967:28). For example, Turner analyzes the meanings associated with the *chishing'a*, a Ndembu hunting shrine consisting of only a forked stick placed in the ground, a piece of earth from a termite hill trimmed into a rectangle and placed at the base of the branch, and a braid of grass. The associated meanings include social relationships between hunters and nonhunters, the hunter's immediate family and matrikin, toughness of mind and body, piety toward the hunter's ancestors, fertility, skill in the use of weapons, and fairness in the distribution of meat—some fifteen different meanings directly associated with this shrine. "This is but a single example of the mighty synthesizing and focusing capacity of ritual symbolism," Turner (1967:298) observes. "It might almost be said that the greater the symbol, the simpler its form." A moment's reflection on the evocative nature of the Christian cross—simply two perpendicular pieces of wood of unequal length—suggests the truth of Turner's observation.

Therefore symbols are "'multivocal,' susceptible of many meanings" (Turner 1974:55), though their meanings tend to cluster around two extremes of a continuum; at one end, there are often a cluster of meanings around physiological and natural phenomena, and at the other, another cluster of meanings about social relationships. For example, the red in the American flag is sometimes explained as representing the blood of those who have died in defense of freedom, the stripes as the original thirteen colonies, and the entire symbol as evoking values of patriotism and respect.

But the important point is that symbols, condensed and multivocal, may speak to different people in different ways; the construction
and reconstruction of meaning occurs with specific, dynamic contexts
of social process. This has profound theoretical implications. If, as so
many anthropologists have argued, symbols are the key to cultural life
and if, as Turner suggests, symbols are dynamic social creations—with
the potential for contradictory, but coexisting interpretations—then
how can a cultural trait or a social structure be abstracted from its
dynamic context? Why should one believe that cultural patterns serve
to create social stability (Radcliffe-Brown) or meet discernible human
needs (Malinowski) when the very nature of cultural life is fluid, contradictory, and dynamic as opposed to stable, congruent, and static?

Turner's insights into symbols touch a central nerve in 20th-century
anthropological thought. Culture exists as experience; it only occurs
insofar as it is practiced. This leads to an anthropology of performance
and a concern with praxis (literally, "action" or "practice," as in the
performance of an art or skill), rather than an anthropology of social
structure. Turner pursued this approach in a variety of investigations,
but one particularly intriguing investigation focused on pilgrimages.

Liminality, *Communitas*, and Pilgrimage

As noted above, Turner borrowed Van Gennep's concept of liminality
and expanded it into a conceptual tool for understanding special
phases in social life when transition is the dominant theme. "If our
basic model of society," Turner (1967:93) writes, "is that of a 'structure
of positions,' we must regard the period of margin or 'liminality' as an
interstructural situation." Periods of transition during rites of passage
or other rituals or during pilgrimages are similar in that they

> . . . are neither here nor there; they are betwixt and between the posi-
> tions assigned and arrayed by law, custom, convention, and ceremo-
> nial. As such, their ambiguous and indeterminate attributes are
> expressed by a rich variety of symbols in the many societies that ritu-
> alize social and cultural transitions. [1969:95]

Liminal periods fascinated Turner because they frequently are characterized by changes in and suspension of normal social relationships.
Liminal periods are not just in and out of time, but are also "in and out

of social structure" (Turner 1969:96), suggesting the existence of two major models of human relationships:

> The first is of society as a structured, differentiated, and often hierarchical system of politico-legal-economic positions with many types of evaluation, separating men in terms of "more" or "less." The second, which emerges recognizably in the liminal period, is of society as an unstructured or rudimentarily structured and relatively undifferentiated communitas, community, or even communion of equal individuals who submit together to the general authority of the ritual elders. [Turner 1969:96]

Turner (1969:106–107) lists a number of binary oppositions which parallel the associated properties of communitas vs. structure: transition/state, equality/inequality, anonymity/systems of nomenclature, silence/speech, absence of status/status, and so on. Such properties are part of rites of passage in traditional societies, but they also characterize moments in the major religions, particularly during pilgrimages.

The imagery of pilgrimage underscores its transitional nature; it is a recurrent metaphor in Christian literature, such as in the most famous pilgrimage in English literature, Chaucer's *Canterbury Tales*:

> This world nis but a thrughfare ful of wo
> And we ben pilgrims, passinge to and fro;
> Death is an end of every worldy soore

and this 19th-century American hymnal:

> This world is not my home,
> I'm just a passin' through.
> My treasures are laid up
> Somewhere beyond the blue.

Christian imagery emphasizes the liminal nature of pilgrimage. After all, Christ was born while in transition, his human existence a brief separation from his true nature.

Outside the Christian tradition, pilgrimages are liminal phenomena exhibiting the quality of communitas in their social relations (Turner 1974:166–167). Such liminality may be communicated by removing the outward symbols of social differences. Turner (1974:243) comments on

> . . . the bond that exists between communitas, liminality, and lowermost status. It is often believed that the lowest castes and classes in stratified societies exhibit the greatest immediacy and involuntariness of behavior. This may or not be empirically true, but it is at any rate a

persistent belief. . . . Those who would maximize communitas often begin by minimizing or even eliminating the outward signs of rank as, for example, Tolstoy and Gandhi tried to do in their own persons. In other words, they approximate in dress and behavior the condition of the poor.

Pilgrimages are a type of social process with basic properties: they are liminal, social relations characterized by communitas and they employ symbols emphasizing the merger or inversion of normal social rankings. Shrines, the objects of pilgrimages, may create a ritual topography in which paramount shrines, related shrines, and the paths between them mark a network of social process. Pilgrimages touched on Turner's basic theoretical interests as he listed them: "the study of 'processual units,' 'anti-structure,' and the semantics of ritual symbols. All these interests converge on pilgrimage processes . . . " (Turner 1974:166).

Conclusion

A brief sketch of Turner's key concepts does not do justice to his vigorous intellect and energetic exploration of such different ideas as the process approach to political anthropology (Swartz et al. 1966) and a study of Noh drama (1984). Edith Turner (1985:8) recalls that during the early 1960s, "It was as if, as his thought progressed, there would come a stage when it was time for him to take a new tack, like a sailboat beating upwind." Turner (1984:19) articulated how his varied interests formed part of a basic research agenda:

> My work as an anthropologist has been the study of cumulative interactions over time in human groups of varying span and different cultures. These interactions, I found, tend to amass toward the emergence of sustained public action, and given my Western background, it was difficult to characterize these as other than "dramatic." ✦

Bibliography

Sapir, Edward
1929 The Status of Linguistics as a Science. Language 5(4): 207–214.

Turner, Edith
1985 From the Ndembu to Broadway. In On the Edge of the Bush. E. Turner, ed. Pp. 1–15. Tucson: University of Arizona Press.

Turner, Victor
1957 Schism and Continuity in an African Society. Manchester: Manchester University Press.
1967 The Forest of Symbols: Aspects of Ndembu Ritual. Ithaca: Cornell University Press.
1969 The Ritual Process: Structure and Anti-Structure. New York: Aldine Publishing.
1974 Dramas, Fields, and Metaphors: Symbolic Action in Human Society. Ithaca: Cornell University Press.
1984 Liminality and the Performative Genres. *In* Rite, Drama, Festival, Spectacle: Rehearsals Toward a Theory of Cultural Performance. J. MacAloon, ed. Pp. 19–41. Philadelphia: Institute for the Study of Human Issues.
1985a The Anthropology of Performance. *In* On the Edge of the Bush. E. Turner, ed. Pp. 177–204. Tucson: University of Arizona Press.
1985b An Anthropological Approach to the Icelandic Saga. *In* On the Edge of the Bush. E. Turner, ed. Pp. 71–93. Tucson: University of Arizona Press.

Turner, Victor and Edith Turner
1978 Image and Pilgrimage in Christian Culture: Anthropological Perspectives. New York: Columbia University Press.

White, Leslie
1949 The Science of Culture. New York: Farrar, Straus & Giroux.

Chapter 19

Clifford Geertz
An Interpretive Anthropology

Clifford Geertz's award-winning book, *Works and Lives,* is subtitled "The Anthropologist as Author," which could serve as a subtitle to Geertz's own career. No other American anthropologist is as authorial as Geertz. He has written or edited some fifteen books including ethnographies discussing his long-term research in Indonesia and Morocco and several collections of essays sketching out an approach to culture that has been called "interpretive anthropology." Geertz's *Works and Lives* was the 1989 winner of the National Book Critics Circle Award for literary criticism, a recognition of the clarity of his prose and its accessibility to educated readers outside the field of anthropology, a discipline not known for its prose stylists. Geertz's essays are published in the *New York Review of Books, Daedelus, American Scholar* and other intellectual journals; his books are widely reviewed; and he contributes to a broader field of intellectual discussion than any other American anthropologist. His eruditeness and clever contrasting of ideas led the *New York Times* book critic Christopher Lehmann-Haupt to coo, "It's invigorating to stretch one's mind on the Nautilus machine of his prose." Clifford Geertz *is* the anthropologist as author.

It comes as no surprise that Geertz's approach to culture is based on the metaphor of culture as text and anthropological inquiry as the interpretation of text. Those ideas, first presented in a collection of essays, *The Interpretation of Culture* (1973), were a catalyst for a debate in American anthropology which turned on key issues such as, What is the nature of culture? How is it distinct from social structure? How is culture understood? What is the relationship between observer and observed?

These anthropological issues arose against the backdrop of a changing world and world view. Unlike earlier ethnographers, Geertz and his contemporaries conducted their research in the new Third World nations that emerged after World War II. The late-20th century is a postcolonial and obviously interconnected world in which there were no uncontacted societies living in Eden-like isolation. As independence movements transformed former colonial subjects into new national citizens, intergroup conflicts intensified as power was reconfigured and new governments exerted their control. In the face of such change, the idea of functionally integrated societies was difficult to maintain since there were no isolated societies and little evidence of equilibrium.

The anthropologist's role had changed as well; instead of studying an isolated society for a year or two and returning to be "the expert" on those people, anthropologists were working in communities and institutions in the United States, Europe, and developing countries among people who had their own stories to tell and the means to tell them (see cases discussed in Brettell 1993). The relationships between anthropologists and informants also changed, sparking a self-examination of the nature of anthropological inquiry. The works of Clifford Geertz have contributed to that examination, and the changes in anthropology are reflected in his own career.

Background

Clifford Geertz was born in 1926 in San Francisco and served in the U.S. Navy during World War II. After the war, he went to Antioch College, pursuing interests in English and philosophy. Except for a couple of economics courses, he did not study the social sciences before receiving his B.A. in 1950. Geertz recalls that "The [philosophical] problems I was concerned with—values and so on—seemed to me to be in need of empirical study" (Johnson and Ross 1991:150), and that led him to anthropology. He enrolled in Harvard's Department of Social Relations, and in late 1951 joined a research project in Indonesia. From 1952 to 1954 Geertz was one of a team of social scientists who worked in Modjokuto, Java, on a project funded by the Ford Foundation (Geertz 1963a:vii). The objective of that research was understanding Third World development, with the explicit goal of improving economic growth (Higgins 1963).

Geertz's works from this period differ from his later writings. His book, *The Religion of Java* (1960), is an example of classic ethnography; Evans-Pritchard could have written it. Another book, *Agricultural Involution* (1963b), is a cultural ecological study of Indonesia, an archipelago comprised of the inner islands (Java, Bali, and Lombok), where 9 percent of the land mass supported 65 percent of the population, and the Outer Islands (Sumatra and Borneo, for example), where 90 percent of the land mass was home to 30 percent of the population. *Agricultural Involution* contrasted the agrosystems of wet-rice, labor intensive, paddy agriculture and dry-rice, land extensive, swidden agriculture, and showed how the spatial distribution of those different agrosystems affected local economies, their colonial economic histories, and their future paths of development. *Peddlers and Princes* (1963a) profiles the very different Indonesian towns of Modjokuto, Java, and Tabanan, Bali, with the goal of understanding the ways local cultural patterns may affect economic development plans. At a time when development projects often ignored local realities for top-down socioeconomic engineering, Geertz (1963a:154) argued that "over-all developmental policies need to be much more delicately attuned to the particularities of local social and cultural organization. . . ." Geertz continued his analysis of Modjokuto in *The Social History of an Indonesian Town* (1965), a synthesis of political and economic development in the community from its mid-19th-century establishment to the late 1950s.

These studies are solid anthropological contributions that advanced scientific knowledge, international policy, and Geertz's career. After a fellowship at the Center for Advanced Study in the Behavioral Sciences at Stanford (1958–1959) and a year as an assistant professor at U.C. Berkeley, Geertz went to the University of Chicago in 1960, where he became full professor in 1964 and remained until 1970.

Geertz's first books do not break with traditional anthropological theory, although some interesting cracks were beginning to show. For example, in *Agricultural Involution* Geertz invokes the cultural ecology of Julian Steward and takes a systems approach shaped by functionalism, although he denies the privileged explanatory role for cultural ecology, arguing that it is important but not all-encompassing (Geertz 1963b:10–11). And the final chapter of *The Social History of an Indonesian Town* introduces an approach called "the document method" (following Harold Garfinkel), which Geertz develops in his subsequent work:

> In this approach a single naturally coherent social phenomenon, a
> found event of some sort, is interpreted not so much as an index of a

particular underlying pattern, as in most quantitative work, nor yet again as the immediate substance of that pattern itself, as in most ethnographic work, but rather as a unique, individual, peculiarly eloquent actualization—an epitome—of it.

The document (which might better be called the "example" or as this method is often referred to as clinical, the "case") is seen as a particular embodiment, a specific manifestation of a more comprehensive pattern which has a very large, in some case virtually infinite, number of such embodiments and manifestations, the one at hand simply being regarded as particularly telling in the fullness, clarity, and the elegance with which it exhibits the general pattern. In it the paradigm is made flesh: the ineradicable specificity of actual events and the elusive generality of meaningful form render one another intelligible. [Geertz 1965:153–154]

With that, Geertz turns to an examination of a bitterly contested election in Modjokuto in a section titled "A Village Election as a Social Document." It is that approach to culture as text, first broached in *The Social History of an Indonesian Town*, which became distinctive in Geertz's subsequent work.

Thick Description and Culture as Text

The course of Geertz's approach was set out in "Thick Description: Toward an Interpretive Theory of Culture," the introductory essay to the collection, *The Interpretation of Cultures*. The essay clearly and forcefully outlines Geertz's view of culture and the nature of anthropological insights. After reviewing the multiple definitions of the word "culture," Geertz states his own position:

> The concept of culture I espouse, and whose utility the essays below attempt to demonstrate, is essentially a semiotic one. Believing, with Max Weber, that man is an animal suspended in webs of significance he himself has spun, I take culture to be those webs, and the analysis of it to be therefore not an experimental science in search of law but an interpretive one in search of meaning. [1973:5]

This is a key, widely quoted passage (e.g. Barrett 1991) with a complex series of implications. In a 1990 interview Geertz said, ". . . that's exactly what I still think. It's just that I didn't know exactly what I was getting myself into by thinking it . . ." (Johnson and Ross 1991:151).

Semiotics is the analysis of signs and symbols, and Geertz argues that cultural behavior is the interactive creation of meaning with signs: ". . . human behavior is seen as . . . symbolic action—action which, like phonation in speech, pigment in painting, line in writing, or sonance in music—signifies . . ." (1973:10). The relevant questions concern the meanings of such signs, as Geertz contends (1973:10):

> Doing ethnography is like trying to read (in the sense of "construct a reading of") a manuscript—foreign, faded, full of ellipses, incoherencies, suspicious emendations, and tendentious commentaries, but written not in conventionalized graphs of sound but in transient examples of shaped behavior.

In *The Interpretation of Cultures* Geertz outlines the notion of thick description, which draws on the work of Gilbert Ryle, especially his "winking" analogy. Ryle used a seemingly silly example—the difference between a twitching eyelid and a winking eye—to show that these similar behaviors were different because the wink communicated meaning and the twitch did not. Building on that difference, Ryle points out that one could see parodies of winks, practice parodies of winks, fake winks, and so on, producing multiple possibilities with even such a simple form of communication; unraveling and identifying those contexts and meanings requires "thick description."

Geertz argues that this is precisely what ethnographic writing does, except most of the time we are unaware of it. To make that point, Geertz reproduces an account from his Moroccan field notes, which, quoted raw, is readable but cannot be understood until it is interpreted.

> In finished anthropological writings . . . this fact—that what we call our data are really our own constructions of other people's constructions of what they and their compatriots are up to—is obscured because most of what we need to comprehend a particular event, ritual, custom, idea, or whatever is insinuated as background information before the thing itself is directly examined (Even to reveal that this little drama [from his fieldnotes] took place in the highlands of central Morocco in 1912—and was recounted there in 1968—is to determine much of our understanding of it). There is nothing particularly wrong with this, and it is in any case inevitable. But it does lead to a view of anthropological research as rather more of an observational and rather less of an interpretive activity than it really is. [Geertz 1973:9]

Asserting that "Culture, this acted document, thus is public," Geertz (1973:9–10) argues that debates over whether culture is materialist or idealist, subjective or objective are misconceived: culture consists of created signs that are behaviors, and anthropology's task is "sorting out the structures of signification" in order to determine "their social ground and import." What makes other cultures different is "a lack of familiarity with the imaginative universe within which their acts are signs" and the goal of anthropological analysis is to make those signs interpretable.

Geertz distinguishes this point of view from other conceptions of culture. Obviously, a semiotic emphasis does not give priority to technology or infrastructure or any other conception of the nature/culture interface as do materialists like White or Harris. Equally, culture does not exist in some superorganic realm subject to forces and objectives of its own as Kroeber suggested; culture cannot be reified. Neither is culture "brute behavior" or "mental construct" subject to schematic analyses or reducible to ethnographic algorithms. Just as a Beethoven quartet is not the same as the score, the knowledge of it, the understanding of a group of musicians, a particular performance of it or a transcendent force, but rather is irreducibly a piece of music (Geertz 1973:11–12), culture consists of "socially established structures of meaning" with which people communicate; it is inseparable from symbolic social discourse.

Javanese Funeral

The implications of interpretation are exemplified in Geertz's analysis of a funeral in Java, a case of social discourse in which shifting political divisions and their symbolic expressions affected core rituals and emotions surrounding death (1973 [1959]). Geertz first outlines a critique of functionalism, focusing on its inability to deal with social change, and then sketches the distinction between culture and social system, "the former as an ordered system of meaning and of symbols, in terms of which social interaction takes place; and to see the latter as the pattern of social interaction itself" (1973:144).

> Culture is the fabric of meaning in terms of which human beings interpret their experience and guide their action; social structure is the form that action takes, the actually existing network of social relations. Culture and social structure are then but different abstractions from the same phenomena. [Geertz 1973:145]

But these two different abstractions are integrated, Geertz argues, in very different ways. Social structure is bound together based on "causal-functional integration," the articulation of different segments which interact and maintain the system. Culture, in contrast, is characterized by logico-meaningful integration, "a unity of style, of logical implication, of meaning and value." It is the sort of coherent unit "one finds in a Bach fugue, in Catholic dogma, or in the general theory of relativity" (Geertz 1973:145). Such distinctions become important in the Javanese funeral when changing associations between symbols and political parties create dissonance in the integration of culture and disrupt the organization of society.

To oversimplify, peasant religion in Java had been a syncretic mix of Islam and Hinduism overlain on an indigenous Southeast Asian animism. "The result," Geertz writes (1973:147), "was a balanced syncretism of myth and ritual in which Hindu gods and goddesses, Moslem prophets and saints, and local spirits and demons all found a proper place." This balance has been upset increasingly during the 20th century as conservative Islamic religious nationalism crystallized in opposition to a secular, Marxist nationalism which appealed to pre-Islamic, Hinduist-animist "indigenous" religions. Those positions became sufficiently distinct that the difference between the self-conscious Moslem and self-conscious "nativist" (combining Hindu and native elements with Marxism) became polarized as types of people, *santri* and *abangnan*. In post-independence Indonesia, political parties formed along these dividing lines: Masjumi became the conservative Islamic party and Permai, the anti-Islamic mix of Marxism and nativism. These differences were epitomized at a specific Javanese funeral.

"The mood of a Javanese funeral is not one of hysterical bereavement, unrestrained sobbing, or even of formalized cries of grief for the deceased's departure," Geertz (1973:154) writes. "Rather it is a calm, undemonstrative, almost languid letting go, a brief ritualized relinquishment of a relationship no longer possible." This willed serenity and detachment, *iklas*, depends on the smooth execution of a proper ceremony that seamlessly combines Islamic, Hindu, and indigenous beliefs and rituals. Javanese believe that it is the suddenness of emotional turmoil that causes damage—"It is 'shock' not the suffering itself which is feared" (Geertz 1973:154)—and that the funeral procedure should smoothly and quickly mark the end of life.

But in this particular case, the dead boy was from a household loosely affiliated with the Permai party, and when the Islamic village religious leader was called to direct the ceremony, he refused citing the presence of a Permai political poster on the door and arguing that it was inappropriate for him to perform the ceremony of "another" religion. At that moment, *iklas*—the self-willed and culturally defined composure surrounding the death—unraveled.

Geertz describes the emotional chaos that ensued, tracing its roots to a central ambiguity: religious symbols had become political symbols and vice-versa, which combined sacred and profane and created "an incongruity between the cultural framework of meaning and the patterning of social interaction" (Geertz 1973:169). Not only is this an interesting point about the dynamic uses of religious and political symbols, but it is a fine example of thick description. Nothing about this case—its selection, its historical background, the political dimension, the cultural expectations, the motives of distraught family and neighbors—none of it can be explained except by exposing

> . . . a multiplicity of conceptual structures, many of them superimposed upon or knotted into one another, which are at once strange, irregular, and inexplicit, and which the anthropologist must contrive to somehow first to grasp and then to render. [Geertz 1973:10]

Conclusion

The process of rendering or evocation is, Geertz argues, the essence of ethnography. Once ethnography moves beyond simple listing, intrepretation is involved as the ethnographer provides a gloss of the gloss that informants provide. Geertz distinguishes the experience-near "native point of view" from the experience-distant realm of social theorists and argues that the ethnographer's task is to explicate the links between the two:

> To grasp concepts that, for another people, are experience-near, and to do so well enough to place them in illuminating connection with experience-distant concepts theorists have fashioned to capture the general features of social life, is clearly a task at least as delicate, if a bit less magical, than putting oneself into someone else's skin. The trick is not to get yourself into some inner correspondence of spirit with your informants. Preferring, like the rest of us, to call their souls their own, they are not going to be altogether keen about such an effort anyhow. The trick is to figure out what the devil *they think they are up to*. [Geertz 1983:58; emphasis added]

And that requires interpretation, distinct from either description or invention. Discerning the connections between multilayered cultural phenomena is not the same as inventing those connections (Geertz 1988:140). The presentation of ethnographic interpretations as observed facts simply reflects the selection of a genre, not an epistemological reality.

Geertz's works, ethnographies and essays, exemplify this kind of self-cognizant balancing act between literal and literary. It is a body of work which draws on developments in neighboring disciplines and speaks to thinkers in other fields. It has also raised some sharp debates about verification: if ethnography is interpretation, then how can we know if the interpretation is correct? Most of us cannot go to Modjokuto or northern Morocco and check the interpretations; we need some other ways to evaluate the ethnographer's claims, but what are they? In traditional ethnographies we could search for various validating points: Is the ethnographer fluent in the local language? Did she live in the culture for an extended period? Was he methodical or biased in his observations? Were the informants "representative" of a larger culture?

But if cultural knowledge is inherently interpretive, how can we invalidate the "truth" of an interpretation since there are potentially as many "true" interpretations as there are members of a culture? And, to extend this logic, if all such claims are equally valid, then the most anthropology can hope for is to create a rich documentary of multiple interpretations, none denied and none privileged. This means that anthropology cannot be a science since it cannot generalize from truth statements or test the statements against empirical data; the nature of culture precludes this.

For anthropology, Clifford Geertz's major contribution has been to force anthropologists to become aware of the cultural texts they interpret and the ethnographic texts they create. He has also touched off a major debate within anthropology about the fundamental nature of the field (see "Postscript: Current Controversies"). Geertz's "evocative metaphor of interpretation as the reading of texts both by observer and observed," Marcus and Fischer (1986:26) write, ". . . has led to the present dominant interest within interpretive anthropology about how interpretations are constructed by the anthropologist, who works in turn from the interpretations of his informants." That key point has triggered a profound rethinking of the anthropological enterprise. ✦

Bibliography

Barrett, Richard
1991 Culture and Conduct: An Excursion in Anthropology. Belmont, CA: Wadsworth Publishing.

Brettell, Caroline, ed.
1993 When They Read What We Write: The Politics of Ethnography. Westport, CT: Bergin and Garvey.

Geertz, Clifford
1960 The Religion of Java. New York: The Free Press.
1963a Peddlers and Princes: Social Change and Economic Modernization in Two Indonesian Towns. Chicago: University of Chicago Press.
1963b Agricultural Involution: The Process of Ecological Change in Indonesia. Berkeley: University of California Press.
1965 The Social History of an Indonesian Town. Cambridge, MA: M.I.T. Press.
1973 The Interpretation of Cultures. New York: Basic Books.
1983 Local Knowledge: Further Essays in Interpretive Anthropology. New York: Basic Books.
1988 Works and Lives: The Anthropologist as Author. Stanford: Stanford University Press.

Higgins, B.
1963 Preface. *In* Agricultural Involution: The Process of Ecological Change in Indonesia. By C. Geertz. Berkeley: University of California Press.

Johnson, A. and W. Ross
1991 Clifford Geertz. Contemporary Authors, New Revision Series 36:148–154.

Chapter 20

Mary Douglas
Symbols and Structures, Pollution and Purity

In a very modest self-assessment, Mary Douglas has said, "I am primarily interested in cross-cultural comparison" (Contemporary Authors 97–100:144); in fact, her works created an important anthropological approach to symbolic classifications and their social contexts. It has been written that "Douglas has been of inspiration to hundreds of social scientists who have felt the need to grasp the symbolic world more effectively" (Guthnow et al. 1984:13). Douglas' contributions have been recognized in honorary doctorates from universities in Sweden, the United Kingdom, and the United States; in 1992 she was named a Commander, Order of the British Empire. Her ideas are presented in a dozen books and scores of articles characterized by probing intellect, modest tone, and sly wit.

Two theoretical traditions are entwined in Douglas' thought. First, she has extended Durkheim's search for systems of classification and the bases of social experience. Like Durkheim, Douglas argues that systems of knowledge are social systems and that their definitional categories express social realities. While Durkheim's point of entry was the nature of the totem, Douglas enters through a commonplace, yet marvelously complex, subject: dirt. If we want to make a cross-culturally relevant definition of dirt, Douglas (1966:35) writes,

> we are left with the old definition of dirt as matter out of place. This is a very suggestive approach. It implies two conditions: a set of ordered relations and a contravention of that order. Dirt then, is never a unique, isolated event. Where there is dirt there is system. Dirt is the by-product of a systematic ordering and classification of matter. . . .

From that deceptively humdrum starting point, Douglas expands her analysis into the larger problems of purity and pollution and their classification.

Second, Douglas employs a comparative method derived from Evans-Pritchard. In her fine study of Evans-Pritchard's work (Douglas 1980; see Chapter 12), Douglas discusses how his exploration of accountability provided a comparative angle which was sensitive to local realities yet recurrent in all human societies. Similarly, Douglas examines two experiences common to all societies: 1) To what extent is a bounded social unit experienced? and 2) To what extent are there specific rules relating one person to another as individuals? These two variables—which Douglas calls 'group' and 'grid'—are variously found in all societies and thus are a basis for cross-cultural analysis, but they also reflect local realities. In this way, Douglas attempts to balance objectivity with attention to local knowledge, simultaneously avoiding uncontextualized comparison and hypersubjectivity.

In her studies of the social bases of knowledge and the comparison of social groups, Mary Douglas has produced a corpus of extremely stimulating ideas.

Background

Mary Douglas (née Tew) was born in Italy in 1921 and raised and educated in Great Britain. After serving as a civil servant in the Belgian Congo during World War II, she returned to Oxford in 1946 to study anthropology under Edward Evans-Pritchard; she received her doctorate in 1951. From 1949 to 1950 and in 1953, Douglas conducted ethnographic fieldwork among the Lele of Zaire. Characterizing her monograph, *The Lele of Kasai* (1963) as "a study of authority—or rather its failure," Douglas describes the existence of aristocratic clans who do not rule or lead, of village headmen "who did not govern, allocate resources [or] adjudicate disputes," and of clans which "had no corporate character whatsoever" (Douglas 1963: 68–85, 202). With its minimal emphasis on overt theoretical statements, *The Lele of Kasai* is clearly influenced by Evans-Pritchard. Most of the book examines the institutions of Lele society and only briefly touches on the issues of pollution that would become prominent in Douglas' later work.

After a brief stint as a lecturer at Oxford, Douglas began teaching at the University College, London where she advanced from lecturer to professor between 1951 and 1977. A spate of articles discussed various aspects of her Lele research (e.g., 1951, 1952, 1955, 1957, 1960), and at various points they presage some of her later interests. For example, an article on Lele social and religious symbolism (1955; reprinted 1975) showed how social form and symbolic systems are linked in Lele culture.

In the mid-1960s Douglas expanded her insights about the Lele into a broader cross-cultural program, considering wider theoretical problems in books like *Purity and Danger: An Analysis of Pollution and Taboo* (1963), *Natural Symbols: Explorations in Cosmology* (1970), and in essays in her edited volume, *Rules and Meanings: The Anthropology of Everyday Knowledge* (1973).

Rules and Meanings collects articles by such diverse authors as philosopher Ludwig Wittgenstein; composer John Cage; novelist Tom Wolfe; anthropologists Evans-Pritchard and Stanley Tambiah; and Mrs. Humphry, the Victorian author of *Manners for Women* (1897), and is a fascinating, though indirect, statement of Douglas' intellectual intentions, as indicated by her selections and brief essays. She prepared the collection for a course taught under the various titles of "Cognitive Anthropology," "Symbolism," or "Religion and Morals," and she admits, "the book expounds more of what this editor believes ought to be accepted in anthropology than what is actually accepted" (Douglas 1973:9). The collection expresses a recurrent line of intellectual concerns that began among late-19th-century social thinkers—most prominently Durkheim and Mauss—who shared

> a common concern with problems of commitment, solidarity, and alienation. They knew only too well that there can be rules without meaning. They also assumed that there can be no meaning without rules. They drove the study of meaning straight to the study of social relations. Formal analysis would reveal the formal properties of a communication system, as a vehicle for meaning: the meanings conveyed would be uncovered only through social analysis. [1973:9]

In spite of this promising start, the cross-disciplinary conversation splintered into specialists' musings and consequently, Douglas (1973:9) argues, "our knowledge of social conventions which make understanding possible remains scarcely advanced from that beginning." The advancement of understanding has been the primary aim of Mary Douglas' work.

Purity and Pollution

"Holiness means keeping distinct the categories of creation," Douglas has written (1966:53), and the social bases of symbolic classifications are central to her work. At the core of religious classifications are the concepts of pollution and purity. Douglas' interest in pollution and purity has two sources. First, these concepts are discussed by anthropologists of religion from Tylor, Frazer, Robertson Smith, and Durkheim on down to her own teachers, Evans-Pritchard and Franz Steiner (Douglas 1966: vii, 10–28, 1968).

Second, and perhaps more important, the Lele were also concerned with pollution (Douglas 1966:vii, 1955 [1975]). *Buhonyi* is the virtue of propriety expressed in shyness, modesty, and shame. *Buhonyi* imbues all status relationships and personal functions. In contrast, all bodily dirt (*hama*) is shameful, the material antithesis of *buhonyi*. The Lele say that insulting a man is like rubbing excrement (*tebe*) in his face (Douglas 1975:9–13). The avoidance of *hama* extends to corpses, blood, excrement, maggots, used clothing, and sexual intercourse. The Lele are horrified by milk-drinking and egg-eating, since milk and eggs are body products and thus *hama*.

By extension, Lele "rules of cleanliness largely amount to an attempt to separate food from dirt" (Douglas 1975:13), and the classification of edible and disgusting foods is shaped by the contrast between *buhonyi* and *hama*. Carnivores, dirty feeders, rats, snakes, and smelly animals like jackals are *hama*. Women will eat most types of monkeys, except for one species that eats the secretions of palm trees; since vegetable secretions, like animal excrement, are called *tebe*, that one species of monkey is also *hama* (Douglas 1975:13–15).

Obviously, Lele symbolism is not about hygiene. It is a system of symbolic classifications which literally distinguish clean/dirty, human/animal, male/female, village/forest, upstream/downstream, and so on, classifications spanning both secular and religious symbols.

What is true of the Lele is broadly true of other human societies, even though the symbols and systems are differently configured. As Douglas wrote,

> Lord Chesterfield defined dirt as matter out of place. This implies only two conditions, a set of ordered relations and a contravention of that order. Thus the idea of dirt implies a structure of idea. For us dirt is a kind of compendium category for all events which blur, smudge, contradict, or otherwise confuse classifications. The underlying feeling is

that a system of values which is habitually expressed in a given arrangement of things has been violated. [Douglas 1968:338]

In a classic, often reprinted chapter, Douglas examines the best-known system of pollution in the West: the Abominations of Leviticus. These Old Testament dietary rules distinguish between what is edible and inedible:

> These are the living things which you may eat among all the beasts that are on the earth. Whatever parts the hoof and is cloven-footed and chews the cud among the animals, you may eat. Nevertheless among those that chew the cud or part the hoof, you shall not eat these: The camel, because it chews the cud but does not part the hoof, is unclean to you. . . . [Leviticus xi: 2–4]

The biblical dietary laws define dozens of unclean animals. Varyingly interpreted as designed to discipline the Jews in their search for holiness or as a primitive avoidance of nonhygienic foodstuffs, Douglas argues that the dietary laws are founded on a model of God as One, Complete, Whole. "To be holy is to be whole, to be one: holiness is unity, integrity, perfection of the individual and of the kind" (Douglas 1966:64). Unclean animals combine elements of different realms: the things that live in the water but lack both fins and scales (eels, shellfish), the birds of the air that live in the water (pelicans, gulls), and any land animal that lacks both characteristics of the paragon of domestication, the cow—chewing the cud and the cloven hoof. "By rules of avoidance holiness was given a physical expression in every encounter with the animal kingdom and at every meal" (Douglas 1966:57). (Douglas' interpretation of Old Testament food taboos differs dramatically from one proposed by Marvin Harris [see Chapter 15] who argues that the food taboos actually serve an adaptive purpose.)

In *Purity and Danger*, Douglas traces the convoluted lines of magic, taboo, mana and contamination, and in the process provides a masterful commentary on anthropological approaches to ritual and religion. But in the last half of *Purity and Danger* Douglas focuses on the relationships between ritual and social systems. For example, Douglas argues that there is a recurrent parallel between the human body and the body politic; rituals designed to protect the human body from outside contamination are mirrored in ceremonies designed to protect the external boundaries of society (Douglas 1966:114–128). Other rituals concern relationships within society. Whether we discuss mana in Polynesia, witchcraft among the Azande, or the curative power of the Royal Touch, "beliefs which attribute spiritual power to individuals are never neutral or free of the dominant patterns of social structure" (Douglas 1966:112). Douglas outlines a clear hypothesis:

> where the social system explicitly recognizes positions of authority, those holding such positions are endowed with explicit spiritual power, controlled, conscious, external and approved—powers to bless or curse. Where the social system requires people to hold dangerously ambiguous roles, these persons are credited with uncontrolled, unconscious, dangerous, disapproved powers—such as witchcraft and evil eye.
>
> In other words, where the social system is well-articulated, I look for articulate powers vested in the points of authority; where the social system is ill-articulated, I look for inarticulate powers vested in those who are a source of disorder. [Douglas 1966:99]

Douglas' interest in the links between symbolic classifications and social systems led to her most ambitious theoretical contribution (Wuthnow et al. 1984:78), a cross-cultural inquiry into group and grid.

Group and Grid, Society and Symbol

Douglas proposed two concepts to frame her cross-cultural inquiry into societies, group and grid. The concepts are simple: "Group is obvious— the experience of a bounded social unit. Grid refers to rules which relate one person to others on an ego centered basis" (Douglas 1970:viii). Group and grid are independent variables. Group and grid also are continuous variables; for example, one could imagine a "group" sliding scale from "no sense of a bounded social unit" to "some sense of bounded social unit" to "well-developed sense of bounded social unit." In Douglas' initial explanations, however, grid and group are simplified as nominal variables—you live in either a "low group" or "high group" society—and their relationships can be presented in a simple 2 × 2 table:

		GROUP −	GROUP +
GRID	+	B	C
	−	A	D

When a society experiences grid and group (Cell C) "the quality of relations is ordered and clearly bounded. If group is found by itself (Cell

D), or grid is found without group (Cell B), the quality of relations is different" (Douglas 1970:viii). Douglas (1982b:191) further explains the two categories:

> The group itself is defined in terms of the claims it makes over its constituent members, the boundary it draws around them, the rights it confers on them to use its name and other protections, and the levies and constraints it applies.
>
> . . . The term grid suggests the cross-hatch of rules to which individuals are subject in the course of their interaction. As a dimension, it shows a progressive change in the mode of control. At the strong end there are visible rules about space and time related to social roles; at the other end, near zero, the formal classifications fade, and finally vanish. [Douglas 1982b:192]

We have previously discussed (see pp. 108–109) the high-grid society of Bajoeng Gede, Bali, as described by Bateson and Mead (1942). In Bali, Mead (1942:10) wrote about the complex rules concerning personal interactions, in which a "fixed and complicated set of regulations, obligations, and privileges" produce a grid in which "space and time and social status form an orderly whole. . . . "

Moving from high grid towards low grid, social "boundaries begin to be arbitrated. Individuals, deciding to transact across them, weaken the classifications" (Douglas 1982b:192). Paradoxically, as grid weakens and as individuals more freely engage in social transactions, the rules governing such transactions may become more explicit, legalistic, and increase in number. For example, one might argue that modern American society is a low-grid society since we elevate the individual and celebrate free choice in economic and social realms; yet we regulate the behaviors and expectations of interactions through the legal system.

Up to this point in her analysis, Douglas' ideas are interesting but not really outstanding: numerous schemes have been used to classify societies. What is significant is the way Douglas links grid and group to other dimensions of culture, such as the economic and political expressions of differing social contexts; symbolic structures relating to the human body and society; and cosmological statements regarding nature, time, human nature, and social behavior (Douglas 1970, 1982a, 1982b).

In situations with strong grid/strong group (Cell C), the individual's social experience is defined first by the social boundary maintained between the group and outsiders and second from the clear rules of behavior between group members. Individual behavior is regulated in the name of the group. Within the group, clearly defined social sectors exist (e.g., classes, castes, age-grades, etc.) which may have specialized roles and unequal access to resources, and a variety of solutions will be used to resolve conflicts between those groups. Strong grid/strong group societies will tend to be larger than other societies and last longer without internal fissioning. Since its members perceive the possibility of "persisting as a group into the future," strong group/strong grid societies can make levies of its members (taxes, corvée, military service) to invest in its continued existence.

Strong group/weak grid societies (Cell D) also emphasize the definition and authority of the group, but because of their low-grid conditions they will lack formalized internal divisions or segregated social sectors. Consequently, relationships between individuals are ambiguous and the resolution of conflicts more difficult. In the face of conflicts, the only penalty for internal disputes is expulsion from the group or the fissioning of the group. This has several consequences: "Disagreement is driven underground" since mechanisms for resolution are ill-developed. Covert factions develop, and group members committed to the maintenance of society will argue for stronger group boundaries to control admission and strengthen the group. Consequently, strong group/weak grid societies will tend to be small and subject to internal divisions (Douglas 1982b:205–206).

The two remaining possibilities, high grid/low group and low grid/low group, have very different social outcomes. In extreme cases of high grid/low group societies (Cell B) the individual is tightly regulated by social rules and individual autonomy is minimized, but so is the individual's affiliation with any social groups, since those groups— by definition—do not exist. The individual's role and behavior are unambiguously defined by powers which are remote, impersonal, and insulating (Douglas 1982b:207).

In low grid/low group societies, "the social experience of the individual is not constrained by any external boundary" and is unregulated by ascribed status classifications (Douglas 1982b:207). All social classifications are potentially negotiable; the relationships between individuals are ambiguous and their mutual obligations implicit. Individuals can transact freely. However, there will be an opposing tendency to regulate transactions which go against social contracts, such as laws that require contracts be honored, laws to protect the freedom to exercise rights, and laws to defend religious minorities. In such societies, rewards go to innovators, economic activities specialize and expand, and the market is controlled by alliances. Nothing succeeds like success in low grid/low group societies, and success is measured by the size of one's following, whether these are customers, political supporters, or fans (Douglas 1982b:207–208).

An analysis of grid and group is linked to broader issues of symbolism. In essence Douglas asks, "If symbols mark systems of classifications, and if classification systems are reflections of social systems, then what types of classifications are associated with which types of societies?" She argues that

> the most important determinant of ritualism is the experience of closed social groups. The man who has that experience associates boundaries with power and danger. The better defined and the more significant the social boundaries, the more bias I would expect in favour of ritual. If the social groups are weakly structured and their membership weak and fluctuating, then I would expect low value to be set on symbolic performance. [Douglas 1970:14]

In strong group/low grid societies, humanity is divided into insiders and outsiders, and nature is similarly classified into two classes: the lovable, vulnerable, cuddly part of nature and the threatening, dangerous, untamable part of nature. The parallel dualities in humanity and nature are more than the extension of metaphors, but reflect "the use made of nature in moral justifications" (Douglas 1982b:210). Outside the village edge, beyond the border of society, evil forces lurk waiting to penetrate the human realm. Within the community, one must find the contaminated agent of evil, drive him out, and purify the realm of humanity again.

In strong group/strong grid societies, the same emphasis on society's borders is present, but it is modified by the presence of strong grid. The explicit rules about the interrelations between group members are justified by a "transcendental metaphysics which seeks to make an explicit match between civilization and the purposes of God and nature" (Douglas 1982b:210). When social relations are confirmed by ritual, the laws of nature are used for moral justification. In strong group/strong grid societies, theoretical models are elaborated, divine sacrifice is highly developed, and social contexts are justified by appeals to "natural law" and cosmological analyses (Douglas 1982b:210–211).

In low group/high grid societies, theoretical notions of society and the cosmos are undeveloped, and cosmologies are incoherent and eclectic "things of shreds and patches" (Douglas 1982b:211). Finally, in low group/low grid societies, the unrelenting competition and selection exercised by individuals is expressed in cosmologies that convey the "excitement and rewards of competition" (Douglas 1982b:212).

And since success is measured by the size of one's following, society is a source of constant concern because approval, once granted, also may be withdrawn. Because following is based on performance, there is intense demand for high standards: our movie stars can never make a flop, our presidents cannot be adulterers.

Nature stands in contrast to the competition of low grid/low group society. Outside the realm of humanity, nature, an oasis of innocence, is not cited to justify social relations since Nature and Society are separate realms. Yet "a wistful sense of alienation from nature never wins against the excitement and rewards of competition" (Douglas 1982b:212).

Building on the framework shaped by group and grid, Douglas (1982b:214–226) offers an amazing list of expectations about such different topics as cookery ("In D the classification of edible foods is likely to assert the prohibition against eating carnivores"), gardening (". . . D will not be specially interested in gardening as a cultural activity, whereas C is likely to use this medium to justify and expand its view of society as hierarchized, trained and compartmentalized"), monuments ("though it has nothing much to raise public monuments to, B respects the burial places of its private dead"), and attitudes about youth and old age, death, personal abnormalities and handicaps, punishment, and justice.

But if we accept Douglas' expectations as plausible, how does one decide where Society X fits on the grid/group diagram? First, grid/group analysis assumes that society is the product of interactions between the individual and her/his environment, the environment consisting of "all the other interacting individuals and their choices." A group does not exist "independently of the volition of its independent members. Their investment of time and energy quickens its life and marks its boundaries" (Douglas 1982b:198). Alternately, as appeals are made to "an ethic of individual value," grid diminishes in force.

Second, the analysis of grid/group occurs at the level "at which people find it necessary to explain to each other why they behave as they do." This level—"the social accounting level, the level of justification and explanation"—can be observed and investigated by the anthropologist. For example, if an individual conducts the varying facets of life—residence, work, shared resources, marriage and kinship—within a common social set, then group is strong. If I spend the early morning as a member of my family, my day as an employee, then return to my family most evenings except for the one night a month I join a poker party and the other evenings I spend as a member of a homeowners association, as a seminar participant, as a PTA member, and so on—then group is weak. Similarly, if I justify my actions by appeals to the rights of the individual or, alternately, to my expected roles as a member of a particular social division, then grid is varyingly weak or strong. None of this requires anthropologists to restructure their basic methods, and it produces tantalizing lines of inquiry.

Fundamentally, Douglas has outlined an approach in which "most values and beliefs can be analyzed as part of society instead of as a separate cultural sphere" (Douglas 1982a:7). Group/grid analysis, Douglas (1982b:199–200) writes,

> is a method of identifying cultural bias, of finding an array of beliefs locked together into relational patterns. The beliefs must be treated as part of the action, and not separated from it as in so many theories of social action. The action or social context, is placed on a two-dimensional map with moral judgements, excuses, complaints and shifts of interest reckoned as the spoken justifications by individuals of the action they feel required to take. As their subjective perception of the scene and its moral implications emanates from each of them individually, it constitutes a collective moral consciousness about man and his place in the universe.

Conclusion

In the late 1970s Douglas moved to the United States where she was Director of Research at the Russell Sage Foundation in New York, a private nonprofit organization sponsoring research in the social sciences. During her time at the Sage Foundation (1977–1981), Douglas coauthored and edited volumes that applied group/grid analysis to modern industrialized societies (Douglas 1982a) and explored the ways they perceived risk (Douglas 1985; Douglas and Wildavsky 1982). In 1981 Douglas became Avalon Foundation Professor of the Humanities at Northwestern University where she was Professor Emeritus in 1985. After two years as visiting professor at Princeton, Douglas returned to England in 1988.

In all her works Douglas has pursued the "study of meaning straight to the study of social relations." Rather than view meanings and social rules as constraints mechanically applied to passive members of human cultures, Douglas argues that humans "holding each other responsible in their dealings . . . attribute to each other voluntary, intended agency." Douglas' perspective is a view of culture that searches "for expectations about human agency," an analytical stance that listens for "the active voice" rather than a passive one. In her works, Mary Douglas (1982:ix–x) has examined a wide range of cultural media—foods and goods, prohibitions and purifications—to listen to the way "people make statements about their life." ✦

Bibliography

Douglas, Mary
1950 Peoples of the Lake Nyasa Region. London: Oxford University Press. (Published under maiden name Mary Tew).
1951 A Form of Polyandry among the Lele of the Kasai. Africa 21(1):1–12.
1952 Alternate Generations among the Lele of the Kasai. Africa 22(1): 59–65.
1955 Social and Religious Symbolism of the Lele of the Kasai. Zaire 9(4):385–402.
1957 Animals in Lele Religious Symbolism. Africa 27(1)46–58.
1960 Blood Debts Among the Lele. Journal of Royal Anthropological Institute 90(1):1–28.
1963 The Lele of Kasai. London: Oxford University Press.
1966 Purity and Danger: An Analysis of Concepts of Pollution and Taboo. New York: Praeger Publishers.
1968a Pollution. In International Encyclopedia of the Social Sciences, Vol. 12. D. Sills, ed. Pp. 336–342. San Francisco: MacMillan and Company and the Free Press. [Reprinted In Implicit Meanings: Essays in Anthropology. Pp. 47–59. London: Routledge & Kegan Paul, 1975.]
1968b Dogon Culture: Profane and Arcane. Africa 38:16–25.
1968c The Social Control of Cognition: Some Factors in Joke Perception. Man (n.s.) 3:361–375.
1970 Natural Symbols: Explorations in Cosmology. New York: Pantheon Books.
1971 Do Dogs Laugh?: Cross-Cultural Approach to Body Symbolism. Journal of Psychosomatic Research 15:387–390.
1973 Rules and Meanings: The Anthropology of Everyday Knowledge— Selected Readings. Harmondsworth, England: Penguin Books.
1975 Implicit Meanings: Essays in Anthropology. London: Routledge & Kegan Paul.
1982a Introduction to Group/Grid Analysis. In Essays in the Sociology of Perception. M. Douglas, ed. Pp. 1–8. London: Routledge & Kegan Paul.
1982b Cultural Bias. In In the Active Voice. M. Douglas, ed. Pp. 183–254. London: Routledge & Kegan Paul.
1982c Preface. In In the Active Voice. M. Douglas, ed. Pp. vii–xi. London: Routledge & Kegan Paul.
1985 Risk Acceptability According to the Social Sciences. Occasional Reports on Current Topics, 11. New York: Russell Sage Foundation.
1986 How Institutions Think. Syracuse: Syracuse University Press.

Douglas, Mary and Aaron Wildavsky
1982 Risk and Culture: An Essay on the Selection of Technical and Environmental Dangers. Berkeley: University of California Press.

Harris, Marvin
1974 Cows, Pigs, Wars and Witches: The Riddles of Culture. New York: Random House.

Wuthnow, Robert, James D. Hunter, Albert Bergesen, and Edith Kurzweil
1984 Cultural Analysis: The Work of Peter L. Berger, Mary Douglas, Michel Foucault, and Jurgen Habermas. Boston: Routledge & Kegan Paul.

Chapter 21

James Fernandez
The Play of Tropes

In many ways the works of James W. Fernandez exemplify a post-modernist approach to anthropology. "Post-modern" is an extremely diffuse concept—perhaps intentionally and inherently so—eluding easy definition. One attempt to distinguish modernism and post-modernism was a schematic list of 32 paired opposites describing "modernism" and "post-modernism" respectively: purpose/play, design/chance, hierarchy/anarchy, selection/combination, and so on (Hassan 1985). Many concepts in the list distinguished the universalizing and authoritative aspects of modernism from the fragmentary, creative, and competitive mosaic of post-modernism. Harvey (1989:44) writes that the most startling aspect of post-modernism is "its total acceptance of the ephemerality, fragmentation, discontinuity and the chaotic." Rather than try to transcend, reverse or reduce that mosaic, the movement revels in "the deep chaos of modern life. . . . " In the humanities and social sciences, post-modernism is frequently associated with thinkers such as Jacques Derrida, Michel Foucault, and Jean-François Lyotard who share a common emphasis on the progressive unraveling of multiple layers of language and meaning, an intellectual process which highlights the shifting nature of truth and truths.

Fernandez's writings are an example of a distinctively anthropological context of post-modernist thought. The post-modern influence in anthropology has had a variety of consequences, but the most central is on the nature of ethnography. Rather than present other cultures as set examples of an overarching theory of functionalism or cultural materialism or structuralism, the objective of anthropological research becomes an ethnography of experience which is deeply emic and may require new forms of experiments in writing about another culture. "These experiments," Marcus and Fischer (1986:46) suggest, "are asking, centrally, what is a life for their subjects, and how do they conceive it to be experienced in various social contexts."

Such concerns are at the heart of James Fernandez's work and are explicitly connected with broader themes in the late-20th century:

> [T]here is just now an especially pronounced awareness that what is done in human affairs is not simply to be taken literally, at face value as it were, but that many such doings, like metaphor itself, stand for something else, so that our sober-minded constructions have obligatorily to be reconstructed. For another thing, we are living at a time when the referential value of language, its ability to provide us with an accurate, transparent view through to and mapping of the reality of things . . . is profoundly questioned. . . . [Fernandez 1991:1]

So the slipperiness of meaning in human affairs requires us to question our views of social life. Our perspectives are not pure reflections of reality—"immaculate perceptions" in Fernandez's term—but are instead refracted through our own, often unrecognized frames of reference. And if this is true as we try to understand our own society, then the distortions are intensified as our gaze turns to another culture.

It is hard to imagine Radcliffe-Brown, Malinowski, Marvin Harris, or Julian Steward worrying about such matters. This is not to suggest that these anthropologists believed understanding another culture was easy, but there is no hint in their works that such difficulties stemmed from the inherent nature of culture. Over the last hundred years, most anthropologists have assumed that understanding another culture—as a coherent set of values, behaviors, and symbols shared by a specific group of humans—was the basis of anthropology. While there was debate whether anthropology was to be modeled after the natural sciences, like biology, or the humanities, like history, there was a recurrent consensus that "the truth" about another culture could be obtained.

Post-modern anthropology severely questions that assumption. First, it argues that there is never one truth, but always several. Second, post-modern anthropologists scrutinize anthropological models as reflecting their proponents' usually Western, often male-dominated, developed societies rather than being images of other cultures. The post-modernist critique often analyzes such models as extensions of domination. Thus, Radcliffe-Brown's portrayal of non-Western societies as "ahistorical" is seen as a not-so-subtle justification of the superiority of

British culture—and thus imperialism—which prides itself on its tradition and written history.

And finally, the opaque meanings of language and behaviors require that anthropologists find an entrée into the way people create and order their own cultural meanings. Rather than reduce reality to imposed, all-encompassing models, the goal is to identify significant concepts that members of a particular society deem relevant.

These issues intersect in Fernandez's work. In 1986 he wrote, "Over the last decade and a half . . . I have been trying to do an anthropology that is alert to the arguments that lie at the heart of our human experience in culture" (Fernandez 1986:vii). But even earlier, Fernandez was concerned with the meaningful construction of culture, a process exemplified by the heated discussions in the men's council house of the Fang of northern and central Gabon.

Background

Fernandez (1982:xx) traces his intellectual genealogy to a group of anthropologists—Malinowski, Benedict, and Evans-Pritchard, among others—who are distinguished by "their embeddedness in the local idiom, their skillful presentation of local points of view." Born in 1930, Fernandez received a B.A. at Amherst College in 1952 and then went to Northwestern University where he studied under the wide-ranging Africanist Melville Herskovits. As a graduate student, Fernandez initiated preliminary research in Spain (a research area he would return to), but in the mid-1950s Africa increasingly dominated his interests. From 1958 to 1961 Fernandez conducted 24 months of fieldwork in Gabon, a Francophone nation on the Atlantic coast of equatorial Africa. After choosing a village, Assok Ening, in the rain forest of northern Gabon as his study area, Fernandez asked permission to stay in the community, a request that triggered a very public debate.

> The room was full. Everyone was anxious to know why a European (*ntangen*) wished to live among them. The speculation was particularly intense because it was said I had come to establish a commerce. Some had heard that I was a *mwan amerika* (a child of America), and since this phrase was often used for Protestant missionaries, some thought I might be intending to set up a mission station. When, as it turned out, I wanted only to live among them to learn their way of life, there was evident disappointment, and some drifted away. [Fernandez 1982:28]

Fernandez's study of Fang religion and syncretism was the basis of a 1962 dissertation and his book *Bwiti: An Ethnography of the Religious Imagination in Africa*, published 20 years later and discussed in detail below. While finishing his dissertation Fernandez started teaching at Smith College where he remained until 1964, at which time he moved to Dartmouth.

Over the next decade Fernandez published widely on the Fang, African religious movements, and the concept of metaphor in cultural analysis. His interest in the cultural ordering of symbols is expressed in articles on Fang aesthetics (1966, 1970, 1972) and architectural design (1977, 1979), and recordings of Fang music (1973). From 1975 to 1986 Fernandez taught at Princeton and after that at the University of Chicago. A fellow of the American Academy of Arts and Sciences, Fernandez has been visiting professor at universities and institutes in Spain, Great Britain, Sweden and the United States.

Beginning in the early 1970s, Fernandez resumed his research in northern Spain. His research on culture change in the mountain province of Asturias continues to the present. Fernandez discusses his research among the miners and cattle herders of Asturias in over a score of articles, each of which takes a specific ethnographic event— boys' schoolyard games, a folklore parade, or a ribald exchange between men and women on a bus—and holds the event up to an analytical light, turning it over like an artifact, examining it from different points of view. From these "revelatory incidents" Fernandez's intention is to "expose the importance of the analysis of metaphors in anthropological inquiry" and the way that such metaphors become adopted by human actors (Fernandez 1986:6). That is the play of tropes.

The Play of Tropes

According to the Oxford English Dictionary, a trope is literally "a figure of speech which consists in the use of a word or phrase in a sense other than that which is proper to it." Fernandez expands the notion to cover "the metaphoric assertions men make about themselves or about others," assertions which influence action (1986a:24). For example, in American society we commonly employ the trope of "the competitive race": "Life's a rat race," "The race for the presidency," "With hard work you can get ahead," "Whoever ends up with the most toys wins," and so on. Life isn't really a race, yet as Americans not only do we use this trope to describe our lives, but we shape our actions based on this conception. The trope is thus a bridge between metaphor and act, and this creates the opening for anthropological insight. Although understanding is not obtained by the simple observation of behavior, neither is Fernandez primarily interested in metaphors as philosophical or linguistic structures. "I am more interested in what tropes do," Fernandez (1986:ix) writes, "than in what they are. . . . " Arguing that anthropology is "essentially a pragmatic and not a platonic or idealist enterprise," Fernandez states,

> It is the kind of study primarily concerned with how humans in real situations get things done such as living together with some sense of fulfillment and satisfaction; mastering an environment, providing food, clothing, and shelter; creating some sense of ultimate meaning to life as well as some sense of humor; bringing up the next generation. [1986:ix]

At that point, Fernandez's argument sounds similar to Marvin Harris' statement (1979:ix; see p. 190) that "human social life is a response to the practical problems of earthly existence," but Fernandez is obviously not a cultural materialist. Fernandez (1986:ix) states that his specific concern is how humans create "identities through the argument of images and the play of tropes."

Fernandez frequently refers to the "movement" in this process, transitions from an ill-defined or vague status to one which is concrete and specific. That movement from the ill-defined to the specific characterizes semantic metaphors ("My love is a red, red rose") and also social metaphors ("Men are dirty pigs"). Movement from the vague to the concrete also characterizes symbolic actions, particularly during ritual. Fernandez (1982b:43) argues that rituals should be analyzed "as a series of organizing images or metaphors put into operation by a series of superordinate and subordinate ceremonial scenes." Thus ritual becomes an acted, public discourse in which meanings are created, referred to, and juxtaposed in actions and words that always stand for something else.

In a very basic sense, that is the play of tropes. But that simple starting point requires enormous ethnographic effort: ceremonial scenes must be described, their relative significances determined, and the polyvalent web of the metaphors' referents untangled. Fernandez (1986b:60–61) outlines a research design to achieve this. Broadly, the research must be based on participant observation, a method that provides "as none other, an awareness of the many different domains of experience in a culture. . . ." Specifically, the research should focus on the way metaphor and metonymy are used to transform vague, socially inchoate individuals into specific, well-defined occupants of particular positions in the social sphere. This process of definition calls on specific sets of signs and symbols ("sign-images") which form a cultural lexicon unique to a particular culture. Rituals which mark such transitions are constructed from that cultural lexicon and refer to a limited number of themes or tropes "to bring about significant conversions in themselves."

Like most anthropologists, Fernandez has arrived at his theoretical position in the process of understanding another cultural reality. The idea of the "play of tropes" emerged directly from Fernandez's efforts to understand the complex meanings of a cult of transformation, Bwiti.

Bwiti

Fernandez's introduction to Bwiti was dramatic: late one night, a loud knock, and a man stood at the door wearing a long flowing robe belted with a red cord. He said, "You do not know me but I am no stranger. I am a child of this village just returned from a long spiritual journey. I have been following the truth!" The night visitor went on, "You must come to the Bwiti Chapel in my father's house." Fernandez (1982:292) writes:

> Suddenly the [man] grabbed my left hand and lifted my arm. "Don't be too sure of yourself. You are not free of all your sins. Look at this arm. You are not without blemishes." He pointed out freckles and pigmented spots. "These are your sins! You have heard the harp at night? While all these villagers are asleep we dance and journey far. They go nowhere here. They wander around in confusion. They don't know where to go. But we go far." He took hold of the red-woven cord around his waist. "You see this cord? This is the Path of Birth and Death. We follow this path. We know life. We know death."

Bwiti is a revitalization movement that developed after World War I, as Fang society experienced the twin pressures of French colonialism and Protestant missionary activity. "The invention and diffusion of religious cults for purposes of protection and revitalization in Africa," Fernandez (1982:292) writes, "is . . . a very old phenomenon antedating European contact. But the pressures of colonial domination and missionary evangelization coupled with the relative inertia, the ennui, that came to prevail among such a previously turbulent people as Fang created particular needs for revitalization." Referring to the "malaise and increasing isolation of parts of Fang culture" Fernandez argues that the Fang "achieve some assuagement and reconciliation in Bwiti" (1982:6). But Fernandez's point is not a Malinowskian reduction of cultural complexes to individual psychological needs. Rather, Fernandez situates Fang cultural malaise and Bwiti's response within specific, local explanations. In so doing he reveals—and revels in—the complexities of the particular ethnographic situation.

Fang experience a garbled, uncertain social order. "Social realities had collapsed while a lexicon persisted" that described categories of social life which no longer existed (Fernandez 1982:87). An egalitarian society lacking specialized genealogists or cosmographers who could establish opinion, the Fang expressed vocal disagreements about the lost meanings of social concepts. "And the Fang were discomfited by these differences. Terminological evidence that clan organization was formerly greater, coupled with present ambiguities about the application of terms, convinced many that their social affairs were in a vestigial state" (Fernandez 1982:87).

Bwiti creates movement from chaos to unity, from divisiveness to common purpose. Intriguingly, it achieves this by multiplying symbolic options rather than reducing them. Fernandez writes (1982:301):

> the Bwiti of the Equatorial Forest, in place of seeking to unify doubled personalities by either conversion to Christianity or nativistic rejection of that message . . . seeks to accustom its members to a much more polyvalent existence by offering them extension into a variety of realms of being.

Given the creative complexities of Bwiti, any summary is inadequate. In the first half of the book (Part I), Fernandez outlines the history of Fang-European contacts and Fang conceptions of the past, time, social and built space, social structure, and world view. He reviews the historical and modern Fang, with particular attention to the aspects of folklore, religion, and legend that had become disarticulated, conflicted, and controversial. It is these elements of collapse which Bwiti reunifies. "In Fang lore we see the roots of Bwiti," Fernandez (1982:73) writes, "but it is a significantly new composition."

In his own composition, Fernandez is intent on placing our knowledge of the Fang within their specific cultural frame. Fernandez organizes his ethnography into conceptual sets that are uniquely Fang (e.g., "Compositions of the Past") rather than into the common chapter titles found in ethnographies (e.g., "Historical Background," "Subsistence," or "Social Structure"). Fernandez uses two other devices to emphasize local knowledge. First, each chapter begins with an ethnographic vignette in which a conversation, an encounter, or a remembered myth opens the discussion of a set of themes. Second, Fernandez consistently provides the Fang word for a concept in English, as in "The overall transformation is from the state of despair (*engôngôl*) to a state of grace (*abora*) . . ." (Fernandez 1982:309). Since relatively few readers understand Fang, this intratextual commentary serves two implicit goals: it bolsters confidence in Fernandez's understanding of Fang culture, and it constantly nudges the reader's attention to the ethnographic detail, to the specifically Fang reality. Fernandez (1982:6) writes, "our interpretation of Bwiti, it should be remarked, has its center of gravity in Fang culture itself."

A complex syncretic religion that originated in southwestern Gabon and spread north (Fernandez 1982:347–367), Bwiti is expressed in a complex all-night ceremony (*engosie*) which travels the path between life and death, from despair to tranquillity, and from isolation to "oneheartedness" (for a description of the liturgical cycle, see Fernandez 1982:436–469). Small doses of a psychotropic plant, *eboga*, which induces "euphoric insomnia," are taken as communion during the *engosie*. Much larger doses are consumed by initiates, and the resulting visions are designed to "break open the head" of new converts (*banzie*) to Bwiti (Fernandez 1982:470–493). Satisfying eboga visions are extensions "into the unseen, the death realm, of the path of birth and death which the all-night ceremonies evoke and follow. Most visions are a following of that path. What the liturgy can only suggest, the taking of eboga actualizes" (Fernandez 1982:485).

Midway through the engosie, a brief sermon from the évangile— often less than 15 minutes long—is dense with polyvalent meanings. The sermons edify, as Fernandez points out (1982:529), but are not didactic or expository. Rather, the sermons create a multilayered "edification by puzzlement" in which "One obtains . . . as indeed one obtains in the architectonic of Bwiti life and in the ritual drama of their celebrations, a sense of reverberation, resonance between levels and domains of interest." In that manner, "we are forced to extend ourselves to larger integrities in wider contexts" (Fernandez 1982:530).

Bwiti is not a set of rules, Fernandez (1982:310) argues, but "a set of projected qualities." Through the combination of dance and action, sermon and vision, Bwiti seeks to move the Fang from despair to grace, from corporeality to spirituality, from sloth to industry, from sexual indulgence to sexual purity, from bad body to clean body, from worthlessness to worthiness—towards the promise of becoming onehearted (Fernandez 1982:309). Bwiti is movement.

> [T]o search for the Bwiti order in codified form, although it may grat-ify a Western need for abstractions of that kind, yet misses the Bwiti moral order where it reposes: in the images and actions of Bwiti myths and legends, in the night-long rituals and accompanying song cycle, in the architectonics of the cult house, and in the midnight "évangiles" of cult leaders. The moral order is more acted out than spelled out, more ritualistic than didactic. . . . It is as much as any-thing a kinesthetic order that is gradually exposed to the membership in the process of their worship. [Fernandez 1982:303–304]

In the process of the Bwiti rituals, actions are based on key sets of metaphor, emphasizing shared communal experience and motivating action. These "performative metaphors" are used in Bwiti to unify, motivate, inspire, and to create "an overarching sense of solidarity in the sacred society of Bwiti . . . " (Fernandez 1982:563).

Conclusion

In his introduction to *Bwiti*, Fernandez previews his idea of explana-tion calling it "basically genetic and semantic." His basic assumptions are that, first, historical experiences create the expectations for revitali-zation and, second, that revitalization is created from "the residue of these experiences." Necessarily this implies that all explanations are based on local knowledge, framed by specific historical circumstances and formed by particular social creators.

Of course this is not enough to make James Fernandez a post-modern anthropologist; Franz Boas' notion of explanation was very similar. But Fernandez's emphasis on local knowledge, the existence of parallel truths (1982:29–73), relations between power and knowledge (e.g. 1986g: 172–173), and a stubborn insistence on the irreducibility of meaning mark the post-modernist themes in the anthropology of James W. Fernandez. ✦

Bibliography

Fernandez, James
1963 Redistributive Acculturation and Ritual Reintegration in Fang Culture. Ph.D. dissertation, Northwestern University.

1964 African Religious Movements—Types and Dynamics. Journal of Modern African Studies 3:428–446.

1965 Symbolic Consensus in a Fang Reformative Cult. American Anthropologist 67:902–927.

1966 Unbelievably Subtle Words: Representation and Integration in the Sermons of An African Reformative Cult. Journal of the History of Religions 6:43–69.

1966b Principles of Opposition and Vitality in Fang Aesthetics. Journal of Aesthetics and Art Criticism 25: 53–64.

1969 Microcosmogony and Modernization. Occasional Papers, Center for Developing Area Studies. Pp. 1–34. Montreal: McGill University.

1970 Rededication and Prophetism in Ghana. Cahiers d'Etudes Africaines. Vol. 10 (38):228–305.

1972 Tabernanthe Eboga and the Work of the Ancestors. In The Flesh of the Gods: The Ritual Use of Hallucinogens. P. Furst, ed. Pp. 237–260. New York: Praeger Publishers.

1975a On the Concept of the Symbol. Current Anthropology 16 (4):652–654.

1975b On Reading the Sacred into the Profane: The Dramatic Fallacy in the Work of Victor Turner. Journal for the Scientific Study of Religion 14:191–197.

1977 Fang Architectonics. Working Papers in the Traditional Arts, No. 1. Philadelphia: Institute for the Study of Human Issues.

1977b The Performance of Ritual Metaphors. In The Social Uses of Metaphor. J. Sapir and C. Crocker, eds. Pp. 100–131. Philadelphia: University of Pennsylvania Press.

1978 African Religious Movements. Annual Review of Anthropology 7:195–234.

1982 Bwiti: An Ethnography of the Religious Imagination in Africa. Princeton: Princeton University Press.

1986 Persuasions and Performances: The Play of Tropes in Culture. Bloomington: Indiana University Press.

1991 Introduction: Confluents of Inquiry. In Beyond Metaphor: The Theory of Tropes in Anthropology. J. Fernandez, ed. Pp. 1–13. Stanford: Stanford University Press.

Hassan, I.
1985 The Culture of Post-Modernism. Theory, Culture and Society 2(3):119–132.

Current Controversies

And the debate continues.

There is a fierce argument within current anthropology about concepts that are at the heart of the discipline: What is the nature of anthropology? Is the idea of culture useful? Should anthropological explanation be modeled on scientific theory-building or on humanistic interpretation? In the wake of these debates, no reigning model is dominant, and thus, as Marcus and Fischer (1986:16) have written,

> there are presently many anthropologies: efforts to revitalize old research programs such as ethnosemantics, British functionalism, French structuralism, cultural ecology, and psychological anthropology; efforts to synthesize Marxist approaches with structuralism, semiotics, and other forms of symbolic analyses; efforts to establish more encompassing frameworks of explanation such as sociobiology to achieve the aim of a more fully "scientific" anthropology; efforts to merge the influential study of language in anthropology with the concerns of social theory. All of these have merits and problems in different measure. . . .

Add to this list the various approaches labelled as "post-modern," and current anthropology appears a swirl of conflicting labels, research agendas, and theoretical frameworks.

Lacking a crystal ball, it is impossible to know the future of these debates, but an interesting glimpse into the controversy is found in a recent electronic forum organized by the American Anthropological Association and published in the *Anthropology Newsletter* from March to September of 1996 (American Anthropological Association 1996a,

1996b, 1996c, 1996d). "Science in Anthropology" was a moderated e-mail discussion between 16 invited anthropologists; their responses provide an interesting cross-section of the debate.

The debate began with a definition of science, but quickly shifted to "science—who's for it, who's against it." Partially this was a rhetorical maneuver, but it highlighted a key issue: should anthropology rely on a scientific mode of explanation—proposing hypotheses, testing them with empirical data, and constructing theory from lawlike generalizations—or are scientific models inappropriate for understanding the symbolic nature of culture and inherently distorting since they treat the more elusive and elliptical aspects of cultural existence as mere epiphenomena, explanatory sideshows that are not as relevant as matters of infrastructure or adaptation?

Michael M. J. Fischer, a prominent post-modernist anthropologist, argues for "the indissolvibility of scientific and humanistic approaches to the study of human societies," charging that humanistic approaches have been ignored and undeveloped in anthropology. Yet, Fischer contends, changes during the late-20th century—the post-modern era—such as "the transnational or global processes that thoroughly rework local cultures," have produced conditions that "challenge anthropology to provide ethnographic accounts in new ways both substantively and formally. They require a greater epistemological sophistication, as well as renewed attention to the relation between form and content in ethnographic writing" (American Anthropological Association 1996b:11).

Absolutely wrong, other anthropologists respond. Science arrives at insights into the world, including the cultural realm of phenomena, through the replicable testing of hypotheses with observable data, the elimination of weak hypotheses, and ultimately the development of theory, which as Eugenie C. Scott writes, "is an explanation of a natural phenomenon, human or otherwise, and is usefully defined as a logical construct based on corroborated hypotheses and repeated observations. The goal of science is theory formation." Further, Scott argues, "no other way of knowing"—*regardless* of the post-modern condition—"will provide us as useful, valid or reliable explanations of humanity as will science" (American Anthropological Association, March 1996a:52).

Initially phrased as an inquiry into the role of science in anthropology, the debate takes a nastier turn. While some anthropologists are content to frame the debate as between "science" and "humanism," Roy G. D'Andrade (American Anthropological Association April 1996b:10) argues that "the conflict is not between humanists and scientists, it is between those who think anthropology should be primarily a kind of political action group and those who think it should be primarily a kind of scholarly study." The political actions are not limited to declarations and signed manifestos about world events, but also affect the practical business of anthropology: hiring for teaching positions, funding of grant applications, acceptance of an article for publication—all may be influenced by academic politics within anthropology, divided and fragmented based on current debates.

Several participants in the electronic forum search for a middle ground. For example, archaeologist George Cowgill writes, "To have any hope of regaining a shared center, we have to shrug off some of the most extreme statements at either end of the spectrum, especially productions that are just not very good in their own terms as either positivistic science, humanities or postmodernism" (American Anthropological Association April 1996b:10). In a series of questions directed to Fischer, Cowgill asks,

> I am genuinely puzzled about how, terminology aside, a hermeneutic approach really differs from a scientific approach. Could Fischer go over this, or at least suggest some key remedial reading? It seems to be that in arguing that what he is doing is not so different from what many self-proclaimed scientific anthropologists are doing, his argument leads toward the idea that at the level of method and theory there is a shared conceptual core to social/cultural anthropology that many or most of us could agree on. (*Fischer responded "Yes" to this.*) [American Anthropological Association 1996a:48; original emphasis and parenthetical]

In the face of such bitter, divisive debate, how can anthropology really offer any insights into humanity? How can knowledge of any depth emerge from such venomous controversy? What comprises the "shared conceptual core" that Cowgill and Fischer believe exists?

At this point, we might recall the undergraduate's very good question that opened this book: "What's the goddamn point of it all?"

It is essential to remember that the shared conceptual core of anthropology emerges from a century and a half of ethnographic investigations and theoretical debates very similar to the current controversy. Boas' attack on racial explanations of behavior was just as strident, just as "political" as any contemporary argument. The debates between Malinowski and Radcliffe-Brown were just as filled with rhetorical maneuvers and personal slights as any present contention. Durkheim's claim of having founded a "science of society" is no more, or less, grandiose than Harris' claim of defining "cultural materialism." And such examples can be replicated endlessly.

Anthropology has always been characterized by debates. For all the fervor of the current "scientist vs. post-modernist" debate, it is not true that anthropology has descended recently from an Edenic, peaceful community of happy anthropologists into the current maelstrom of despise and dissent. Such an idea is an unrealistic glorification of the past. It ignores the history of anthropologists and their ideas.

But how can any knowledge develop from such a contentious discipline? The knowledge anthropologists have gained in the last 150 years has been generated because of controversy, not in spite of it. It is a simple fact that we know much more about ourselves and other cultures than was known in the mid-19th century. It is undeniable that we know more about human culture than our great-great-grandparents did. This is partly due to controversies which have caused anthropologists to rethink ideas and restudy specific ethnographic cases. There is no doubt, for example, that Trobriand Islanders' culture was much better documented after Malinowski's work than before, but even deeper knowledge of Trobriand society has come with the many restudies by anthropologists like Annette Weiner (1976, 1988), Melford Spiro (1982), and others (Battaglia 1986; Brindley 1984; Hutchins 1980). These restudies were provoked by controversies, and, in turn, led to greater knowledge.

But in addition to the accumulation of knowledge about individual cultures, anthropology has gained basic insights into human nature. A partial list includes:

✦ Race does not account for variations in human behavior.
✦ Other cultures are not "fossilized" representatives of earlier stages in human evolution.
✦ There is a complex dialectic between individual and culture in every society. Individuals are shaped by and shape the culture they experience.
✦ Culture is not a thing of "shreds and patches," but neither is it a smoothly integrated machine. Different elements of culture meet the adaptive requisites of human existence, express the creativity of human actors in their use of symbols, and reflect the transmitted experiences of humanity.
✦ Our knowledge of other peoples is shaped by our own cultural experience. There is nothing simple about understanding another culture.

Anthropology generates controversy because we are our subjects. Fields where there is a clear-cut division between observer and observed— like entomology where the difference between entomologist and fly is obvious—do not provoke the same controversies that anthropology does. At a more fundamental level, we humans are simultaneously phenomena governed by the laws of nature *and* chaotic self-creations with endlessly complex ideas about the meanings of existence. Any field that studies an organic actor like a human is bound to experience conflicts.

The anthropologist Eric Wolf observed that anthropology is the most humanistic of the sciences and the most scientific of the humanities. This is a catalyst of our controversy, but also the basis of our intellectual contributions. Recently Gregory Reck has written:

> [A]nthropology's uniqueness and contributions [has] resided, as always, in its simultaneously comfortable and uneasy location between things, between the sciences and the humanities, between history and literature, between ourselves and the other, between objectivity and subjectivity, between the concrete and the abstract, between the specific and the general.

> Living in the cracks between these worlds comes with the territory. It is our nature and strength. For as long as we are anthropologists . . . we will retain the primary goal of understanding the human species, realizing that multiple routes lead to that understanding. [Reck 1996:7]

The pursuit of that understanding is reflected in anthropology's multifaceted, multidimensional visions of culture. ✦

Bibliography

American Anthropological Association
1996a Commentary: Science in Anthropology, Anthropology Newsletter, 36(3).
1996b Commentary: Science in Anthropology, Anthropology Newsletter, 36(4).
1996b Commentary: Science in Anthropology, Anthropology Newsletter, 36(5).
1996d Commentary: Science in Anthropology, Anthropology Newsletter, 36(6).

Battaglia, Deborah
1986 Bringing Home to Moresby: Urban Gardening and Ethnic Pride among Trobriand Islanders In the National Capital. Boroko, Papua New Guinea: Institute of Applied Social and Economic Research.

Brindley, Marianne
1984 The Symbolic Role of Women in Trobriand Gardening. Pretoria: University of South Africa.

Hutchins, Edwin
1980 Culture and Inference: A Trobriand Case Study. Cambridge: Cambridge
     University Press.

Marcus, George E. and Michael M. J. Fischer
1986 Anthropology as Cultural Critique. Chicago: The University of Chicago
     Press.

Reck, Gregory
1996 What We Can Learn From the Past. Anthropology Newsletter 36(4):7.
     American Anthropological Association.

Spiro, Melford
1982 Oedipus in the Trobriands. Chicago: University of Chicago Press.

Weiner, Annette
1977 Women of Value, Men of Renown: New Perspectives in Trobriand
     Exchange. Austin: University of Texas Press.
1988 The Trobrianders of New Guinea. New York: Holt, Rinehart and Winston.

Index

A

American cultural anthropology, 18, 42–43, 65–67, 113–115, 165–167
Ancestor worship, 148–149
Andaman Islanders, 142
Animism, 62
Arapesh, 107
Aristotle, 15
Australian Aborigines, 54, 61–62, 121–122, 129, 147–148, 183
Azande, 152, 154, 158–159, 160

B

Bali, 108–110
Bateson, Gregory, 104, 108–10
Benedict, Ruth
    on Apollonian and Dionysian archetypes, 84–85
    background, 79–81
    on configurations, 82–85
    criticisms of, 192
    on deviations, 85
    fieldwork, 80, 81
    on individual and culture, 66–67, 192
    writings of, 81–83, 86
Boas, Franz
    background, 44–48

criticism of cultural evolution, 42–43, 48–50, 169
fieldwork, 44–45
historical particularism of, 43, 49–50, 169–170
influence of, 42–43, 51, 65, 169–170
linguistic studies, 45, 46, 89–90
physical anthropology of, 45, 46–47
on race and racism, 47–48
Bohannon, Paul, 59, 60
Brazilians, rural, 190–191
British social anthropology, 18, 113–115, 149–150, 166
    criticisms of, 140–142, 152–153, 161–162

C

Communitas. *See* Turner, Victor
Comparative method
    Boas on, 48–50
    defined, 22–23
    Durkheim on, 56–57
    Mauss on, 121
    Radcliffe-Brown, 144
    Tylor on, 22–23

About the Author

Jerry D. Moore received his Ph.D. in anthropology from the University of California, Santa Barbara. He has directed archaeological research in Peru, Mexico, and the United States, and has conducted ethnoarchaeological and ethnohistoric research in Peru and Mexico. Moore has been a Fellow in Precolumbian Studies at Dumbarton Oaks Research Libraries and Collections, and a Visiting Research Fellow at the Sainsbury Centre for the Visual Arts, University of East Anglia. He is the author of *Architecture and Power in the Prehistoric Andes: The Archaeology of Public Buildings* (Cambridge University Press) and articles and professional reviews in anthropological journals. Moore also writes book reviews and articles on culture and related topics for newspapers and magazines. He is associate professor of anthropology at California State University, Dominguez Hills. ✦